SEX

THE WHOLE PICTURE

NICOLE BELAND

SEX
THE WHOLE PICTURE

The Ultimate How-To for Lovers

SEX &
HEALTH
PUBLISHING

This book is dedicated to Dr. Ruth Westheimer,
the woman who took the stigma out of talking and learning about sex.

Commissioned photography by Philip James.
Front cover photograph by Ghrislain & Marie de Lossy/Getty Images.
For other credits, see page 304.

Produced for Sex & Health Publishing by Hydra Packaging, 129 Main Street, Irvington, NY 10533, USA

Printed in the U.S.A.

ISBN-13 978–0–7394–9396–0

Notice
This book is intended as a reference volume only, not as a medical manual. The information
given here is designed to help you make informed decisions about your health. It is not intended as
a substitute for any treatment that may have been prescribed by your doctor. If you suspect that you have
a medical problem, we urge you to seek competent medical help.
Mention of specific companies, organizations, or authorities in this book does not imply endorsement by
the publisher, nor does mention of specific companies, organizations, or authorities imply that they endorse this book.
Internet addresses and telephone numbers given in this book were accurate at the time it went to press.

SEX &
HEALTH
PUBLISHING

PART 1: sex

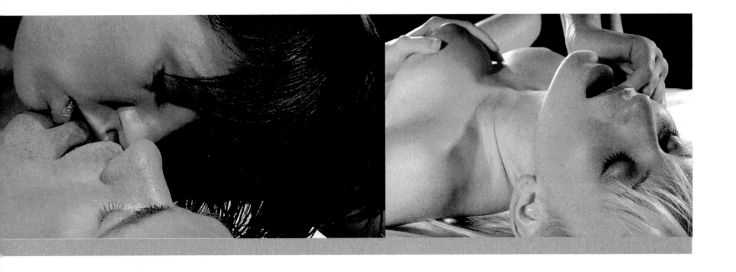

preface

There are two types of people who typically fail to reach their full sexual potential. The first think that they're already so fantastic in bed that there is no room for improvement. The second think that they'll never be fantastic in bed so they shouldn't bother trying. I assume you're flipping through this book (1) to see the gorgeous and tantalizing photographs of people having sex; and (2) because you're smart enough to know that great sex requires a good deal of knowledge and skill, and that acquiring both can be a simple matter of looking, reading and then doing it yourself. It would be wonderful if we all had a sexual partner who was a virtuoso between the sheets and could show us every possible way to give and get pleasure, but such virtuosos are few and far between. Better to become one yourself.

Given the major role sex plays in our lives, colleges and universities should offer courses based on the *Kama Sutra*, but they don't. Therefore, it's up to us to seek out information about sex on our own. We find out about sex from our friends, from television, movies, magazines, instructional video tapes, from the people or person with whom we sleep, and from books. What makes this book a particularly good source of information is that almost every tip and move that I describe is illustrated in careful – and red-hot – detail, making the 'instructions' easy to understand, remember and put into practice the next time you get it on.

Another element that makes this book different, and I think better, than any other how-to book about sex, is that it takes a realistic approach. For example, most books separate kissing and caressing into a chapter on foreplay, as though kissing and caressing weren't major component of every stage of a sexual encounter. (The idea of 'foreplay' itself is more than a little out of date. A sexual encounter doesn't have any kind of fixed schedule.) Most books about sex also make

assumptions about men and women that are completely antiquated; for example, assuming that women never enjoy frenzied, high-energy sex, or that men never like the slow, romantic kind. Today's women are often as confident and active in bed as men. Modern women enjoy sex because it feels good, not just because it's a way of becoming more emotionally connected with their partner. And many of today's men enjoy sex as much for the intimacy as for the physical pleasure. As the sexes become more equal out of bed, their attitudes and actions in bed reflect that equality.

I've also included chapters entitled 'Fast Start' and 'Slow Start', in keeping with my belief that the sex techniques and positions a couple will choose have everything to do with the kind of sex they want to have. On those nights when you feel the urgent desire to hit the sheets in a hurry, you're not going to seduce your partner the same way you would when you want to make slow, sensual love. How you're craving to be touched, and crave to touch your partner, is deeply connected to your mood. In each of these chapters you'll find tips specific to the sexual scenario you want to create.

Another reality of sex ignored by most other books is that in most positions, one partner controls the action more than the other. Someone is on top and/or doing the majority of the thrusting and grinding. For that reason, the positions pictured and described in this book are divided into two categories: 'She Drives' and 'He Drives'. But no matter who is at the wheel, there are tips for both partners about how to make the most of every coital configuration, whether it's a hand move that will make your partner moan, or one that will up your own level of excitement.

As we compiled this book, the designer, photographer, editor and I have done our best to leave as little as possible to the imagination. Of course, there are some things that we can't show in this book (if we did, we'd have to wrap it in plastic and sell it only in adult bookstores), but where we've had to hold back we've included detailed illustrations that should make the message crystal clear. Another of our goals was to make the book erotic as opposed to sterile or solely instructional. I think we've accomplished that, and I hope you agree.

Ultimately, we – a handful of twenty-, thirty- and forty-something men and women who have had our share of sexual experiences – wanted to create a sex book that we would want to relax with on the couch on a Saturday evening, picking and choosing new things to toss into the mix that (or any other) night. That's why we went to great lengths to add moves and techniques that were more advanced and unique than the same old advice most sex books regurgitate. All the basics are here, but we've tried to give advanced lovers plenty of new material as well. There's information about sex toys, erotic games, bathing and massage, and even having sex in the great outdoors.

This book is 100-per cent couple friendly. I understand that the best sex usually occurs when two people care about and trust each other enough to get creative, communicate and relax to the point where they can let pleasure take them over completely. I hope you'll consider leaving this book on your partner's pillow to give him or her a fun, sexy surprise. I also hope that you'll agree that it is the ideal gift for engagements, weddings, birthdays or even for your parents' fortieth anniversary (just kidding, sort of).

It's impossible for this, or any book, to cover every aspect of sex in complete detail, so in the name of doing one thing and doing it well, we decided to focus the first half of this book on vaginal sex for heterosexual couples. In the second half of this book, we've provided an extensive reference section about sexuality, which includes information on subjects ranging from birth control to sex and from ageing to the nature of sexual attitudes around the world.

Please browse these pages at your leisure, garnering a tip or new idea here and there as you go. And please also feel free to use it as a form of erotica, allowing the vast variety of two-dimensional images to get you in the mood for some three-dimensional fooling around.

sex

The photographs, descriptions and tips on the following pages have one purpose, and that's to help you have exciting, satisfying sex every time. In my opinion, that's a goal well worth working toward. One's sexuality is very simply a part of the fabric of our being, and if we aren't expressing ourselves sexually, we aren't living life to the fullest. Sex stimulates us physically and mentally. It makes us healthier – it's terrific exercise, it relieves stress and it enhances sleep. It creates feelings of intimacy with our partner. Sex is just good, clean, delicious fun.

If you think that hot sex is somehow beyond your reach, think again. A fantastic sex life begins with your thoughts and attitudes about sex. And not only is it within your power to have satisfying sex, but it's your responsibility. Not your partner's responsibility – yours. The fact that you picked up this book shows you understand that you have an enormous amount of control over the quality of your sex life.

Don't wait to be turned on. Turn yourself on. The more active you are in seeking and giving pleasure, the more you'll get in return. Know that the more you think about sex, the sexier you feel. And the sexier you feel, the better sex will be. Studies have shown that men and women with high self-esteem enjoy sex more than those who

don't feel good about themselves. We can't really put ourselves out there sexually, or in any other way, unless we're proud of who we are.

I hope you'll use this book to enhance your private fantasy life. It's hard to flip through these pages without getting turned on. Which is definitely part of the point. If that happens, go with the flow. Don't be embarrassed about masturbating, or 'solo sex' as I call it. Exploring your sexuality alone is very healthy – I can't think of a better way to release tension at the end of a long day – and it can be a great way to jump-start a flagging libido. Masturbation is also a good way to learn about what you like. And, of course, masturbation is crucial to enjoying your sexual self between relationships.

You can also save up your excitement about what you see in this book and surprise your partner with all you've learned. Or, make a date to read it with your partner and tell – or better yet, show – each other what turns you on. Afraid your partner wouldn't be into it? You won't know until you try. Most people are secretly hoping that their significant other will take the lead and spice things up in bed. The only rule is to treat yourself and your partner with respect. Don't try anything that makes either of you uncomfortable. Great sex is just another way of communicating with your partner, so

make sure to keep the lines of communication open. Don't be reluctant to talk about what you find hot, and what isn't your cup of tea. Not everything here is for everyone, but I guarantee that everyone will find something that will seriously enhance their sex life, no matter how steamy it already is.

You may also find that the more time you spend 'working' on improving your sex life, the more your inhibitions and preconceptions about what you would or wouldn't do change. We are all sexual creatures. Our bodies have a way of telling us what they want. The more time you spend with this book, both by yourself and with your partner, the more comfortable you're both likely to become with experimenting. Practise leaving your inhibitions outside the bedroom door, and soon enough you'll be ready and willing to try just about anything once.

This part of the book, the nuts and bolts, if you will, is meant to instruct, inspire, to

fire-up the libido and to increase intimacy with your partner. Read it with an open mind. And get ready to learn things you didn't know about your own and your partner's body. If you ever had any doubt about how to give the perfect hand-job, or just exactly where a woman's g-spot is, you will be confident in your technique and placement after reading about them here. And remember, practise makes perfect. It's true that the more sex you have, the more sex you want, so get prepared to spend more time in bed – or in the kitchen, or the backseat of your car, or wherever or whenever the urge strikes you.

As you're about to see, we've included tips for every stage of the sexual process. We acknowledge that sex seldom begins in the sack. It begins with flirting, with feeling turned on, with kissing on the corner or in the car. Then take your pick. What will it be tonight, 'Fast Start' or 'Slow Start'? That all depends on whether you want to take off her panties in one quick move (we'll tell you how) or unbutton his shirt one excruciating button at a time. Do you want to do it standing up against the refrigerator? Or move slowly from room to room? Is tantric sex for you? Is it a night for intense eye – and body – contact and inch-by-inch exploration of her body? Or is this the time to have sex with most of your clothes on, a highly underrated erotic experience that brings back all of the thrill of your first teenage sex sessions. It's up to you, but I recommend you try it all.

Continuing down the list, we have, naturally, 'Going Down'. Read it for positions and his and her oral pleasuring techniques. Next, read about how to give the perfect hand-job and for fingering techniques that will make her see stars.

Some nights the man is in the driver's seat, some nights it's the woman. Flip straight to 'He Drives' and 'She Drives' to see how to take charge tonight. Ladies, are you shy and passive in bed? Tonight is the night to ask for what you want. Whether or not you're on top, you can call the shots. And men, don't confuse sensitive with submissive. When you're in the mood to get in touch with your inner Tarzan, you'll certainly find an obliging Jane for the techniques we offer in 'Thrusting 101'.

In 'Sexy Extras', learn about better ways to get wet with a variety of lubricants, and check out our toy chest: vibrators, dildos, cock rings, pearl thongs and all manner of racy items you can use to make sex even more fun. Have you ever been curious about using props like blindfolds, handcuffs

and scarves? Satisfy your curiosity here. Read about and try role-playing, sex games, fun with food, and then take your sexual picnic outside for a titillating, naughty and natural setting. And then you can discover the many wonders of orgasm, his and hers. Rest assured, you'll be seeing a lot more of these in the very near future. Afterglow, too, has its place in these pages – that time when you are ready to drift off into a peaceful sleep, or even better, to start all over again, but this time more slowly and sensuously.

I've also included information about erotica, including novels, magazines, videos and strip clubs. Don't knock it until you try it. You might even get a few new ideas about how to do it on your own. Just because you're alone, doesn't mean things should be boring or routine. You're worth the extra time and attention. And I wouldn't dream of forgetting 'Bathing and Massage'. You could stop with standards like rubbing the feet, but why would you want to? Learn massage techniques to drive your partner wild with desire. Your bathtub will never look quite the same after it's been the setting for a hot and steamy sexual encounter. Just use common sense, and a non-slip bathmat!

As you read through the following pages, or even if you just look at the sumptuous and sexy photographs of the various sexual positions and illustrated tips, congratulate yourself for empowering yourself sexually. Being shy is simply a waste of your precious time. Sex is as natural, and as necessary, as laughter. So dim the lights. Slip into something more comfortable. And read on. But don't feel any pressure to read this cover to cover. Under the covers would be far more appropriate.

1 temptation

One minute, sex is the furthest thing from your mind. The next, your brain is blissfully in the gutter. All it takes is a single cue— an underwear ad gliding by on the side of a bus, the mischievous smile of an attractive stranger, the aroma of a favorite cologne or perfume, a hand on your thigh—and that visceral ache to touch and be touched takes over. Sights, sounds, smells, flavors, sensations—there's absolutely no limit to what might flip your sexual switch. Although much has been learned about what floats most people's boats, there are no hard-and-fast rules, and no rights or wrongs. Realizing that everyone has his or her own specific turn-ons (that are bound to change over the course of a lifetime) is the first lesson to being a good lover. The only way to know what really excites a new partner is to engage in some playful trial and error—or, if you have the guts, to come right out and ask. But before you start searching for a person's sexual buttons, you need to engage in the flirtation that makes them want to sleep with you in the first place. From intense eye contact to suggestive body language, tempting a member of the opposite sex is an art anyone can master. And contrary to what supposedly went down in the Garden of Eden, giving into a lustful urge with a willing partner is far from sinful—it's heaven on earth.

visceral thrills

Would you believe that a turn-on is an innocent thing? You should. Being excited by the sight of an open mouth, the feel of a breast brushing against your arm (or of an arm brushing against your breast), or the way someone's body moves as they walk down the street is hardly the result of an intelligent decision. Yes, you can choose whether or not to let your eyes linger or savor the sensation, but that sexual jolt hits you whether you like it or not. In a word, it's visceral—a complicated combination of instinct and conditioning. And between the two, it's hard to say which has the greater influence. You can't argue with biology, but there are scores of individual childhood and adult experiences that strongly shape an individual's idea of what is and isn't sexy.

Although practically every man on the planet is attracted to breasts, the degree and nature of that attraction depends on how he's been conditioned. Early exposure to images and experiences that sexualize large-breasted women might cause him to get more excited by a D cup than an A cup. Yet, later in life, after having intimate experiences with small-breasted women or encountering additional conditioning that causes him to think of less curvaceous women as more desirable, his subconscious concept of sexy breasts may change or—more likely—broaden. Similarly, a young woman might be attracted to square jaws, only to find that by her thirtieth birthday she associates superhero chins with a former lover who left her, and now finds them completely unappealing. In sexuality, as in all other aspects of being human, nature and nurture don't battle—they simply merge.

In exploring what gets you fired up, try not to be critical. Your sex drive is like a console with thousands of buttons that you've played only a small part in programming—there are bound to be plenty of clichés as well as some strange and wonderful surprises.

(Above) A long, lithe neck is considered a classically beautiful feature in women. To draw even more attention to the area, spray or dab just a little perfume around your neck.

(Top, left) As for jawlines, strength and confidence—two stereotypically attractive male traits—are highly associated with a square jaw. In the past, comic book superheroes and Hollywood leading men almost always had chiseled chins. But as sensitivity and emotional availability have become more desirable male characteristics, the square jaw isn't as idealized as it used to be.

(Opposite, top left) Is there any question about the appeal of barely there panties? Not only do they make a woman feel sexy, but—when revealed to her special audience—skimpy undies are a real turn-on.

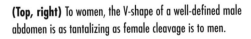

(Top, right) To women, the V-shape of a well-defined male abdomen is as tantalizing as female cleavage is to men.

(Above) Wearing a pair of high, strappy heels is a sign that a woman wants to be seen in an erotic light. The heels change her posture, accentuating her backside, and also make walking difficult—communicating that she is willing to be vulnerable.

(Right) When an attractive person bends over, a few heads usually turn in that direction. It's a moment when the observer is free to check out and admire a shapely backside without risking being seen. Of course, the act of "bending over" is also associated with sex.

(Top) The mouth is a perfect erotic trigger, and biting your lip definitely enhances the come-hither look.

(Right) Dancing is a healthy and sexy way in which people lower their inhibitions and cut loose. A person's actions while dancing might be more forward and suggestive than when standing at the bar. So unless you've already been flirting, don't assume that all the bumping and grinding in public will lead to a racier version of the same in private.

(Bottom) The taste of alcohol on our own or our lover's lips is often perceived as sexy for a very good reason. We drink to relax, have fun, and feel sexy. We drink when we want to party, and possibly hook up.

(Opposite) Some textures are considered sexier than others. When it comes to women's clothing, soft and fuzzy sweaters beg to be felt. So does clothing made of materials such as silk, suede, lace, and leather.

are you flirting with me?

Flirtation always hints at the possibility of a sexual encounter—even if that possibility is so farfetched that neither person imagines it will ever happen. When we flirt, we play with our own and others' desire for sex to make socializing more fun and, occasionally, to have an easier time getting what we want. Many people believe that playful flirtation is harmless, while others view it as misleading and potentially hurtful. We all must decide for ourselves how we want to use the power of attraction in situations in which no real sexual intention exists. But keep in mind that while we can refrain from emphasizing our sexuality, it's always on display via our bodies. An attractive person is likely to discover that any amount of friendliness toward the opposite sex is interpreted as flirtation. There's no controlling another person's attraction to you, or their wishful thinking.

It's when flirtation involves a strong, mutual desire for sexual contact that the fun really starts. Eye contact is probably the single most important element of showing romantic interest. There are very few times in life when we stare a person directly in the eyes for more than a second or two at a time. It's only during moments of intense emotion that we catch a man or woman's gaze and hold it for several beats, before letting our

(Top) The intertwining of legs and touching of hands are signs that both people are attracted and engaged. While hand contact is intimate in a romantic sense, leg contact is more sexually charged, as is a hand placed on the thigh.

(Right) Laughter and smiling are signs of flirtatious approval.

(Opposite) Leaning into your partner creates closeness and emphasizes sexual focus. This woman is making it obvious that her interest is exclusively in the man she's looking at. By closing off his view, she's also communicating that she wants him to focus on her just as intently. And the proximity she's created increases intimacy.

eyes move away. Combined with an inviting smile or sexy smirk and a touch on the hand, leg, or arm, lasting eye contact becomes distinctly flirtatious.

Fidgeting, hair-flipping, hair-twirling, pulling the label off of a beer bottle, tearing a napkin to shreds, stirring a drink again and again…. These are all signs of tension, which is common when we are with a hot member of the opposite sex. When a woman plays with her hair or lifts her chin and tilts it to the side to expose her neck (a sign of vulnerability) she's emphasizing her femininity.

(Opposite) The beginning of a first date opens the door to all sorts of possibilities; experiencing the anticipation is half the fun.

(Top) Moving close to the object of your affection will make it clear whether or not he or she is interested.

A gentle touch to the hand is probably all you'll need to find out.

(Right) It's electrifying to realize that attraction is mutual. You feel a combination of exhilaration and nervousness—it's like being on an amusement park ride.

it's in the kiss

The first few kisses of a romantic encounter are like the opening credits of a movie. They set the tone for everything to come. Lips can touch softly to begin a night of romantic sensuality wherein every move is fully enjoyed. Or they can crash frantically, tongues delving into the other person's mouth. How your partner responds to your kiss tells you instantly whether they're feeling the moment or wanting something different. Being a sensitive kisser who notices when your partner is pushing forward or pulling back will allow you to adapt until you're both kissing with the same intensity and purpose.

(Top) A French kiss will develop its own rhythm. Heads tilt one way and then the other. Tongues move in and out. Hands wander below the neck. You'll begin to anticipate each other's moves and respond accordingly.

(Left) Sometimes it's nice to just wrap your arms around your partner and focus entirely on their mouth—especially when the kiss is the main course of the night, and sex isn't expected. Simultaneous stroking and caressing add electricity.

Perhaps the single most useful lip-locking tip is that when you first kiss someone there should be nothing on your mind other than the feel and taste of their mouth. Even if your hands wander to stroke their cheek or neck, to touch their hair, or travel passionately over their body, concentrate completely on their mouth. Feel the shapes of your lips and tongues and notice how they're coming together and moving apart. Pretend that at that moment your mouth is the center of your body, the very center of the universe. This may sound dramatic, but a great kiss always is.

The obvious erogenous zones are treated to kisses all the time. But a savvy lover knows that the feel of a soft mouth against the skin of any part of the body can be wonderfully erotic. The collarbone, the neck, the spine, the insides of the wrists and knees, the lower back, the inner thighs are sensitive and yield great pleasure. Body kissing is also a wonderful way to surprise someone whom you've had sex with for years. Break the routine by kissing him or her from head to toe.

(Right, top) Don't underestimate the power of a gentle kiss. The feeling of soft lips on her neck is enough to drive almost any woman mad.

(Right) The moment when you both lean in for a kiss can be as exciting as the kiss itself.

(Opposite) Take time to linger during a kiss just to enjoy the feeling of your lips brushing together.

2 fast start

Sometimes the urge to have sex is a spark that slowly builds into a fire—and sometimes it feels as though a lightning bolt has just electrified your crotch. In the latter instance, what you don't want is sex that progresses one careful step at a time. What you're craving is something far wilder and out of control. Gentle kisses and lingering caresses go by the wayside as the drive to grope and thrust takes over. In the passionate rush, shirts are left half-unbuttoned, pants drop around the ankles, and bra straps are left dangling in the wind. This is not to say that hurried and urgent sex isn't emotional or romantic, because it certainly can be. It's just a different kind of romance. As long as both partners are in the same sex-crazed mood, it can provide as deep a sense of connection as a candlelit, soap opera-style sex scene.

The following pages reveal positions and moves that make for fantastic frenzied sex from beginning to end. And, speaking of endings, a fast start doesn't necessarily have to lead to a fast finish. Stopping and starting, slowing down here and there for a moment or two of manual or oral stimulation—can all prolong the ecstasy and add to the overall excitement.

accelerate

If you want sex sooner rather than later, it helps to communicate that fact to your partner in a way that will get him or her as fired up as you are. Both men and women love to feel lusted after, and many get an erotic jolt just from hearing their partner confess that they're horny as hell.

To get things started, whisper in your partner's ear that (1) he or she is incredibly hot, and (2) you want desperately to get him or her naked—or something along those same lines. Some people love a dirty word thrown in for emphasis; others find X-rated talk off-putting and prefer a less graphic come-on. The better you know your partner, the more likely you are to hit all the right notes. Those words, combined with some well-executed touching and some tantalizing visual cues, should quickly create a hot and heavy atmosphere. Watching how your partner responds to your advances will clue you as to whether they're good to go, or need some time to get there. If they pull away or stop your hand, you know they need to be seduced more slowly.

(Top) For him: Don't beat around the bush if you want to get your woman's attention fast.

(Right) For her: A five-fingered grip on your man's package will get the results you're looking for—as will a smooch smack-dab on his zipper.

(Above) Fast sex doesn't have to be aggressive; it can also be fun and lighthearted. Coming on to each other playfully, but still blatantly, can be as effective as a more serious attitude. Guys should try the fireman's carry to start things off with a big bang.

(Left) Just undressing can be enough to set off your partner. Making direct eye contact as you do so will let him or her know that you're not just getting ready for a shower. If you begin touching yourself after stripping, you can expect a sexual ambush within seconds.

easy access

Having sex with your clothes on can feel much naughtier than doing it totally naked. It gives the whole encounter a more spontaneous, more forbidden, more erotic vibe. Nipples peeking out from a bra beg to be kissed and touched. A thigh that flashes into sight before disappearing again under a skirt seems even more desirable for being partly hidden.

We also associate certain clothes with certain activities. Having sex with someone in a suit can be thrilling, because it suggests that you're misbehaving—getting it on when you should be working. Not bothering to bare your entire body adds to the overall charge of fast sex because it's yet another sign that you aren't willing to wait.

(Opposite) One of the best parts of leaving a woman's bra on is the way it pushes her breasts up and together. Pull the cups below the nipples to make them stand at attention.

(Top, right) Leave on a pretty pair of panties to create a tantalizing challenge. Pull them aside and slide the penis in. (It's best to hold the fabric away from the penis to prevent chafing.) You can always stop and take them off at any time.

(Left, top and bottom) Suddenly coming on to your partner in an unusual place will instantly end a sexual rut. Make the most of your surroundings. Caress them in a hallway or gently nudge them back onto a table.

fifth-gear positions

High-octane intercourse can certainly take place in the bedroom, but to maintain a real sense of spontaneity and urgency, it's much more effective to finish right where you start—as long as you aren't breaking the law.

Having sex standing up, with the man entering from behind and the woman bent over a solid piece of furniture, is an ideal position for fast sex, in part because it already has an animalistic feel to it. Although this configuration does make for deep penetration, it doesn't provide much clitoral contact. Using a hand to stimulate her clitoris makes up for the drawback.

(Top, left and right)
For her: In positions like these, your bottom needs to be quite close to the edge of the furniture to allow for full penetration.

(Right) For him: Help support your partner's

weight and aid her balance by holding onto her thighs as you thrust.

(Opposite) For him: You can also rely on a sturdy countertop to help support your partner's weight during these positions.

Against-the-wall sex is more challenging—and more erotic—than it looks. At first, it requires the man to lift his partner's full weight (hands under the thighs, very close to the butt is the best grip), but once in position, the wall acts as a partial support. It usually lasts for only a few breathless thrusts before it becomes too much effort—unless the woman is very petite, or the man is very strong—but every moment is well worth the momentary strain. Totally freestanding sex is also beyond fantastic, but not for the out-of-shape. It just might be the single best reason for a guy to hit the gym.

Having sex standing up is easiest in a narrow hallway. **For her:** Once lifted into position, you can press your feet against the opposite wall to help support your weight. **For him:** Press your body against hers to support her against the wall. Place your hands under her butt to balance her weight.

3 slow start

The best sexual encounters tend to begin with a slow, soft kiss. As that kiss gets deeper, bodies move closer, minds become more focused, and hands start to roam. Even if you've had sex with your partner hundreds of times, you can still feel the incredible thrill of slowly progressing to a climax. The perks aren't just that you're bound to feel each wonderful sensation for a little longer than you would during a quickie—you're also more likely to feel a vaster variety of sensual thrills. By taking your time, you have a chance to pay attention to how you both respond to different touches, kisses and licks, positions, thrusts, and pressures. You have more opportunities to try new things, make small adjustments, and build toward a state of heightened arousal that rocks both of you from head to toe. And, during slow sex, you're more likely to look each other in the eyes, to communicate what you want, and to tap into more profound emotions. A lengthy sexual encounter is like a gourmet meal. It's not just about satisfying your hunger; it's about enjoying every single, delicious mouthful.

sexy beginnings

When you're in the mood to savor sex, start with soft kisses and caresses, letting your lips and hands glide at first, then slowly add more pressure. These first small moves set a precedent for your partner to follow—they let him or her know that you're in the mood to let every sensation linger.

Starting in first gear doesn't mean you have to kick off the night with a mouth-to-mouth kiss. It isn't *where* you direct your attention first that sets the mood for leisurely loving, it's *how*. You can start below the waist and still inspire long, romantic sex with soft kisses, light touches, and gentle licks. And, the more time spent caressing each other over your clothes, the more you'll both anticipate the fabulous sensation of skin against skin.

(Opposite) Feel her nipples become erect one at a time, as your fingertips circle each one over her shirt.

(Above) Romantic, frilly clothing can inspire a slower-paced response from a man than something tight and naughty.

(Right, top) For him: Treat a woman to the most classic romantic move—sweep her off of her feet and carry her to bed.

(Right, bottom) A little kiss on her panties can provide a provocative preview of things to come later on.

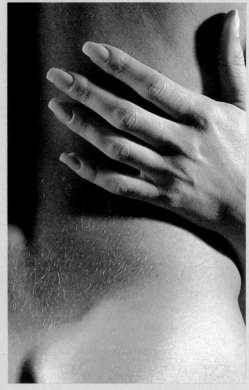

savor every spot

Peel off your partner's clothing piece by piece. Notice each freckle and curve as it's uncovered, then kiss or stroke it.

When one person is still partially dressed and the other is naked, the results can be extremely racy. Keep all or a few pieces of clothing on after stripping your partner to let them know that, for the moment, their bare erogenous zones are the sole focus of your attention.

Pay attention to those seldom-appreciated areas—a man's nipples, for example. The surprise of feeling fingertips, lips, or a tongue in these sensitive areas will shoot tiny shivers of pleasure up your partner's spine. Be sure to use more pressure in typically ticklish places to keep the touch, kiss, or lick sensual as opposed to silly.

intense connection

In a long-term relationship it's easy to fall into an eyes-closed routine in which first this happens, and then that....You stop talking, or really looking at one another, and just get physical. At that point, sex is about as intimate as a wrestling match—and that can be unsatisfying and boring, because you feel that you're just going through the motions. Prevent this from happening by taking a minute to be still, looking your partner in the eyes, kissing them carefully, stroking their hair and complimenting them, or telling them how you feel. When you begin to touch each other again, things will feel different, better, more intense, and fulfilling.

(Top) For him: Take control of the action while still being gentle by cradling her head in your hands.

(Right) For her: To intensify this position, wrap your arms and legs around your partner's body and pull him closer to you for deep penetration. Match the rhythm of each thrust so that your bodies move together.

(Opposite, top) Holding hands during sex is surprisingly intimate and loving.

(Opposite, bottom right) Grasping your partner's hands is also a romantic way for you to provide added support and balance when he or she is moving up and down on top of you.

This move is guaranteed to take a woman's breath away. Encourage her to straddle you on the edge of the bed and give her neck and breasts plenty of loving attention as she moves on top of you.

When you're ready, lift her by placing your hands under her thighs, slowly turn her around, and lay her back on the bed. If you can handle multitasking, try kissing her continually as you do it.

tantric tricks

Feeling more connected to your partner doesn't always require touchy-feely conversation. Try slowing down and increasing eye contact instead. Inspired by tantric sex (which has a significant spiritual component), these simple techniques can help raise the intimacy factor of your sex life.

(Opposite) One night, have sex while maintaining eye contact. You'll be surprised how close you will feel to your partner, and how much can be communicated by eye contact alone. If you have a hard time keeping your eyes open during sex or making direct eye contact, this extreme exercise can help you conquer that phobia in a single night.

(Top) If sex often feels like a race to orgasm, consider taking a long time-out to catch your breath, reconnect, and relax. Lie back and let your level of arousal fall considerably. Talk a little. Massage each other's neck, shoulders, back, or feet. After fifteen or more minutes, slowly start becoming sexual again. Everything will feel even better the second time around.

(Right) Sit comfortably and breathe into your partner's mouth for a few deep breaths. Feel the energy of their breath.

4 going down

An anytime treat, oral sex can be the high point of foreplay, the main event of the night, or a *bonne bouche* that you and your partner return to over and over again during a long and luxurious sexual encounter. Warm, wet, and intimate, oral sex can be just as fun and satisfying as full-on intercourse. As a matter of fact, some men and women prefer oral sex to all other forms of fooling around. Lying back and having someone go down on you is the ultimate in sexual pampering. You're literally allowing yourself to be consumed. And being the consumer is equally enthralling. There's something about feasting your eyes and mouth on your lover's genitals that can make you drunk with the eroticism of it all. But, in spite of the fact that the sensation of a tongue on the vagina or penis is usually enough to make any person frantic with pleasure, performing skilled oral sex isn't as simple as one might think. Men often complain that women aren't careful enough with their teeth, don't realize that they need to incorporate variety, or don't know to move in a steady, consistent rhythm. And women complain that men don't lick in the right places or for anywhere near as long as it takes to make them come. This chapter aims to teach all of the basics of fantastic oral sex—from how to lick and suck in all the right ways, to where to put your fingers and hands while doing it—plus a few extra special techniques that will make you a bona fide guru of going down.

clitoral kissing

There are many sexy ways to head south with your mouth. One is kissing a slow path from her knee up to her inner thigh, or from her navel down to her clitoris. If you have any doubt that a woman wants you to go down on her, this is a great technique—it will give her time to intervene. It's also a nice way to tease her into wanting more oral sex. To that end, you can kiss from one knee, up the thigh, directly on the labia and clitoris, and then continue to kiss down the inside of the other thigh. Several small kisses and flicks of the tongue directly around the clitoris will have her begging for you to hit the spot. Another approach is to immediately, and with no hesitation or other contact with the vagina, treat the clitoris to a long, wet, firm lick, or a few short flicks with the tip of your tongue. Whether you're starting slow or jumping right in, remember that the more you enjoy giving oral sex, the more likely your partner will love getting it.

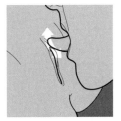 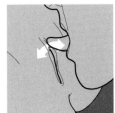   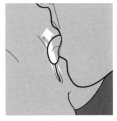

Tonguing Techniques: Use the tip of your tongue to flick the clitoris in an up and down and/or side-to-side motion. Try it slowly, and then quickly, and even more quickly. The flick can be light or firm. Some women may be able to come from this kind of contact; others may find it too intense or even ticklish.

The figure 8 is a fabulous technique for covering the entire surface of the clitoris. Some men also report excellent results from drawing the letters of the alphabet with their tongue.

Circle the clitoris with the tip of your tongue. Try doing it lightly, and then with increased pressure.

When a woman's clitoris is very sensitive, she'll prefer the kind of wide licks you would use when eating an ice cream cone.

(Opposite) A woman's inner thighs are very sensitive. Starting your journey to the clitoris by kissing them will not only give her intense pleasure, but will also build her anticipation for the thrills to come.

(Above) Requesting that your partner hold her legs up and out of the way allows you better access to the vagina. If you want to be able to hear whether or not she's moaning with pleasure or asking for something different, it also helps to not have her thighs sandwiching your ears.

(Top and left) To earn an ovation, go down on your partner while she stands on a chair. She'll feel in control—it gives her a lot of freedom to move and respond—and pampered at the same time. In addition you'll have a fantastic viewpoint and full access.

(Opposite) Nothing impresses a woman like the ability to finger her during cunnilingus. The best way to do this is to steadily lick the clitoris while very slowly sliding one or two fingers in and out of the vagina (so that your palm is facing up). As she gets more excited, try maintaining a steady, gentle, pulsing pressure on the front (pubic hair side) inside wall of the vagina, which is where the g-spot is believed to be.

Another technique that helps some women reach orgasm is to lick the clitoris while simultaneously rubbing the area just above it. Few people realize that the clitoris includes a 9-centimeter shaft and a two wishbone-shaped arms that extend down the labia majora.

the blow job

The best blow jobs are given by women who love giving blow jobs. It's a huge turn-on for a man to know that the woman sucking on his penis is enjoying the experience (almost) as much as he is. In spite of the name, there is no "blowing" involved (unless you feel like blowing on his penis just for fun). There should also be no teeth involved—when giving a blow job, always cover them with your lips. The main movement of fellatio consists of sliding your mouth up and down on the head and shaft of the penis, letting your saliva provide the moisture necessary to do this smoothly. Besides the mouth, carefully placed hands also enhance the experience. Like the clitoris, a man's penis responds to different types of contact at different times on different days. Sometimes, fast and hard will turn him on the most; sometimes, he'll prefer slow and soft.

On the outer side of the penis just below the head and in the center is the frenulum—the most nerve-packed spot on the shaft. Licking and rubbing this sensitive area will send shivers up your partner's spine.

You can bring a man to orgasm simply by sliding the head of his penis and an inch or so of the shaft in and out of your mouth. There's no need to take in any more than what is comfortable for you.

With just the head of the penis held loosely between your lips, tilt your head first to one side and then the other so that your mouth massages the penis with either a quick or slow circular stroke.

What's the best position for giving a blow job? Any one that works! **(Top and bottom, left; and top right)** Whether you're facing your lover's feet or his head, there are lots of simple things you can do to intensify the fantastic feeling of fellatio. Caress his balls, play with his pubic hair, or stroke his thighs. You can also enhance the pleasure by pressing on his prostate gland, which is about an inch inside his body, directly up from the area just behind his testicles. To do this, place the pads of your fingers (no sharp nails!) just behind his testicles and apply gentle pressure. Let him know what you're trying to do and ask what feels good.

(Opposite) Kneeling in front of your partner is a classic position for giving a blow job.

Men love it when a woman plays with their penis as though it's her favorite toy. Anytime during a blow job, you can take a few seconds to lick or suck it, hold and squeeze it, bat it from side to side, rub your face against it, or use your hand to slap it gently against your tongue. Of course, too much of this kind of play will get silly, but it's fun to mix it up. Another option is to slide a saliva-moistened penis over or between your breasts. By pushing your breasts together, you can create a fleshy groove for his penis to slide up and down in. And don't over-look the foreskin. This highly erogenous tissue responds to many different kinds of stimulation. Slide your tongue underneath it, or suck it into your mouth and gently nibble. As always, you can tell from his reactions what works.

Testicles, as every man knows, are sensitive to both touch and temperature, so having a hot and wet tongue slide over them is extremely pleasurable. For the ultimate lick, a woman should start at the bottom or even behind the testicles, and keep lick-ing upward until she gets to the tip of the penis, at which point she can slide it into her mouth.

To increase the intensity of a blow job at any time, a woman can wrap her domi-nant hand around the shaft of the penis and move it up and down. With the other hand, she can cup the testicles gently but firmly. When a man approaches orgasm, his testicles pull up close to his body. By simu-lating this motion, you bring him closer to the brink. Remember to be gentle.

(Above) This blow job technique isn't for beginners. Lie on your back and have your partner kneel above you so that his penis can slide into your mouth. Placing a pillow under your head will improve the angle. It's impor-tant in this position to grasp the bottom of the shaft of the penis with your hand so that you can control how deeply you take the penis into your mouth at all times. You can hold your head still on the pillow and let him thrust or, if you have the neck strength, you can provide the motion. Use your free hand to grasp his butt, or stroke his testicles and the area just behind them. If he likes attention to his anus, you can slide a hand between his legs and circle it with your finger.

(Opposite) Lying on your side with your head on a pillow as your partner lies on his side next to you makes for an absolutely effortless oral sex experience. For the ultimate in laziness, have him thrust his hips back and forth to move his penis in and out of your open mouth.

69

Going down on each other at the same time results in an incredible number of different sensations pulsing through your body at once. It's easy to lose track of what your partner is doing to you or what you're doing to your partner as your attention flits from what's in front of your face to what's happening between your legs. The best 69 is a little wild and sloppy, with lots of moments when you or your partner take a break just to enjoy what the other is doing or to let them know how you feel. A simultaneous orgasm during 69 is a little like a yeti sighting—there are reports of it, but few people have come across one themselves. The reason is that, because you're preoccupied with your own performance, it's difficult to completely let go and enjoy what's being done to you. Men also find it difficult to hold back an orgasm while having such a glorious thing pressed against their mouth at the same time their penis is being sucked. Don't worry: she won't hold it against you.

(Top, left) If you and your partner are close in height, Sideways 69 is a real treat. Rest your head on the inside of your partner's thigh so you can lick and suck comfortably. The likelihood of simultaneous orgasm is highest in this variation of the 69 position, because it allows you to relax and let go much more easily. **For her:** Tilting your head back slightly and guiding the shaft of the penis with a firm hand will help you take more of your partner's penis into your mouth.

(Above) Sitting 69 isn't as hard as it might look. Any woman who's taken a yoga class or two will probably be able to pull it off. If you're a couple who loves to try challenging moves, this is the position for you.

For her: Stand so that your legs are on either side of your seated partner's thighs. Then bend all the way forward, bending your knees, if necessary. **For him:** It's important for you to grasp your partner's waist to help her keep her balance and stop her from rolling forward off the couch and onto the floor, or falling backward onto your face—unless you'd like that, of course.

(Opposite) Having your partner on top during oral sex can be very exciting. Try to switch who is on top and explore the different angles of each position. Having the person who is on top rest their weight on their knees and shoulders will make the position more comfortable, too.

The granddaddy of all oral sex positions is—drumroll, please—standing, upside-down cunnilingus. A man needs to be strong to flip a woman upside down so her legs are on either side of his head. He can then bend his head forward and go down on her. Clearly, this move is for advanced lovers. Only the strongest men will be able to maintain this position for long, but even just a minute of upside down oral sex will *really* impress a woman

For her: When your partner is lifting you, help him by swinging your legs to the side and keeping your abdominal muscles contracted. Grasp his thighs to help feel more secure.

For him: The trick to flipping your partner into this position is to bend at the knees, your left hand on her right hip and your right hand on her left hip. Then, in one motion, lift and twirl her body around.

5 hands on

Like kissing, using your hands is one of the crucial skills of getting it on. Great lovers know how, when, and where to touch, and seldom have idle hands—unless they happen to be tied to the bedposts. From the moment you start making out, you should already be grasping your partner's hips, stroking their arm, back or thigh, or sliding your fingers around to the nape of their neck. From caressing to grabbing to scratching, there are countless ways that you can increase the pleasure of any given moment by getting your hands involved. In addition to using your digits to enhance every aspect of doing the deed, bringing your partner to orgasm via manual stimulation is a highly underrated experience. Most couples who quickly move from making out to oral sex or intercourse forget how fun a fantastic hand-job or thorough clitoral rubdown can be. Manual stimulation allows you to lean back and closely watch his or her reactions—which can clue you in to the kind of stimulation he or she needs to climax during oral sex and intercourse. And then there are all those handy tricks that get your partner in the mood in the first place—like sneaking lusty feels over and under clothes. The thrill of being felt up never fades, no matter how old you get. Nothing teaches like experience, but the next few pages are filled with tips and techniques that will help you become more skillful in the sack.

joy stick

When you want to get your mitts on your man's penis, there's no reason to be shy about it. Bring his member to attention by rubbing it deliberately through his pants or by working your hands down the front of his jeans, wrapping your fingers around it, and beginning to stroke—do it softly, so that you're not pulling at the skin. While you can be playful and gently squeeze his penis or even wag it from side to side, you should never be overly rough or rub it too quickly or too tightly without adequate lubrication. This is especially true for circumcised men. An intact man will have tissue (the foreskin) that you can slide up and down using his own natural lubrication. Some men don't like a woman to touch their penis until it is already hard, but this is not usually the case. Most men enjoy it when a woman is eager to help it reach its full potential.

For couples who love public displays of affection, the hand-job is one of the few sexual acts you can pull off on the sly. A little under-the-table groping can be a lot of fun, as long as the waiter doesn't notice. It's a great way to get hot before taking the action some place more private. If you take it all the way, have a napkin close by for quick clean up.

Make a ring with your thumb and index finger and slide it up and down over the head and the very top of the shaft—these are the most sensitive parts of the penis.

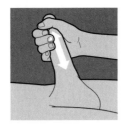

Wrap your entire hand around the penis for a fuller, slightly less intense, yet equally enjoyable, sensation.

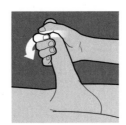

This twisting motion can be very erotic as long as it's done with a lighter grasp to avoiding pulling the skin.

Many men enjoy having their prostate gland stimulated during a hand-job. Locate the area of skin directly behind his testicles and push upward with the pads of your fingers.

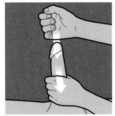

Stimulate the penis from top to bottom with both fists descending one after the other, so that instead of an up-and-down motion, there is a continual downward stroke.

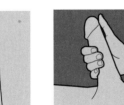

Tugging gently on the skin between the testicles can give a hand-job some extra oomph. When trying new moves like these, be sure to ask your partner.

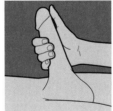

The frenulum, located at the center of the underside of the head of the penis, is loaded with nerves. Make sure that it gets plenty of stimulation with every stroke by holding your hand so that the length of your thumb rubs against it.

Create a ring around the base of the penis with the thumb and index finger of one hand. Hold it there, squeezing gently, while stroking the rest of the penis with the other hand. This helps to engorge the penis.

(Opposite) Sliding your hand down to your partner's crotch during sex is romantic and oh so stimulating.

(Top, right) It's easy to sneak in a hand-job while having sex in almost any position.

Give your guy the kind of attention you would want him to give you. Caress his penis carefully, not absentmindedly. Pay attention to how he's responding—give him more of what makes him breath faster, moan, or sigh. If your guy is circumcised, use a slow, light, up-and-down stroke when his penis isn't lubricated. You can also just trail your fingers up the length of the shaft, and over and around the head. With lubrication, you can grasp the shaft more firmly and slide your hand with a smooth up-and-down stroke. If he is intact, then you have some other options. Feel free to gently tug on his foreskin (it feels good!) or to grasp him firmly, moving the skin up and down over the penis. This kind of play can change depending on how erect he is. When he grows fully erect, slide the thin and delicate foreskin back and forth over the hardened shaft, for a delightful contrast in sensation.

slippery fingers

Manual stimulation is incredibly important for women. To have an orgasm, most need a little more clitoral contact than intercourse generally provides. During sex, reach down and rub your partner's clitoris whenever possible, and you're guaranteed to increase her chances of having an orgasm. For some women, manual stimulation is the only way they can come. Rubbing the vagina the right way isn't something a guy just knows how to do. It's something he has to learn. If a woman's vagina isn't yet lubricated, handle the labia and clitoris *very* gently to avoid hurting her. And never try to insert a finger into a dry vagina. To stimulate the clitoris when the vagina is dry, exert gentle downward pressure on it and the surrounding area with the pads of one, or two, or three fingers, and then move it from side to side or around in a circle. This non-abrasive stimulation will likely help her to become more aroused and wetter, at which point you can spread that wetness from her vagina over her labia and clitoris. Some women love it when men begin stroking their vagina very early in a sexual encounter. Other women prefer that their partner focus on kissing and giving their breasts plenty of attention before going farther south.

(Above, right) For him: Having your hand under her skirt is as exciting for her as it is for you. Stroke her clitoris through her panties to build the anticipation of feeling your fingers against her wet skin.

(Right) For him: Even if you've seen your girlfriend or wife naked a thousand times, don't rush to take off her panties every time. Take the action to the next level by sliding your hand under her panties.

There's more to the clitoris than meets the eye, so don't just rub the nub.

Stimulate the clitoris and surrounding area with the pads of all four fingers. Apply light to firm pressure using an up-and-down motion.

Slow circles provide a wonderful sensation and can be very helpful in bringing her to orgasm. Vary pressure and speed, depending on what your partner likes best.

When fingering a woman, insert your fingers so that your palm faces up. The natural curve of your fingers will stimulate the sensitive front (pubic hair side) inside wall of the vagina.

Finger your partner and stimulate her clitoris single-handedly by using the thumb, as pictured. To drive her wild, use the other hand to rub her pubic mound.

(Left) Like receiving oral sex from behind, being fingered from behind is a thrilling twist. Bend your partner over the table or the couch and massage her bottom while you stimulate her clitoris and vagina.

(Opposite) For him: Experiment with how you stimulate your lover's clitoris. She'll let you know what works.

The vagina can seem complicated if you've never gotten up close and examined what you're working with. To get to know it well and learn how best to please your partner, situate yourself between her widely spread legs to get a good view, and then rub her clitoris (and the very sensitive area around it) in different ways. Watch what she responds to best. Notice the prepuce, or clitoral hood—the flap of skin that sometimes covers the clitoris. This is similar to the male foreskin. You can pull it back to expose the clitoris completely. Some women will prefer that their clitoris be rubbed from over the hood, others will want more direct contact, and still others would rather you rub the area directly above the clitoris than the clitoris itself. Asking your partner what she likes is the only way to know for sure.

To finger your partner and stimulate her clitoris with two hands, use the thumb of the opposite hand, as shown.

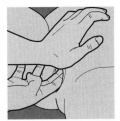

Some women like very intense pressure on the entire area around their clitoris. The best way to give them exactly what they want is to use the heel of your hand.

6 she drives

Woman on top? Yes, please. More women in more cultures are reveling in their sexuality than ever before. Shaking off the good girl/bad girl dichotomy, members of the fairer sex are embracing the reality that they can be shy and submissive one night, and brazen and unbridled the next—or change from moment to moment. And rather than respond to a man's desire for them to be one way or the other, women are making the decision based on their own mood, the nature and setting of the encounter, or on nothing more than a whim. Women are also becoming increasingly comfortable initiating sex, asking for what they want, and controlling the action. All of this is very good news for men—it's those wonderful women who have the courage to fully express themselves sexually who are the most skilled, creative, and exciting lovers. This chapter illustrates how a woman can get behind the wheel in bed and steer the action in ways that heighten both her own pleasure and that of her partner. From positions that let her dominate, to bold hand and mouth techniques, the moves featured on the following pages will help her show off her skills and unleash her passion.

ladies night

If you want to take the lead, use signals that send that message loud and clear. Wearing lingerie that's more fit for a courtesan than a coquette—think black stockings, tiny panties, and a push-up bra—will make it obvious that you're not in a subtle or submissive mood. Of course, the sight of you in black lace is also likely to make your partner pounce immediately, so come right out and tell him that you want him to lay back and let you have your way. He isn't likely to argue.

For him: Encourage your partner to be more forward, by asking her to get on top during sex and telling her how much you love it when she's in control. When touching her, ask if she wants it faster, slower, softer, or harder. Many women put their partner's needs first, almost without thinking. Let her know that doing what she wants is just as enjoyable for you as it is for her.

(Left) For her: Don't be afraid to use slightly aggressive or playful moves like beckoning him with your finger to "come here," slapping his butt, pushing him down onto the bed, or presenting your nipples to his mouth to be kissed and sucked.

(Opposite, top left) For her: Press your man's hands up over his head against the wall or bed to make him feel dominated—a feeling men are surprised to discover how much they enjoy.

(Opposite, right and far right) Have fun being the boss. Decide whether you want to fully or partially undress your man; whether you'd prefer to keep on your lingerie (pushing the fabric aside to allow access where and when you want to) or peel it off slowly; whether you crave long extended foreplay or would rather plunge his member inside of you immediately. You should try everything. Change your mind. Indulge your desires.

lips, teeth, and fingertips

Ladies, there's no end to the list of devilishly delicious things you can do with your mouth, teeth, tongue, and hands. Nibble and suck on a man's ears, neck, nipples, lips, fingers, and penis. Grab his butt cheeks and squeeze or spank them. Run your nails gently up and down his back. Kiss him from head to toe. When his testicles are within reach, cup or stroke them softly. Most men find it extremely pleasurable to have the sensitive skin between their testicles and anus stroked (some men like to have their anus stimulated gently, while others enjoy penetration—always ask before forging ahead). And you shouldn't hesitate to touch yourself. It's pleasurable for you, and men find it intensely erotic. Caress your breasts, pinch your nipples, rub your clitoris, slide a finger into your vagina or anus, or do whatever else feels good at the moment.

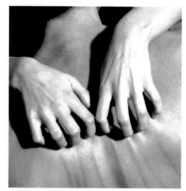

(Above) You don't want to cause pain or leave marks, but scratching a man's back during sex can be incredibly sexy. Trail your nails from the top of his bottom all the way up to his shoulders in one long, shiver-inducing scratch.

(Top, far left) A man's butt is very sensitive and responds well to stimulation. During sex, squeezing his butt cheeks apart can increase the intensity of the thrust and show him you aren't afraid to get a little rough.

(Top, right) Sucking a guy's fingers is a great way to tease him before a blow job.

But finger sucking also feels exhilarating in its own right. Fingers are extremely sensitive and the sensation of having them inside someone's mouth delivers a warm, soft thrill.

(Above, right) Nibble your lover's nipples or take one between your teeth for a very gentle bite. Men's nipples aren't as sensitive as women's but they still get erect when licked, kissed, and bit.

(Opposite) The openmouthed kiss feels far sexier than the close-lipped peck. Let him enjoy the feeling of your hot breath and wet tongue against his skin.

cowgirl

There's more to the Cowgirl position than a woman simply sitting upright and grinding her hips back and forth or raising and lowering her body straight up and down on a man's penis. By leaning forward or backward she can change the angle of his penis inside her body and feel it exerting pressure in different spots inside her vagina. Leaning back will bring the head of his penis in closer contact with the g-spot, which can trigger an amazing orgasm.

(Top) By leaning back in the Cowgirl position, a woman allows her partner access to her clitoris.

(Right) Of course, she can also attend to her own clitoris in this position.

(Opposite) For him: Give her breasts plenty of attention by massaging them with your hands or kissing and sucking her nipples.

(Above) For her: To begin, straddle your partner facing his head, lowering yourself onto his penis. Once there, you may choose to sit and enjoy the feeling of him filling you. When ready, place your feet flat on the surface of the bed or whatever you are on, and move into a squatting position, for a greater range of motion. If your quadriceps muscles and knees can handle the stretch, leaning back can be surprisingly comfortable and romantic. Movements in this position are small, but the man can thrust upward to penetrate deeper. The woman's hands are free to stimulate her clitoris. Ride your partner, keeping your body fairly upright to make sure that you're not bending the penis in an uncomfortable way. Move up and down, with an occasional side-to-side wiggle. Squatting also allows for a greater range of up and down motion. Slow, steady strokes are better than fast, as it's possible for the penis to slide out and slam into the pubic bone by accident, which can be quite painful. Try rotating your hips in a small circle or moving very slowly from side to side as you raise and lower yourself onto your partner. Press your hands against your partner's chest to help shift your weight forward. This frees your hips, letting you move in a way that pleases you and enhances your pleasure.

For him: When she's on top, follow her lead. When she moves down on you firmly to achieve deeper penetration, thrust up slightly. When she's moving quickly or erratically, stay still and let her have her way with you.

(Opposite) The Cowgirl is the classic woman-on-top position. Not only does having sex in this position put her in charge, but it also allows for a different kind of intimacy.

rear view

The female bottom is a work of art that many men love to watch moving gracefully—or gyrating wildly—during sex. The following positions also provide an eye-opening view of the penis sliding into the vagina, as well as deep, intense penetration.

(Above) For her: Lean far back to make your clitoris a focal point for pleasure either by stimulating yourself, or asking him to do the honors.

For him: Stimulate the clitoris directly with the pads of your fingers or your thumb. Use a side-to-side motion and light to firm pressure. Caress her breasts and legs, brush your fingers through her pubic hair, and give her clitoris gentle attention. If she leans forward, you can sit up and kiss her spine and caress her buttocks, maybe even give her a small massage. To help her balance, place your hands on her hips, or slide them under her buttocks and help lift her up and down.

(Opposite) By sitting up straight you not only vary penetration, you can give your partner a stimulating view and caress his testicles.

(Above) Great balance allows a woman to squat completely upright in backward Cowgirl, which is particularly erotic for her audience of one. In addition to feeling fully empowered, she's getting a great workout.

(Right) For her: Resting your hands on your partner's legs allows you to use one hand to rub your clitoris or stroke or cup your partner's testicles.

(Opposite) For her: Try this position to give your partner a pleasant surprise. When you've been straddling him, facing his feet, lean all the way back, supporting yourself with your arms in a "crabwalk" position, then move your hips up and down, using your legs to help you thrust. He'll love watching your bottom in action and—if it's long—feeling your hair tickle his chest. In this position, the penis rubs against the front wall of the vagina in a way that can be very stimulating.

For him: In this position, a hand or two under her bottom can help give a woman support, balance, and more thrusting power.

lap dance

Full frontal seduction can make a woman feel incredibly sexy and in control. These positions are also fantastic for inducing orgasms, because they give a woman a chance to dictate how and when she wants to change positions, and to grind as quickly or slowly as she needs to come.

Climb on top of your partner as he sits in a chair. Let your legs fall comfortably on either side of his body and grab the back of the chair, using it to rock your body back and forth. Confidence is crucial. Don't second-guess what you want to do, just do it. And don't hold back when it comes time to grind with gusto. If your clitoris requires a lot of friction to get off, then go ahead and move at the speed of light. Your partner will be thrilled to see you getting into it and letting go. Sit in a way that allows for the deepest penetration and then alternate tucking your butt forward and then thrusting it back to create friction between your clitoris and his abdomen, and simultaneously move his penis inside your vagina.

(Far left) Any time you stand to change position, give him a full, close-up view of your breasts. Press them together, push your nipples into his mouth, or invite him to move his face between them—something many men love to do but might feel a little shy about requesting.

For him: Encourage her to put on a show with her breasts by telling her how beautiful they are and how much you love watching them move, and feeling them against your body.

(Left, top and bottom)
For her: Stand in front of your seated partner, facing the same direction, and bend your legs to lower yourself onto his penis. Place your hands on his thighs for balance and support, then raise and lower yourself onto his penis. Lean back against your partner to change the angle of penetration and to give your quads a break. You can continue to raise and lower yourself to create short strokes that provide for deep penetration.

For him: Reach around to caress your partner's breasts or just hold tightly onto her hips.

the rock

Luxurious and intense, this sitting position gives both partners full, exciting views of each other's bodies as well as of the action happening between their legs. Arranging herself in his lap as though doing the crab-walk, the woman rocks back and forth, allowing his penis to slide in and out of her vagina. Quickening the pace can take this position from calm to climactic. At any point during sex, the couple can lean forward to engage in deep, passionate kissing. With weight distributed between her arms and legs, the back-and-forth swinging movement of her hips is surprisingly easy—even for women without particularly strong arms.

For him: Use your arms to help support your partner's weight as she leans backward and eases into the thrusting motion. By leaning backward yourself to different degrees, you can change the angle of penetration and have a better chance of stimulating her g-spot.

For her: As you reach climax, wrap your legs around his waist and your arms around his shoulders, grinding your pelvis against his, or bounce gently up and down. Sitting still and hugging in this position is wonderful after climax or during breaks in the action.

the slide

Women who appreciate a lot of clitoral stimulation will love the Slide. It's like a naughty amusement park ride.

For her: Straddle your partner with your feet flat on the bed, holding onto his shoulders for balance. By pushing with your legs and pulling yourself forward with your arms, you can move up and down on your partner's body. The angle of your partner's abdomen in this position gives you the ultimate in clitoral friction. Try long, slow movements, and then shorter, quicker thrusts.

For him: Sit back on your heels, supporting your weight with your arms extended behind you. Thrust your hips upward to meet her downward stroke, or just provide a strong, steady surface for her to move on.

the wraparound

To create a romantic, passionate mood during sex, a woman can straddle her partner as he sits upright, and wrap her legs around his back and her arms around his shoulders.

(Above and right) The Wraparound is the perfect position for a deep, long, intense kiss, enhanced by sporadic attention to each other's necks and earlobes.

For him: Wrap your arms around her torso and pull her against you.

For her: Make small back-and-forth movements with your hips, or simply enjoy the sensation of his penis inside you and the closeness of your bodies.

the ramp

This is the closest sex can get to hanging out in a lounge chair.

The Ramp is the perfect position for morning sex, when you're both a little sleepy and just want to relax— yet enjoy an intimate sexual experience.

(Left) After climbing astride your partner, lean back against his bent knees. Push your self up with your legs in small, short movements. Rub your clitoris with one or both hands. If and when you want more friction, lean forward and grind with more force.

(Below) For her: Flip over for an extremely hot angle change.

the cobra

Lying flat on top of one another with legs extended, this position allows for delicious, full-body contact. Deep kissing and eye-gazing make the Cobra an extremely intimate position.

For her: Enter this position by straddling your partner, sliding his penis inside of you, and then lying forward and swinging your legs back and together. To create friction, slide your entire body back and forth, contracting the muscles of your vagina to increase sensation. If you and your partner are the same height, you can easily hold his hands back over his head. This will give you a greater sense of dominance and him the permission to lie back and do nothing but enjoy the sensation. Raising your torso with your arms gives your partner a gorgeous view of your breasts and helps you to move more freely. You may find that you can easily reach orgasm is easily reached in this position, because the clitoris rubs against the abdomen, and the penis may hit your g-spot.

under control

A woman doesn't need to be on top to direct the speed, intensity, or direction of a sexual encounter. By moving her hips and body and allowing the man to follow her cues, she can direct just as well from below. While moving beneath a man, a woman can experiment with being aggressive. She should move with strength and confidence, thrusting with as much force as would a man. If she falls into a steady rhythm, he can anticipate her movements and both can build to an exciting climax.

(Opposite) You can use thrusting or rotating hip action to control penetration in any position in which your partner is entering you from behind, including standing and kneeling.

(Top) For her: Hold onto his shoulders and use them to help slide your body back and forth beneath him. **For him:** Exert a little pressure on your partner, but not so much that she can't move. Stay still in this position to help her achieve orgasm more easily.

(Above) For her: Lie on your stomach while he enters you from behind and supports the weight of his torso with his arms. Slide your hands between your legs and over your clitoris while thrusting your hips up and down.

For him: When your partner is moving her hips underneath you, try to take your weight off her lower body, allowing her more freedom to move. It will allow you both to maintain deep and controlled thrusting.

7 he drives

The idea that men are perfectly happy doing it the same way every time is, and always has been, completely false. (Who started that rumor anyway?) Men want and need variety, and being on top is one great way to get it. When a guy is in the lead, a woman will look to him to direct the speed and pressure of the action, giving him the power to make sex as dynamic and erotic as he wants it to be. Obviously, the more a man knows and does, the more exciting his sex life will be. Even guys who have been doing it for decades and whose repetoires include a long list of fine-tuned moves, can rest assured that there are always new positions and tricks to try. And new tricks lead to bigger, better orgasms. A major component of an explosive climax is opening your mouth—to ask for exactly what you want. Men who don't make direct requests in bed are doing themselves and their partners a disservice. When a woman is happily rolling around in bed with you, she's more than eager to please, but she can't read your mind. A few clear directions will make her better able to fulfill your every fantasy.

man power

As empowered as women are, many prefer a man to do the seducing, especially early in a relationship. From making her feel sexy and pampered to getting her clothes off gracefully, the more slick moves a guy has up his sleeve, the better. From the first kiss, a woman can tell whether he's confident in the sack. So men, don't hesitate. Be forward and precise. Let her know from the start that you know exactly what you're doing.

There are plenty of hot moves you can make that will send sexy shivers up her spine. Take her in your arms, dance with her for a few steps (music not required), and then dip her gently, planting a kiss on her chest or neck. Or lift her off of her feet as you kiss her. Both will make her feel sexy because you're letting her know that you can move her entire body, and do it well.

Unless you're both in the mood for a quickie, a woman will assume that a man is skilled in bed if he starts slowly and takes time to build anticipation. Run your hands up her torso and caress her breasts outside of her clothes to steadily raise her level of excitement. Pinch her nipples through her shirt. And when you kiss her, do it softly at first and then up the intensity by using your tongue and lavishing her neck with kisses.

(Top, left and right) When you play the role of a take-charge man, don't be hesitant. Place your hand (gently) on her breast, lavish her chest with kisses. In short, sweep her off her feet—figuratively, anyway.

(Left) Unclasping a woman's bra with one hand is easy. Most bras have a hook-and-eye closure in the back. When you push them toward one another, the hook comes loose. Use your thumb and forefinger for the most control. If your first attempt isn't successful, use both hands to get it done quickly, rather than continuing to fumble. If she's wearing a front-closing bra or an over-the-head bra, just ask her to "take this thing off" so you can see her beautiful breasts.

(Opposite, top to bottom) You can pull a woman's panties off with one or both hands with this incredibly hot and very impressive move. While you're both lying down side by side, reach your hand between your partner's legs and grasp the back center of her panties and pull them down her legs and off of her feet in one fluid motion.

the classic

The most popular man-on-top position is the Classic, aka the missionary position, in which the man's legs are extended out between his partner's and some of his weight is pressing down on her chest. Many women find the sensation of their lover's body on top of them highly erotic—as long as he's not so heavy that she feels squashed. Large men should always distribute some of their weight by propping themselves on their elbows or hands.

(Top) For him: In this position you can dig your knees or feet into the bed to help add power to your thrusts. You can also thrust at slightly varying angles to treat yourself and your partner to different sensations.

(Above and opposite) For her: Although you can let your lover have total control, it's much more erotic for you both if you show your enthusiasm by stroking his back, grabbing his buttocks, and letting him know what you like by moaning or just saying what feels good. To help him penetrate deeper, raise your legs and hook your ankles around his waist.

(Opposite) For him: A sexy option is to lift yourself onto your hands and feet so that the only part of your body making contact with your partner's is your penis. If you are able to support your weight with one arm, take a minute to reach between her legs and give her clitoris some loving attention.

victory

You'll both feel like winners in this high-intensity, deep penetration position.

(Opposite) For him: While kneeling in front of your partner, lift her legs into a wide "V". Keep in mind that some women are more flexible than others, and she may need to bend her legs slightly to make this position more comfortable and sustainable.

(Top) For him: To get even deeper, lean forward and let her legs fall to either side of your waist.

(Above) For her: Hold your calves or thighs and lift your bottom slightly to help your partner thrust as deeply inside you as possible.

the rabbit

The Rabbit is an extremely comfortable position that provides an exceptional feeling of closeness because the partners' bodies are huddled tightly together.

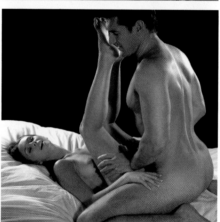

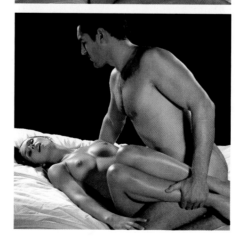

(Right, top to bottom) This variation, legs over to one side and then the other, offers its own distinct sensation because it changes the position of the vagina.

For him: Sitting back on your heels with knees spread, you can lean slightly forward against your partner's knees while you pump your hips back and forth. Charge up this position by lifting your partner's legs straight up.

For her: Lie back with your knees tucked and your feet pressed against your partner's chest. You'll be able to feel every inch of his penis as it moves in and out of you.

(Opposite) Choose one variation on this move and enjoy it only, spend several minutes in each position, or move her legs from left to right as you thrust, for a twisting treat.

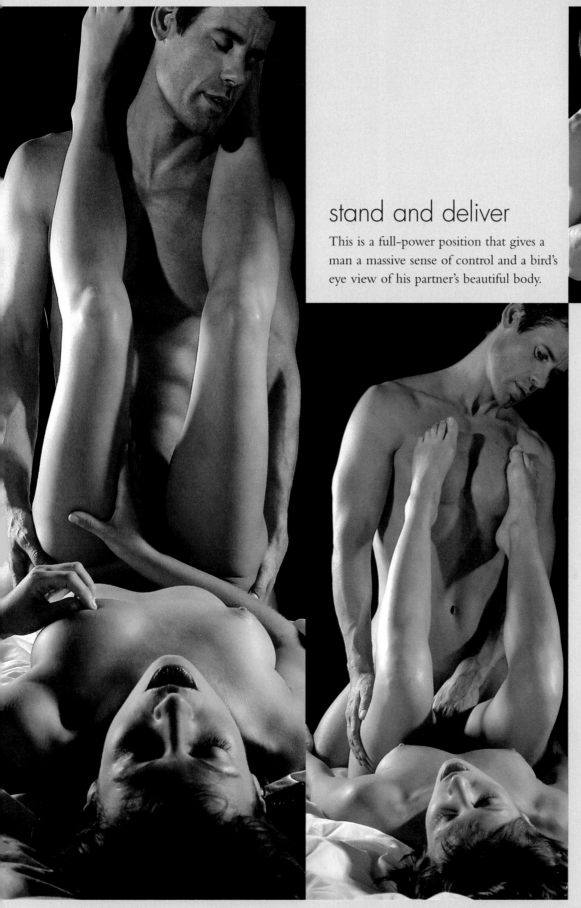

stand and deliver

This is a full-power position that gives a man a massive sense of control and a bird's eye view of his partner's beautiful body.

(Opposite) For him: Stand beside the bed between your partner's legs as she lies back, then lift her lower body to meet yours by holding onto her butt or upper thighs. **For her:** Relax your body. Let your legs hang loosely over the edge of the bed. Soften your stomach muscles and let your partner take over.

(Far left) For him: To deepen penetration, lift her legs and raise them onto your shoulders. **For her:** Use your hands to caress your own breasts, thighs, abdomen.... Not only will it provide heavenly sensations for you to enjoy, your partner will love watching your every move.

(Left) For him: While in this position, take time to stimulate your partner's clitoris.

(Top) Kiss her ankles and calves in this position to make her feel ultra-pampered.

the superhero

Lift her up, up, and away with testosterone-fueled upright sex. A relatively easy way to get into this position is for the man to lift his partner from a sitting position. How long you can maintain upright intercourse depends on your strength. Doing it while standing next to a bed is a good idea, because you can gracefully fall onto the mattress at any time.

(Opposite, top) For him: Bend at the knees and grasp her just beneath the butt when lifting. If you doubt you can pull off this position, it's better not to try, because you could both end up on the floor. Avoid arching your back to support her weight, so you don't injure yourself. You'll have to support her body almost entirely with your arms. If she wraps her legs around your waist and her arms around your neck, it will make moving her up and down on top of your penis much easier.

(Opposite, bottom) For her: Help your partner support your weight by grasping his waist with your legs and holding on to his shoulders.

(Top, right) The two-chair version of standing sex offers a similar thrill with far less muscle strain. Start with two chairs set side by side. The woman should stand with one foot on either chair, with her legs slightly bent so that her vagina is at the proper level to meet the penis. The man thrusts from between her legs, and can slide his hands around and under her butt to help keep her at the proper height.

(Bottom, right) Another option is for the man to prop his bottom on the edge of a high sofa while his partner straddles him. From this position, he can lift her occasionally for a few moments of free-standing fun.

jackknife

A cinch to segue into from missionary position, the Jackknife offers several tantalizing angles of penetration.

(Opposite) For him: Your partner's flexibility will determine how far forward you can lean into this position. Because her leg is bent, it's actually more comfortable for her than it might look. First, lift her left leg and place it on your right shoulder. After enjoying that sensation, you can return her leg to the bed and lift her right leg onto your left shoulder. You should feel a variation in the angle of pressure on your penis inside her vagina. Placing her right leg on your right shoulder or her left leg on your left shoulder in a scissor -like position will add yet another sensation to the mix. At any time you can move your partner's leg down onto your thigh to lessen the intensity. The angles are exhilarating.

(Top) For her: Relax your hamstring muscles—breathe deeply and imagine them melting—to make this position even more pleasurable.

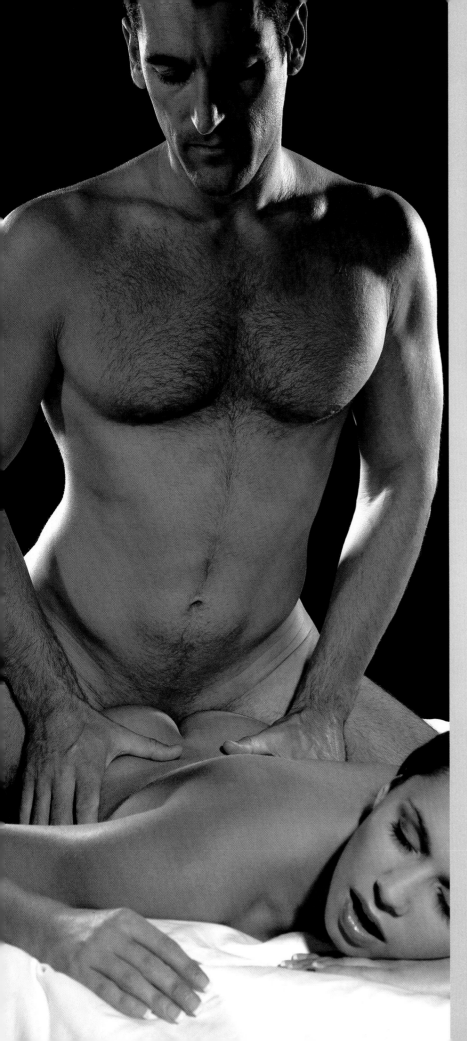

(Left) The most underrated variation on Dog Style is with the woman lying flat on her belly while the man straddles her upper thighs. From here, a couple can transition easily into The Arrow (see page 128).

(Top) Dog Style with both of you on your knees is both comfortable and highly erotic. **For him:** Reach around and stimulate your partner's clitoris as you thrust in and out of her.

(Top center) For her: Let your torso drop so that your chest lies flat, but your hips are raised. Spread your arms and relax, enjoying the sensation.

(Opposite, far right) For him: Have your partner bend over a bed, another piece of furniture, or just in an open area of the room so you can enter her from behind while standing. **For her:** Bend over farther and hold onto your legs. From this position you can make a narrow "V" shape with your fingers and place it over your vagina, giving his penis another tight slot to slide through.

dog style

This position should be called Lion Style, because whether you're power-thrusting or slow-grinding, it makes a man feel like the king of the jungle—not some eager-to-please puppy dog.

the arrow

This position is very romantic, yet because the man penetrates from behind and above, it's anything but tame.

(Bottom) For him: Raise and lower your hips to gain a small but powerful range of motion. Raising yourself onto your arms and digging your knees into the bed increases your thrusting power. For her: Place your feet on your partner's butt and pull him deeply inside you. Allow your back to arch naturally. This position provides your partner with a sensuous curve he can kiss and caress.

(Right) Having sex in the Arrow position with the woman on her back instead of her belly is fantastic for clitoral stimulation. The man may have to enter his partner with her legs spread at first and then maneuver so that his legs straddle hers. He can then thrust his hips up and down. By slightly tilting his body forward as he thrusts, he'll be ensuring that his penis slides against her clitoris.

sidewinder

Sex while you are spooning can be a middle-of-the-night treat or a fun way to spend a lazy afternoon. It is incredibly intimate because it allows the man to hug his partner from behind, kiss her neck, caress her breasts, or let his hand slide between her legs and over her pubic mound.

(Top, right) Do it face-to-face while lying on your sides for a relaxing encounter with plenty of opportunity for romantic eye-gazing. **For him:** Hold your partner's leg up and out of the way to penetrate her more deeply.

(Bottom, right) For her: Throw your leg high over your partner's hip to allow him to enter you more deeply.

thrusting 101

Varying the intensity, depth, and angle of your thrusts will make sex far more sensational than continually thrusting at a steady pace. In the same way that the shaft of your penis is not as sensitive as the head, the inside of a woman's vagina is not nearly as sensitive as her clitoris. But there is an area—known as the g-spot—on the front wall of the vagina (the wall behind her pubic hair) that when stimulated provides an electric sensation. Angling your penis so that it rubs against this area will add to the intensity of your partner's pleasure and help bring her to orgasm. Keep in mind that both shallow and deep thrusts can feel amazing, especially when you alternate between one and the other in the same position. Pushing very deeply into your partner and then maintaining that depth is another big woman-pleaser, especially if you then grind your hips slowly from side to side or in a circular motion. Pushing in the penis deeply and then using short thrusts allows you to pump quickly without worrying about the penis disengaging in an awkward or painful way. Use a variety of thrusts over the course of a sexual encounter and then stick to a steady rhythm as you both reach your peak. And there will no doubt be times when sliding your penis slowly in and out of a vagina, stopping and starting as you get closer and closer to coming, is nothing less than awesome.

(Opposite, top) Sex in the Classic (page 114) position allows for the full range of thrusts, from deep and vigorous to slow and languorous. Slide the penis head and a bit of the upper shaft in and out between the labia to take advantage of the extra sensitivity of the coronal ridge. By tucking your hips slightly you can increase the upward angle of your penis, helping it to hit a woman's g-spot.

(Opposite, bottom) Dog Style (page 126) is a great position for fast yet controlled thrusting. When pumping vigorously, it's very important to slide the penis in and out at a straight angle. Moving quickly and unpredictably may end in a painful clash. Bending forward in Dog Style will help you angle your penis downward so that it comes in contact with a woman's g-spot.

(Above, left) With your partner on top, you can thrust upward to deepen penetration and increase the overall intensity of sex. Try thrusting upward every other or every third time that she starts the downward stroke of her vagina onto your penis. The alternating sensations can be extremely hot.

(Above, right) Having sex in any position in which the woman's legs are bent toward her chest, allows the penis to penetrate the vagina more easily. Some women enjoy this feeling; others find extremely deep penetration uncomfortable. And even women who enjoy it most of the time may have days when it feels a little too intense. It's always best to start with shorter strokes in such positions and then push deeper in increments, watching your partner's reaction.

Tuck your hips in missionary position to angle the penis toward the g-spot.

Lean forward to angle the penis downward toward the g-spot during dog style.

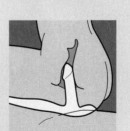

When she's on top, thrust upward to help increase the force of the friction.

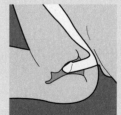

For deeper penetration, angle the penis downward during missionary position.

8 sexy extras

You don't need props, toys, or games to have incredible sex, but like whipped cream atop a hot fudge sundae, *need* has nothing to do with it. From lubricant, or lube, that heats up when you blow on it to vibrators with remote controls, sex enhancers simply add an additional level of excitement to an already satisfying sexual relationship. It isn't necessary to buy anything to start playing dirty, although there are tons of great toys on the market. You can pour chocolate sauce over your lover's nipples, run an ice cube up and down his spine, tie her wrists to the bedpost with a necktie, or read him an erotic story you've written yourself. The point is to do something different, something fresh, something saucy, that will give you both a little extra erotic buzz. Many people are reluctant to tell their partner that they'd be interested in occasionally bringing a toy to bed or playing a sexy game, but raising the topic in a playful way—as if you were suggesting, say, a round of mini-golf or a dip in the pool—is likely to meet with a smile and a seductive "maybe" from even the shyest bedmate.

wetter is better

If there's one sex enhancer that every couple should always have in their bedside table, it's personal lubricant. Even when a woman has enough natural wetness to make sex perfectly comfortable, a little extra can make intercourse feel even slicker and more luxurious. For long sessions, the extra lubrication is crucial for preventing painful friction. Dildos, vibrators, and other toys usually provide more pleasure when properly lubed; manual stimulation is far more fun and enjoyable when fingers are slippery enough to roam freely; and anal sex should never be attempted without lots of lubrication. So go out and buy a tube or bottle of lube and keep it within easy reach. *Note*: Be sure to check the label of any lubricant to make sure that it is safe to use with condoms or any sex toy you might be using. Only water-based and silicone-based lubes should be used with latex, as oil causes latex to deteriorate. (That means no baby oil, petroleum jelly, lotions, moisturizers, massage oil, or any other products that contain oil when using a rubber.) Also keep in mind that silicone-based lubes are not compatible with silicone sex toys. The safest and most non-irritating lubes are water-based.

Try different varieties of lubes to discover which kind you like best for which activities. Water-based lubes vary in texture from very watery to slightly thick.

Silicone-based lube is usually thicker than water-based lube and lasts much longer than any water-based lubes. They also stay slick under water, making them a better option in the shower, tub, or any other watery environment. Silicone-based lube is also the best option for anal sex and will not harm latex, so is safe to use with condoms. One drawback is that silicone lubes wash off only with soap and water.

For her: Lubricants that contain glycerin, which is a form of sugar, taste sweet, but can increase your chance of developing a yeast infection. If this a concern for you, check the label to make sure the lube is glycerine-free.

(Top) Since most of your sexual action probably takes place in your bedroom, keep lubricant handy in a nearby drawer, or transfer it into a pretty pump bottle that you can leave on top of your bedside table. It will look like an innocent bottle of moisturizer to visitors, and will always be at the ready when you need it.

(Left) Applying lube to your own and your partner's genitals can be a very sexy experience. Do it slowly with a few sensual strokes. Keep in mind that too much lube may reduce friction to the point where there's very little sensation. After one or two tries, you'll know how much to use and will have no trouble getting it right every time.

toys

Sex toys come in all shapes, sizes, and colors. Some vibrate. Some can be controlled by remote. Some bear a startling resemblance to actual body parts. Others have been made to look like cute animals. Flipping through a sex-toy catalog is sure to put a silly grin on your face and raise your eyebrows. One thing is for certain: if it can make your body feel good in a sexual way, someone has designed it, packaged it, and put it up for sale. Here is a selection of some of the best-loved items currently on the market. (*Note:* Always clean your sex toys properly after every use.)

(Above) The right toy can make good sex even better.

Cock Ring (Left)

A cock ring is a metal, leather, or rubber device shaped like a ring, usually 1½ inches to 2 inches (4 to 5 cm) in diameter. Some leather cock rings have snaps or other closures to make them adjustable. The testicles and the erect penis are slipped through the ring, which fits tightly, putting pressure on the dorsal vein in the penis. The idea is that the cock ring stops the blood that has engorged the penis from flowing out as quickly as it might, helping a man to retain his erection longer. Some men also just like the feeling of having it wrapped around the base of their penis.

Anal Plug (Bottom, right)

You may have heard about anal (or butt) plugs. This model is accompanied by a multi-function controller. One button controls the speed or intensity of the vibration and the other controls the vibration patterns. This particular model has five settings: vibrating, pulsating, surging, escalating, and roller coaster. What more could one want?

Anal Beads (Below)

The thrill of anal beads is not slipping the beads into the anus, though a person might find that erotic. The big pay-off is pulling them out one by one at the exact point that a person reaches orgasm.

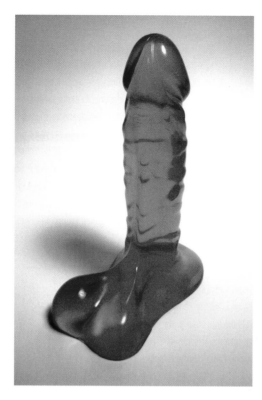

Vaginal Sleeve (Middle, left)

Vaginal sleeves are male masturbatory devices that are made to feel like a woman's vagina. A man lubricates his penis and then slips it inside the sleeve. Some also vibrate for extra sensation.

Cock Tie (Bottom, left)

On those nights when you want sex to be a formal affair, don this bolo-tie style cock ring. This one is made of black PVC, which warms quickly to body temperature. It's designed so that you can arrange the clasp to brush your partner's clitoris or perineum. The best part of this ring (aside from the fact that it goes well with a tuxedo) is that you can adjust it to apply the right amount of pressure.

Clitoral Tickler (Bottom)

Clitoral ticklers stimulate the clitoris during intercourse. They come in many different shapes, but usually have a hole through which the penis fits. With each thrust, the tickler moves against the clitoris, adding considerably to a woman's pleasure. Some clitoral ticklers vibrate for more intense friction.

Vibrator (Opposite)

A vibrating rubber duckie could turn out to be your favorite bath mate. This model features a round head, pointed tail, and a nubby beak to massage all your favorite areas. Of course, vibrators come in all sorts of shapes and sizes.

G-Spot Massager (Top, left)

The shape of the g-spot massager allows it to directly stimulate the front wall of the vagina, which many women find leads to earth-shattering orgasm.

Dildo (Top, right)

Dildos are devices that are made to look and feel like an erect penis. Some companies offer a woman the opportunity to design a dildo that looks just like her partner's penis—a great idea for those times when she's feeling frisky but he's not around.

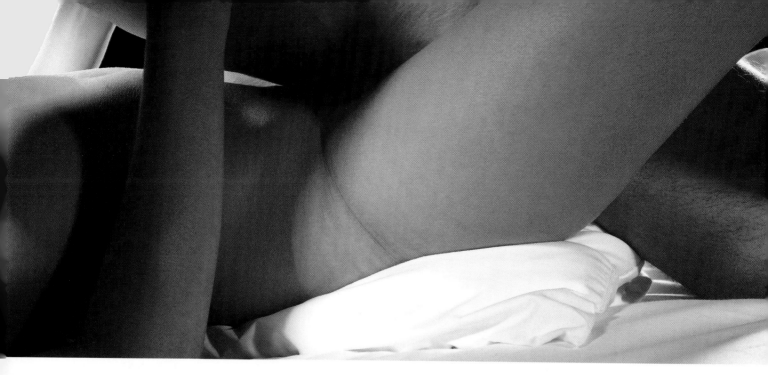

props

A sexual prop can be just about anything that you use before or during sex to make the experience more arousing or pleasurable. It can be as simple as a pile of pillows or as complicated as a sex swing. A pair of leather boots can serve as a sex prop, as can a piece of furniture that you use for support. Great lovers see the world around them as filled with items that can make sex more interesting, exciting, and enjoyable. The question is not what, but how.

Pillows (Above)

Soft, fluffy pillows make excellent sex props. Slide one under your knees if you're on the floor. Guys can put them under a woman's bottom when she's lying on her back to make her vagina more easily accessed during oral sex or intercourse. Both partners can use them anytime during sex to gain a slightly different angle or support any part of their body that needs it. Large, wedge-shaped sex pillows are designed to help couples have sex in a variety of positions.

Blindfold

Covering your partner's eyes with a blindfold made distinctly for that purpose, or any other piece of cloth that happens to be on hand, allows you to treat him or her to surprise kisses, touches, and licks. Because your partner can't see, his or her other senses will be heightened. It can be fun to tease your partner in this state, slowly building arousal so that sex itself is an overwhelming release. Try caressing his or her body with different textures—a feather, a leather glove, a silk scarf or a velvet scarf.

Fuzzy Handcuffs

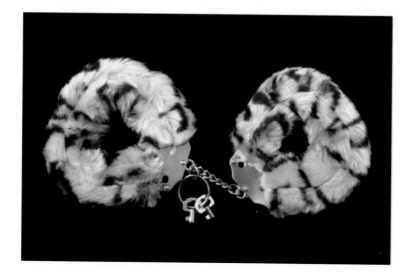

(Left) What could be more fun than a little bondage with the object of your affection? We're not suggesting anything too serious, just some fun and games with a pair of fuzzy handcuffs. A bonus is that these cuffs feel oh-so-good against your partner's skin. Of course you can play cops and robbers, but use your imagination and come up with some other fun ideas, too. For instance, cuff your partner to the bed and then have your way with him or her.

Naughty Talk

Whispering randy nothings in your partner's ear can be a big turn-on for two reasons. The first is that simply saying or hearing slang that is taboo in everyday life—words for erotic actions and body parts—is enough to give most people a shot of sexual adrenaline. The second is that the mere sound of your partner's breathy voice speaking your name can set off sparks. Whisper your secret desires into your partner's ear and have them come true.

Dress-Up (Right)

Playing dress-up doesn't require a store-bought costume, although it can be a treat to surprise your partner in a nurse's outfit or a police uniform. For women it can be as simple as scouring the closet for a sexy little outfit and matching it with a pair of high heels. Wearing a wig can also make the encounter feel more daring and risqué. Dress-up for guys is a little more difficult to pull off without looking more silly than sexy. But a pair of black silk boxer shorts may be enough to get your partner going. If you have a sense of humor, try a thong that makes your penis look like an elephant's trunk.

Stripper Gear

Strippers are always ready and willing to flaunt their sexuality. So when a woman dons anything a stripper might wear—leather lingerie, elbow-length satin gloves, or a masquerade mask—it can get both her and her partner fired up. By stealing their look for a night, you can also borrow their lack of inhibition.

Fire

Whether it's a fireplace, a campfire, or a single candle, fire taps into our primitive sense of pleasure. It instantly makes you feel more relaxed and sensual. Just be sure to keep flammable items away from the flame so that your passion is the only thing ignited

Body Paint (Left)

More playful than erotic, body paint is a great tool for taking sex a lot less seriously. Consider playing tic-tac-toe on someone's thigh, attempting a self portrait on your partner's belly, or drawing an "X" on every spot that you want caressed. You can have as much fun smearing paint around during sex as brushing it on, or wait to get your sexual satisfaction in the shower as you help each other wash it off.

Randy Rugs (Opposite, top)

Thick, plush rugs—especially sheep skin rugs—are a pleasure to roll around on naked. The idea of a nude woman on a white, fuzzy rug also has status as a common male fantasy image. That's one fantasy that is easy for any couple to fulfill that will feel great, too.

Pearl Thong (Below)

This sexy thong creates a tingling sensation as the pearls slide between your labia. It has the added side effect of driving your partner mad with lust.

Ice (Right)

Use it to cool the back of your lover's neck, the insides of their elbows and wrists, or the back of their knees on a hot night. The sensation can also awaken erogenous zones, especially nipples, and get them ready for a nice wet, hot tongue.

Sexy Decor

Throwing a set of extra-special sheets—linen, silk, satin— on the bed may be all it takes to inspire extra-special sex. Create a bedroom that feels open and uncluttered, with plenty of soft, rich textures and room to move. A large floor-length mirror can also be a lot of fun. Pull it in front of the bed to watch yourselves in action.

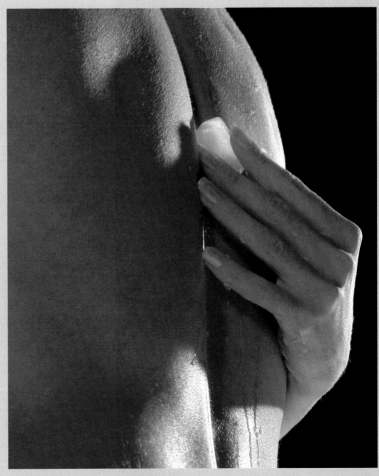

have some fun

A couple who can laugh, tease each other, and be ridiculous before, during, and after making love will, without a doubt, have a smokin' hot sex life. That's because it takes a lot of trust and comfort to really fool around together. And if you're still nervous or self-conscious around your partner, playing a few games will help you lose that baggage. Playing is all about letting go of the serious issues we deal with every day and being spontaneous, bold, and stress-free.

(Above) Spanking is a playful aphrodisiac. For both the spanker and the spankee, light love taps are a fantastic source of tension release and can be extremely sexy. This isn't S&M—it's just good, healthy fun.

(Left) If you have a pair of dice around the house, you have the makings for any number of sexy games. Just designate one act for each possible combination of rolls from two to twelve. For example, roll a two and you owe your mate a kiss; a three and he or she gets a French kiss; a twelve could mean…well, use your imagination. It's also fun to throw a couple of duds into the mix—for instance, if you roll a seven, you get socked with a pillow.

(Opposite) Pull out the cards and play a game of strip poker. Whoever ends up naked first has to be the other's love-slave.

There are plenty of naughty adult board games for you and your partner to break out on a weekend night when you're looking to spice things up. A bottle of wine will turn the game into a party for two. Or you can just pull out any old game, from checkers to Twister, and amend the rules to include some sexual prizes and penalties.

take it outside

Given how natural it is, doing *it* in the great outdoors feels surprisingly forbidden—in a very sexy way. Plan a vacation that involves getting away someplace private and beautiful where you can have sex on a blanket in the grass, gazing at a breathtaking view the entire time. Do it on a mountain top, on the beach, in the woods, and in every other wild, yet private, place or situation you can imagine. Until you can get away, sneak some loving in to a few of these less exotic yet still exciting locales.

Public displays of affection are a great way to heat things up so that by the time you get home, you're ready to rip off each other's clothes with your teeth.

Make out passionately on a busy street corner. Press your partner against the wall of a restaurant or bar for a heated kiss. Grab a feel when no one is looking. Pushing the limits has a way of seriously raising libido.

(Above) Pick a dark alley or just get up against your house for some risky yet racy action.

(Right) When you were a teenager you probably had sex in the back seat of cars because you had to. Doing it now of your own volition will bring back that flood of adolescent anticipation and crazed horniness that leaves the windows covered in steam.

9 climax

All orgasms are not equal. Some happen so fast and resonate so little that you can barely tell that they even happened. Others rock your world to the point where you can't move or speak for minutes afterward. Most orgasms fall somewhere between. Coming may be the grand finale of getting it on—if there wasn't a point at which our nerves went into overdrive and couldn't be touched anymore, we'd probably continue humping forever—but it doesn't have to be the main goal of recreational sex. Far better goals are to give each other pleasure, grow closer as a couple, and celebrate each other's bodies. Ideally, climax is just a nice exclamation point at the end of an already satisfying sentence. That said, getting to orgasm is an important part of sex, because without it, something would certainly be missing. Although there are some general moves that are likely to bring a person to orgasm, every individual is different and may require a particular kind of stimulation to trigger their climax. Couples need to communicate openly with one another to discover what each partner likes and doesn't like as they get closer to coming, because doing the wrong thing at the wrong time can easily throw someone off track. And since many women have difficulty reaching orgasm to begin with, the more their partner understands their preferences, the better.

her orgasm

Whether a woman has an orgasm during any sexual encounter depends largely on whether she's had enough stimulation to become completely aroused. On the whole, a woman's body takes longer to work up to climax than a man's. Starting slow with plenty of kissing and touching to warm her up will help a woman to start a steady climb toward her peak.

For him: Some women are driven wild by breast stimulation and others could take it or leave it. If you know it's something your partner likes, lavish her chest with attention at several different points during sex, not just at the beginning. For a good sense of what turns on a woman, a combination of manual stimulation and good communication is your best teacher. Ask your partner what feels good, and what might feel better. Encourage her to talk as you touch her. While this kind of exploration won't provide a formula that works every time, it will provide an enormous amount of information about the kind of friction your partner prefers.

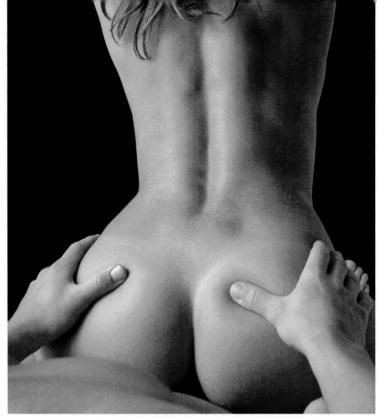

(Above) Oral sex is an amazingly intimate way to bring a woman to full arousal and orgasm. As your partner becomes more excited, pay attention to what is turning her on the most—is it fast, light flicks from your tongue directly on her clitoris, or firm licks over the entire clot and surrounding area? When you know, stick to that move and slide a finger (with your palm facing up) into her vagina and keep it still. If she reacts positively, slide in a second finger. Keep them still, pressing only slightly against the front wall of her vagina as you continue to massage her vagina with your mouth. By fingering her at a point when she's already stimulated, you can bring on a fabulous orgasm.

(Top, right) For him: Many women feel self-conscious about grinding their lower body as fast as they'd like to get off. Grasp your partner's butt or hips during sex and pull and push them back and forth to encourage her to move them quickly. It may be all the encouragement she needs to take off.

(Bottom, right) For her: Don't be shy about pushing and grinding hard or just gliding your body lightly against your lover's if that excites you. When trying to come, make your own pleasure the priority. Having an orgasm requires concentration, so if you're worrying about anything or anyone else, it won't happen. Sometimes the only way to get the stimulation you need to reach orgasm is to use your own hand. This is true for many women, so don't hesitate to get your digits involved.

(Opposite, top right) For her: Cowgirl position (see page 88) is a favorite because it allows you to press your clitoris against your partner's abdomen and slide it back and forth in fast, rhythmic thrusts, slow, circular grinds, or whatever motion feels best (might as well try them all).

(Opposite, bottom) When you're about to come, let your lover know it!

his orgasm

In his teen years, a guy may be able to come in seconds, but as men get older, orgasm becomes less a knee-jerk reflex and more a response to skillful erotic stimulation. Anything from work stress to fatigue to performance anxiety can make it difficult for a man to let go and explode. There are many little moves that help get a guy over that hump, and the more a woman knows, the better she'll be at bringing him to climax. Even if a man can come at the drop of a hat, that doesn't mean that a woman shouldn't treat him to tricks and techniques that give his orgasm extra oomph. Here are a few to use when he gets close to coming.

Some men love having their testicles caressed or cupped and others prefer not to have them touched. Men who do love this kind of contact will get a thrill from a woman's hand sliding over their scrotum as they near orgasm. The prostrate gland is another favorite spot for many men.

(Left) For her: Men love to watch and sexy visuals have a way of making them come like gangbusters. As you see your partner getting more excited, start caressing your breasts and nipples to give him some eye candy. Or move into a position that allows him to watch his penis sliding in and out of your vagina in vivid detail. This "look-while-I-touch" technique will turn him on even more.

(Opposite, top) Just as a woman should rub her clitoris at any time that she wants more direct stimulation, either partners can grasp the base of the shaft of the penis with their hand and stroke it to make intercourse more intense.

(Opposite, bottom) For her: The sound of you enjoying yourself will turn your partner on. Don't resist any urges to moan or sigh.

(Top) Anal stimulation is tricky business. While some men and women love to have their anus touched and/or penetrated, others would be very turned off if their partner were to go there. It's always best to ask whether that's something he or she likes, rather than surprising them during a heated moment with a move that could make them jump ten feet into the air and ruin the moment.

(Opposite) For her: The best way to learn what kind of testicular touch your man likes best is to play (always gently, never roughly) with his balls during oral sex or while giving him a hand-job. Run your fingers over his scrotum, gently tug on the skin between his testicles, push them toward his body, or just cup them in your palm. Pay attention to what makes him moan or causes his penis to become more engorged, then use those moves as he approaches orgasm. To stimulate his prostate, push up firmly (about an inch) with the pads of two fingers on the area just behind his testicles. In the few seconds prior to orgasm, most men's entire bodies will become extremely tense, causing their toes to curl. When you feel his muscles tightening, be sure to continue exactly what you're doing without changing or stopping.

afterglow

Make the most of post–sex relaxation by using it as a time to bond with your partner and exchange some mutual praise. This is the time to say, "I love you," and tell him or her how attractive they are and how much you enjoy their body. The intimacy and openness created by sex can strengthen a relationship and increase levels of trust and comfort.

Just because sex is over doesn't mean you have to stop touching. Continuing to kiss and caress each other softly will keep you feeling close and help transition from the intense connection of intercourse to being two separate people again.

For him: After you've spent some time lavishing your partner with post-coital TLC, ask her if she would like a clean towel. This is especially nice if you haven't used a condom, because your semen has probably already started to drip out of her vagina and onto her thighs and the sheets.

A little tenderness goes a long way in bed. Look your partner in the eyes, brush strands of wet hair off their face, kiss non-sexual parts of their body like their shoulder, cheek, or forehead, and otherwise make it perfectly clear that you adore them. It's the perfect ending to your sensual experience.

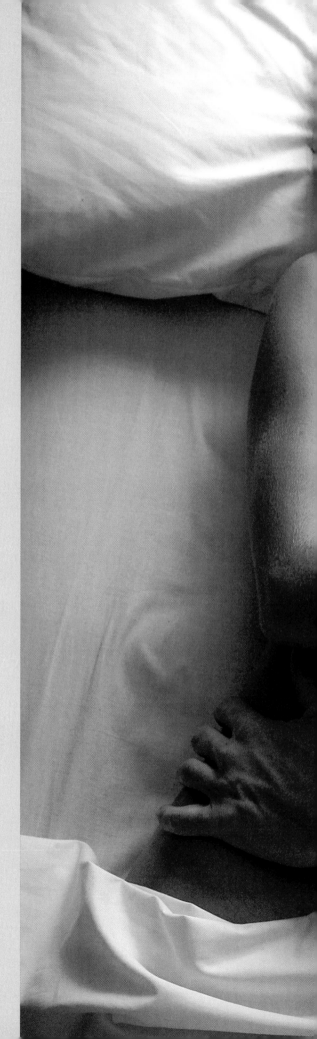

Taking some time to cool down and doze together will help the transition from the intense connection of intercourse to being two separate people again.

10 erotica

To fit into the category of "erotica," material such as film, photographs, audio recordings, or stories must have been created with the specific intention of causing sexual arousal. There is seldom a deep emotional or intellectual component to erotica. For that reason, the sexual satisfaction people get from it is usually short, sweet, and rather meaningless. This isn't necessarily a bad thing. Like an insubstantial snack that holds you over until dinner, erotica can be a nice treat between real romantic encounters with the opposite sex. The nature of erotica can be merely suggestive—a photograph of a woman licking her lips—or intensely graphic—a photograph of a woman licking a penis. What, if any, type of erotica you enjoy is determined by your personal tastes and ability to feel comfortable responding sexually to stimuli like movies and books. In some cultures, erotica is considered a healthy part of a person or couple's sex life, and nothing to be embarrassed or ashamed of. In other cultures, erotica is illegal. From a sexual health perspective, as long as your use of erotica does not affect your life or relationships negatively, there's no reason not to feel comfortable using it while masturbating or with your partner as added stimulation for you both.

words and images

If you like to read, you might get a thrill from erotic stories or novels. There is no end to the variety of available sexual plots. Chances are that all of your favorite fantasies have been written about in careful detail. If they haven't, consider writing a fantasy yourself and maybe even reading it to your partner.

Phone sex is something you can do with your partner when you can't be together or with a stranger via a pay service. Although it can be arousing, it can also be expensive, as most phone-sex lines charge by the minute. If it's the sound of breathless voices talking dirty that you like, a less costly option is to buy erotic audio tapes that involve the scenarios that turn you on the most.

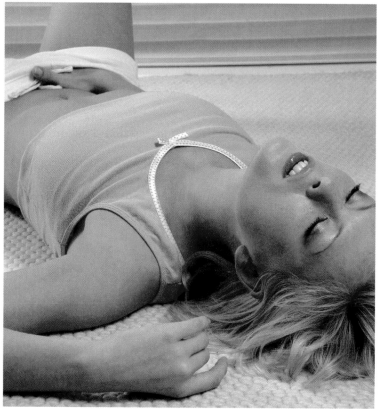

Erotic stories are meant to turn you on, so let them. Let go of your inhibitions as you read and enjoy picturing the scene in your head. When you feel turned on, start to touch yourself. Some people can bring themselves to orgasm simply by staring at a particularly racy word while they masturbate.

Both men and women can enjoy looking at sexual images. Again, what you like is purely a matter of taste. The only way to find out what visuals rev your sexual engine is to do a little browsing in an adult bookstore or online.

strip clubs

Strip and sex clubs are places where human sexuality is put on display, where watching naked women and/or men dance or engage in sexual play or actual sex acts is not only condoned, it's their raison d'être. In societies where nudity or sexuality is oppressed, some people may find this atmosphere refreshingly unrestrained. To others, it can seem degrading to either the performers or the audience or both.

Determining whether visiting a strip club is healthy or unhealthy sexual behavior has a lot to do with an individual's reasons for going, and how it affects the rest of his or her life. If a person is looking for real fulfillment of any kind, he or she will likely be very disappointed and frustrated. And if his or her romantic partner or family is upset by commercial sexuality, going to a strip club could be more disruptive than the superficial titillation is worth. As a general rule, if a sexual behavior poses serious negative consequences, it should probably be avoided. If it has only positive effects and is a source of pleasure, it should be embraced. Many couples enjoy going to strip clubs as a way to become turned on together.

There are many different kinds of strip clubs that range from dark and seedy bars to large, well-lit, multi-floor complexes that feel like X-rated amusement parks. The cleanliness and overall pleasantness of the place reflects what kind of women work there and how enjoyable your experience is likely to be.

Rules differ among strip clubs. Often, patrons may be touched by the strippers, but the patrons themselves are not allowed to put their hands on the strippers. Customers frequently have the option of paying a particular stripper to give them a lap dance that involves plenty of grinding, writhing, jiggling, and possibly more, depending on the club. A few establishments allow patrons to interact much more intimately with the women working there, in ways that might include showering with them, mud wrestling, mutual massage, or other hands-on activities. Keep in mind that strip clubs are businesses and strippers are looking to make as much money as possible. Nine-and-a-half times out of ten a stripper who says that she "really likes you" in a way that's "different from how she feels about all those other customers," or who hints at possibly getting together later for sex or a date is just trying to get you to empty your wallet.

11 solo sex

Bringing yourself to orgasm is a great way to get your blood pumping, to reduce stress, to clear your mind, to help you sleep, to alleviate boredom, and just to see and feel your sexuality in action. It's also a wonderful way to pamper yourself. Think of it as giving yourself a massage, or as an at-home spa treatment for your erogenous zones. As for when and where to masturbate, as long as you have privacy (a locked door is your safest bet) and aren't breaking any laws, the sky's the limit. Masturbation at its best is not a fast or frenzied act, but rather a slow and luxurious one in which you really take the time to arouse yourself completely and delay orgasm until you're just about ready to explode. Instead of just using a single hand to get the job done, consider using lubrication, letting your hands roam over other parts of your body besides the obvious hot spots, adding a sex toy or erotica to the mix, or using a strong showerhead to do your handiwork for you. Think of it as having enough fun for two people all by yourself.

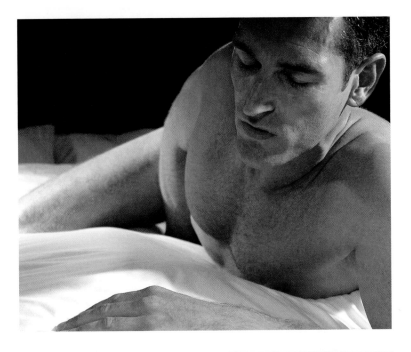

on his own

When you were younger you may have thought of masturbation as a necessary chore to release some of that pent up sexual energy. Although you can still use solo sex for that purpose, it can accomplish much more. With time on your hands and no one else to please, you have a chance to experiment with different strokes and pressure to find out just how intense an orgasm you're capable of. As easy as it is, don't just play with yourself the same way every time. See how different hand techniques affect the length and power of your orgasm.

Give your testicles plenty of attention. Try tugging on them with one hand while you stroke your penis with the other. This is a technique that sex experts suggest for helping to prevent orgasm. Give it a try as you reach your peak. If it works, it may be a helpful trick you can use during intercourse. Conversely, cupping your balls and pulling them snugly against your body can often help trigger orgasm. You can also try stimulating your prostate by pressing up on the area of skin directly behind your testicles.

(Opposite) Morning masturbation is a great way to start the day.

(Top) There is no single position in which to enjoy some solo sex. Sometimes simulating the pose you would take with a partner can get you off

(Far left) The shower is an all-time favorite place for masturbation. Try using a loofah or wash cloth in addition to your hand.

(Left) Is there a lock on your office door? If you have complete privacy, then there's no reason why you shouldn't take a mid-afternoon break that will make you a much happier and revitalized worker than if you just had a cup of coffee.

on her own

Masturbation is even more private for women than it is for men. Unlike men, women seldom make jokes with their friends about jacking off—and it's something parents seldom discuss with their daughters. As a result many women feel embarrassed about solo sex, when there's no reason to be. It's perfectly healthy and good for a woman's sex life because it helps her become more familiar and comfortable with her body and her sexuality.

Fantasy can be a very exciting component of masturbation. Imagine your ideal sexual encounter and touch yourself in all the ways that you'd want your partner to touch you. Grab and caress your breasts and butt. Pinch your nipples, rub your vagina over your panties. Close your eyes and picture it happening while your hands make it feel real. Or you can focus completely on the here and now and the way your hands feel on your body. Completely concentrating on each sensation can be as erotic as letting your imagination go wild.

(Opposite) If you like solid, steady pressure on your clitoris, ride the arm of a stuffed chair or couch, or the edge of a table or desk with a thick towel or blanket folded over it.

(Top) A popular way that women masturbate is to lie on their belly with their hands thrust between their legs, grinding their hips up and down so that their clitoris and pubic mound rub against their firmly held fingers.

(Right, top) Keep plenty of batteries around so that your vibrator never dies at an inopportune moment.

(Right) For fast, constant stimulation, vibrators that slide onto your finger are a fabulous option. Most women come very easily when they use one. Experiment by moving the vibrator around your labia and inserting it into your vagina.

12 bathing and massage

Stress, tension, and worry are the archenemies of great sex. When you're distracted or wound up, it's impossible to be fully present in your body. That's why bathing and massage are such valuable parts of a satisfying sex life. They help put distance between the problems you face every day and the time you spend getting physically intimate with your partner. They return your focus to what you're feeling instead of what you're thinking. Water, all by itself, is refreshing, relaxing, and very sensual. A cold shower can give you renewed energy and mental clarity for a night out. A warm bath can bring you into your skin, slow you down, and make your body more sensitive to touch. And bathing with your partner opens doors to all kinds of slippery fun. Sex in the bath or shower can be a challenge because of limited space and hard surfaces, but it's one worth taking. You can lather each other and feel your bodies sliding against each other completely friction free. On those nights when immersing yourself in soothing H_2O isn't enough to calm your racing mind, or when you want the ultimate in tension relief, ask your partner for a head-to-toe massage.

hot & steamy

When someone isn't in the mood for sex, it's usually because they're too stressed out to feel sexy. If you're looking to get it on but your partner isn't, suggesting they take a hot shower or long soak in the tub is a better game plan than pawing them and hoping they come around. The same goes for you. Don't dismiss the idea of sex until you've given yourself a chance to catch your breath surrounded by some hot, tension-melting steam or stress-busting bubbles.

First, prep the bathroom for a spa-style soak. Light a candle and play some soothing music. Then run a bath as warm as you can take it, and soak for at least ten minutes to let your muscles fully relax. Close your eyes and just be. Try not to think at all. Breathing deeply will help you feel even more at ease.

Let a stream of hot water blast the tightness out of your neck and back. Roll your head forward and from side to side. Lather your body slowly, giving yourself a massage in the process. Rub biceps and calves, knead your lower back, and massage your feet and toes as you wash them. Massage your scalp as you shampoo. Then just lean back against the wall and let the water fall on your skin.

(Opposite, top left and opposite, bottom) Just because you're showering or bathing alone doesn't mean it can't be a highly stimulating experience. Soak, rest, and relax, and then follow that up with a little solo sex.

(Opposite, top right) Washing your partner's hair is a wonderful way to treat them with some tender loving care.

Massage their temples and scalp as you work the shampoo into a lather. Be careful to keep the suds out of their eyes, and work your hands gently though their hair as you rinse it. As an adult, it can be both relaxing and stimulating to be handled like a child.

(Left) Take turns scrubbing each other's backs with firm, circular strokes.

(Above) When it's time to start soaping up each other's erogenous zones, do it slowly and sensually, letting your fingers slide over every inch of each other's skin.

(Opposite) Standing sex from behind is easiest in a small shower stall. The wall of the shower can be used for support (never lean on a glass shower door). If there's more room, the woman can bend over at the waist and hold on to the side of the tub for balance.

(Left) One fun-filled position for having sex in the tub is to lie side-by-side with your partner. The warm water and slippery soap is bound to add some extra spice to the experience. It's even more comfortable if you place a rubber mat on the bottom of the tub.

(Above) For her: Squeeze warm, soapy water from a sponge onto your partner's penis, aiming right for his extra-sensitive frenulum (the strip of skin that attaches the foreskin to the shaft of the penis on the undersurface of the glans), then follow up by stroking the entire shaft and head with a soapy hand.

(Far left) For him: Use the showerhead to squirt a steady stream of water at her clitoris. Many women masturbate this way, and you may discover that it can bring your partner to orgasm.

the rubdown

Giving a good massage is like any other sensual activity: the more focus and energy you put into it, the more pleasurable it will be. The simplest way to position yourself when giving your partner a massage is to straddle his or her buttocks. Using massage oil will help your hands slide smoothly over their skin. Don't use too much; your hands should move without friction, but shouldn't feel sloppy. Start by laying your palms on your partner's shoulders and sliding them down to the buttocks in one smooth stroke. Repeat several times to warm the skin. You could also do this long, warming stroke over the buttocks and down the legs and feet to wake up the entire body.

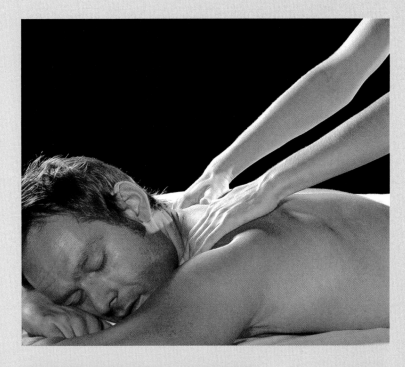

(Above and left) Knead the base of your partner's neck and upper shoulders.

Use your palms, thumbs, or knuckles to make firm circles along either side of the spine.

(Far left) Use your body weight to add more pressure if needed.

(Bottom, left and right) Explore outward from the spine, using little to no pressure over bones and deeper pressure over muscle. Listen to your partner. They'll clearly indicate when you've hit a spot that needs attention.

Work your way down the back, starting on either side of the spine, and then moving outward toward the sides of the torso. Continue using firm, fluid, circular strokes. Your right hand should make clockwise circles; your left, counterclockwise circles.

(Opposite, clockwise from top left) Kneading your partner's buttocks will send them to heaven. Knead your own butt to learn how much pressure to use.

Work your way down to the thighs and calves. The back of the legs may be tight and sensitive, so use light pressure. Avoid tickling feet by massaging with the heel of your palm instead of your fingers. Massage the thick, round pads of each toe individually.

(Counter clockwise from top left) When you work the front of your partner's body, start from the shoulders and gently massage the pectoral muscles. This is where the massage turns from therapeutic to sexual. Circle his or her nipples with your fingers. Slide your hands down the back and side of the torso with long, smooth, gentle strokes.

Be a tease; get closer without actually touching your partner's hot spots. Build anticipation for the moment when your hands finally reach a very hard penis or soaking wet vagina.

part 2

sexuality

Although sophisticated moves and skillful techniques can certainly improve your sex life, an understanding of sexuality will make it even better—and safer. That's what *Part 2: Sexuality*, is all about.

Much of what we know about sex can be traced directly to the Kinsey Institute, a division of an American university that is devoted to the scientific research of sex and sexuality and the training of sexual therapists. The institute is the outgrowth of the groundbreaking work of zoologist Alfred C. Kinsey. In 1938, Kinsey was asked to coordinate a course about sex for students who were preparing for marriage or who were already married. Kinsey and his peers began to conduct research and their first publication, *The Kinsey Reports: Sexual Behavior in the Human Male*, was released in 1948. The institute still exists and continues to provide invaluable information.

The joint efforts of William H. Masters, a gynecologist, and Virginia E. Johnson, a psychologist, have also been a major source of knowledge about sex and sexuality. Beginning in 1957, Masters and Johnson designed research tools that allowed them to measure the physical aspects of sexual response. The results of this research were published in 1966, in a book entitled *Human Sexual Response*, which quickly became a bestseller. In 1970, Masters and Johnson published *Human Sexual Inadequacy*, which discussed clinical treatments for sexual impotence, premature ejaculation, and other sexual problems. Others followed. In 1976, cultural historian, Shere Hite published *The Hite Report: A Nationwide Study of Female Sexuality*. The 478-page book contained not only statistics about women's sex lives, but also anecdotes from the women who participated in her research. A decade later, Hite updated her first study in *The Hite Report on Women and Love: A Cultural Revolution in Progress*. Her most controversial finding was that 98 percent of American women were unhappy with their sex lives.

For those individuals who are interested in this fascinating subject, many universities now offer courses on human sexuality. Most also frequently support in-depth studies on specific sexual topics.

The more effort an individual makes to discover his or her own sexuality, the more comfortable, confident, and satisfied he or she is likely to be with his or her sexual encounters. Learning about sex is also the best remedy for embarrassment or shame. Many people are surprised to discover how common their concerns and questions about sex are. If you are confused or curious about an aspect of sex or sexuality, chances are the answer you are seeking are in this section.

Her Anatomy

Although male anatomy may play a significant role in the daily life of a man, and perhaps his sexual partner, it has inspired nowhere near the number of paintings and sculptures, sonnets and songs, sermons and parental lectures—the veneration and the fear—that the female body has.

Many aspects of the female anatomy evoke wonder. Unlike the primary organs of male sexual anatomy, which are essentially external, a woman's organs are covered physically and, for many women, emotionally. And the clitoris, unlike the penis, has only one purpose: to give pleasure. Even the medical terms for the sexual features of a woman's body reflect the mythological and mysterious quality of the feminine. The hymen, named for the Greek god of marriage, is also called *maidenhead*, and for centuries has played a significant role in the course of a young woman's life (see page 202).

Although cultural attitudes toward women have changed dramatically in much of the world during the past 100 years, it is possible that the mystery, and therefore the continuing fear and misunderstanding, associated with female sexual anatomy is rooted in the fact that it is, for the most part, hidden. The first step toward understanding female anatomy is to acquire the knowledge of its internal and external components. This technical information may dispel some of the mystery of a woman's body, but it probably will also deepen your appreciation of it.

External Genitals

Not all of a woman's sexual organs are hidden, and the parts that can be seen—the external genitals—as a group are called the *vulva* or *pudendum*. The appearance of the vulva and the size of its diverse parts vary from one woman to another, and in fact it is common for the two sides to not "match" exactly on one woman. Looking at them from the belly side to the back side they appear in the order listed here.

Mons Pubis

The soft mound at the front of the vulva is the *mons pubis* or the *mons veneris* (see illustration, page 199), which in Latin means the mountain of Venus. It's an evocative name for a structure that can be sexually sensitive in some women, but its primary purpose is to protect the woman's pelvic bone during sexual

Q+A

Q: Sometimes after a long session of lovemaking with my husband, my clitoris feels sore. Could it possibly be getting injured?
A: Intercourse, no matter how vigorous, cannot injure your clitoris. And neither will contact with hands or the mouth or even a vibrating sex toy. The soreness you feel is a result of overstimulation, which can be uncomfortable, but not dangerous. The best way to avoid the discomfort would be to pay attention to how your body is responding during sex and limit the amount of stimulation your clitoris gets by shortening your lovemaking sessions somewhat or taking breaks. If the irritation occurs without sex or gets worse, the problem may be unrelated to intercourse and you should see your health care provider.

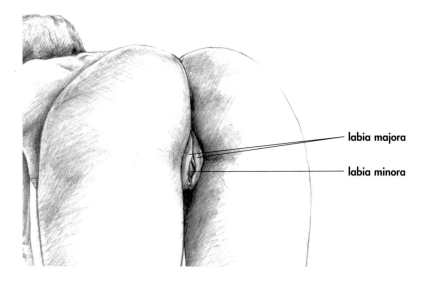

labia majora

labia minora

intercourse. After puberty, the mound is covered with a triangle of pubic hair (unless a woman chooses to remove it partially or totally).

Labia Majora

Latin for "large lips," the *labia majora* are pads of fatty tissue that extend from the mons pubis to the perineum (see illustration, page 198) and vary somewhat in size from woman to woman. They completely or partially hide the other parts of the vulva and often are covered with pubic hair. Their color can range from something close to a woman's overall skin tone to a more pink or brown hue. During sexual arousal the labia majora swell and flatten, moving away from the vaginal opening. After menopause, the lips become thinner and do not change as dramatically during sex.

Labia Minora

The companions to the labia majora, the *labia minora* (Latin for "small lips") are thin stretches of tissue that lie directly inside the larger lips, but may protrude beyond them

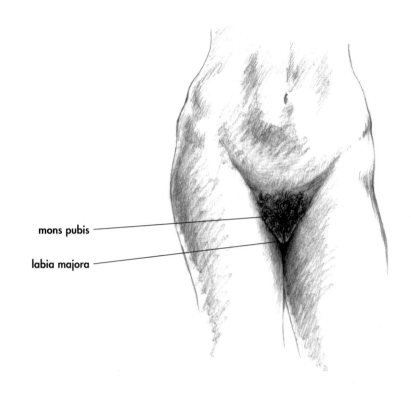

mons pubis

labia majora

(see illustration, page 198). The labia minora vary widely in size, color, and shape, but the most common metaphor used to describe them is a flower. They are soft, thin, and flexible, and the way they sometimes fold can be reminiscent of the petals of a tropical flower. When a woman becomes sexually aroused and is

about to reach orgasm, the labia minora swell and change color. In women who have had children, they change from dark red to a deep wine color; in women who have not had children, the change is from pink to bright red. Shortly after climax, the lips return to their normal size and color.

Clitoris

The most sensitive of a woman's sexual organs, the clitoris (see illustration, page 201) has one purpose—to provide sexual pleasure. It is a small area, but it is filled with nerves, making it highly sensitive to touch. Sex therapists often advise women to explore their clitoris (and discover its responses) through masturbation so they can share with their sexual partners what will give them the most pleasure.

Q+A

Q: I sometimes have a strong urge to urinate immediately after sex. Is there anything wrong with me?
A: The urethra and bladder lie among the reproductive organs and are slightly stimulated or irritated by the pressure and movement associated with sexual intercourse. Both men and women may respond to sex with an urge to go to the bathroom. If your bladder is full or nearly so when you are having sex, it's likely you will have the uncomfortable feeling you may urinate during intercourse because pressure on the bladder triggers the urge to urinate. Avoid the problem by urinating before you have intercourse, if you can.

her anatomy

Q: Sometimes when I have sex I don't get very wet and intercourse can hurt at first. Can I do anything to help that?

A: Vaginal lubrication depends on several factors, including level of sexual excitement, physical condition, and emotional state. Make sure you and your partner are taking enough time for you to become sufficiently stimulated before intercourse proceeds. Don't rush your body—let it respond in its time. If the problem is physical, it may be caused by a hormone imbalance (possibly due to the type of birth control pill being used) or a vaginal cyst or infection. If so, you may just require simple medical treatment. Either way, consult your health care provider.

An emotional or psychological basis for the problem could be a sign that you are under too much stress or that you have some doubts about your relationship. Many people respond to anxiety in a physical way. If the problem lies just in you, you may want to examine your lifestyle and make some changes to relieve stress. If your response is based on problems in your relationship, you need to talk with your partner and try to deal together with whatever is bothering you. If you feel you need more help, you can see a counselor by yourself or possibly a sex therapist with your partner. Take the opportunity your body is giving you to look at your relationship and make it what you need.

Note: Natural lubrication decreases as a woman ages, and doesn't indicate a physical or psychological problem. Any woman who feels she'd like more lubrication can use a personal lubricant. (If you are using condoms for birth control, make sure to use a water-based lubricant; oil-based lubricants can damage latex.) For more information about lubricants, see pages 138–139.

The clitoris consists of three nerve-packed parts: the *glans*, which is the visible tip; the shaft, which is hidden behind the *clitoral hood* and the tissue of the labia minora; and the *crura*, which are two arms attached to the base of the shaft that curve down the sides of the labia majora and back toward the thigh muscles. Clitoral tissue is erectile (like the penis) and as blood flows into the region during sexual arousal, the whole structure enlarges—the glans can double in size. During the excitement phase (see pages 230–232), the clitoris may move out from under the clitoral hood, but as a woman is about to climax, the clitoris retracts. If a woman does not have an orgasm, the clitoris may remain enlarged for a few hours, which can be uncomfortable.

Female Circumcision. Female circumcision is a term that refers to a number of procedures performed on the female genitalia for cultural, rather than medical, reasons. The consequences of female circumcision vary depending on the form practiced and the conditions under which it takes place. If the procedure is carried out without anesthesia in unclean conditions, a girl or woman may experience extreme pain and serious long-term health effects; it sometimes results in death. Female circumcision is widely used in certain parts of the world, but has been rejected almost completely by Western countries as barbaric, where it is sometimes now referred to as female genital mutilation.

Just like people, no two vaginas are alike. The difference in appearance can be quite marked, as shown by the illustrations at left.

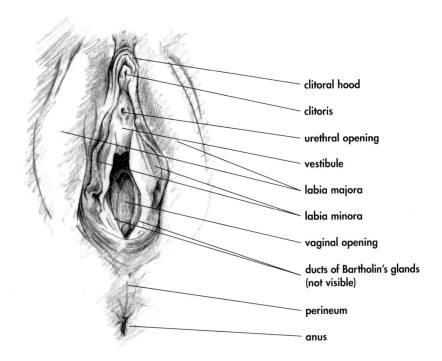

clitoral hood

clitoris

urethral opening

vestibule

labia majora

labia minora

vaginal opening

ducts of Bartholin's glands
(not visible)

perineum

anus

Vestibule

The area inside the labia minora is sometimes referred to as the *vestibule*. The openings to three different internal structures lie within this area: the opening to the urethra (the tube through which urine travels to leave the body); the opening to the vagina (see illustration, above), and the ducts of the Bartholin's glands (not visible), which secrete lubricating fluid during sexual stimulation.

Perineum

The short stretch of skin that lies between the vaginal opening and the anus is called the *perineum*. This area is sensitive and can be a source of pleasure for men and women when it is stimulated during sexual intercourse. This is also the area that frequently tears (or is cut) during childbirth to accommodate the passage of the baby from the birth canal to the world.

Anus

The anus is located at the end of the digestive tract and is the place from where solid waste leaves the body. It is sensitive to touch in both men and women and can be a source of pleasure when stimulated during sexual intercourse.

The structures of the vulva correspond to the anatomy of the male genitals (see illustration, page 215) and they share common developmental roots in an embryo. For instance, the clitoris glans corresponds to the glans penis, and the shaft of the clitoris corresponds to the corpora cavernosa. The labia minora, labia majora, and the clitoral hood correspond to the scrotum, and the vestibular bulbs that lie beneath the skin of the labia minora correspond to the corpus spongiosum. Lastly, the Bartholin's glands correspond to the male Cowper's glands (see illustration, page 218).

Q+A

Q: My grandmother died of cervical cancer and now my mother has been diagnosed with it. How can I keep from getting it?

A: Besides maintaining a healthy lifestyle that includes a good diet, exercise, and no smoking, there is little a person can do to prevent cancer. However, an important tool in early detection and treatment of cervical cancer is a test called a Pap smear or Pap test. Named for Dr. George Papanicolaou, who developed the test, a Pap smear is a procedure that your physician performs during a gynecological exam. The doctor uses a cotton swab to remove a sample from your cervix, the cells of which are examined by microscope to look for abnormal cells. The procedure usually causes little pain, but some women experience slight discomfort.

If the results of your Pap smear show abnormal cells are present, the test should be repeated to confirm the initial results. Abnormal cervical cells do not always indicate cervical cancer or any other serious disease. Many kinds of infections can explain the cells and may be treated without surgery. If the irregular cells are deemed highly suspicious or premalignant, your doctor may recommend the removal of the area where the cells are present. If the cells are malignant, the doctor may recommend a hysterectomy, but such a step needs to be thoroughly discussed and confirmed by a woman and her doctors before proceeding with surgery.

her anatomy

Q: My cousin has endometriosis, which has made it impossible for her to get pregnant. What is it? What causes it?

A: Endometriosis is a condition in which the kind of tissue that lines the uterus also grows outside the uterus and attaches to other organs in the abdominal cavity, particularly the ovaries and Fallopian tubes (see illustration, page 203). It is a progressive disease that tends to worsen and recur after it has been treated. Symptoms of the disorder include painful menstrual periods, abnormally heavy menstrual bleeding, and pain during or after sexual intercourse.

The endometrial tissue outside the uterus responds to menstrual cycle hormones in the same way as the lining of the uterus (it swells with blood, then is shed). Unlike the uterine lining, which is passed out of the body through the vagina, the tissue in the abdominal cavity has nowhere to go, which results in pools of blood in the abdomen, causing inflammation, which in turn causes scar tissue. This scarring can interfere with ovulation or block the Fallopian tubes, both of which may cause infertility. Endometriosis may also cause ovarian cysts.

The cause of endometriosis is not known, but theories do exist as to possible causes. One such theory suggests that during menstruation, endometrial tissue migrates back through the Fallopian tubes and into the abdomen, where it attaches and starts to grow. Another theory suggests that the disorder is the result of a genetic abnormality that causes endometrial cells to grow outside the uterus during fetal development.

Not every woman diagnosed with endometriosis is infertile or guaranteed to become so. Physicians categorize endometriosis as minimal, mild, moderate, and extensive, based on the amount of scarring and diseased tissue found upon examination. Depending on the stage a woman's endometriosis has reached, she will be treated with medication, surgery, or both.

Internal Genitals

The internal sexual organs of a woman offer a place for a man to participate in the creation of new life. Here, the sperm and egg have the opportunity to meet and join, and they ultimately make a home for an unborn child, delivering that child into the world. It's no wonder that ancient civilizations saw a woman's reproductive system and ability to conceive as sacred, and that even in contemporary times a pregnant woman is often viewed with awe. The structures that make up a woman's internal genitals include the hymen, Bartholin's glands, vagina, cervix, uterus, Fallopian tubes, and the ovaries.

The urethra is located among the sexual organs, but it does not serve any purpose in reproduction (unlike a man's urethra) and is not considered part of the reproductive system. However, because the urethra can affect and be affected by sexual activity, issues related to its functioning are discussed later in this section.

Hymen

Sometimes called maidenhead, and named for the Greek god of marriage, the hymen is a membrane that partially blocks the opening to the vagina. Almost all women are born with a hymen, but the size of the membrane varies widely. In many cultures the condition of the membrane is thought to indicate virginity, but the hymen can be ruptured during medical examinations, injury, and activities such as sports and exercise. Also, the insertion of a tampon and any masturbatory activity that involves inserting fingers or other objects into the vagina can rupture the hymen. All this clearly shows that a ruptured hymen is not an indication of having had intercourse or the loss of virginity.

If a girl is born with a hymen that completely blocks the vagina, she will have to undergo a procedure called hymenectomy before the onset of menstruation. If the hymen is not opened to some degree to allow the outflow of menstrual blood, illness and even death can occur. Some women have hymens that are too small or too flexible to be fully opened by normal activity and they may have to have the remaining tissue removed prior to having a child.

Bartholin's Glands

Lying on either side of the vaginal opening, the Bartholin's glands secrete some fluid when a woman is sexually aroused. The amount of fluid released is small, especially compared with the lubrication provided by glands farther inside the vagina, but it may assist somewhat

internal reproductive system

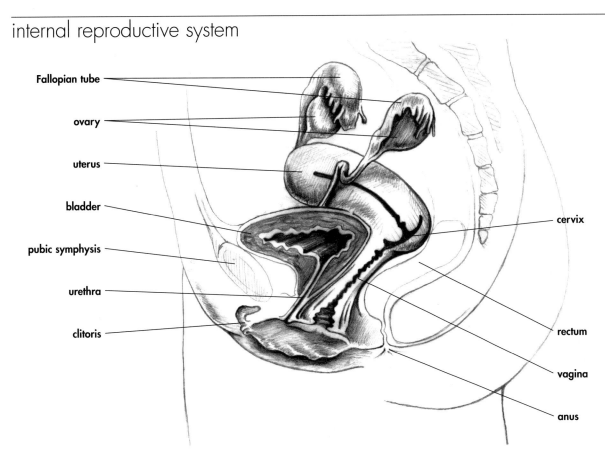

Fallopian tube

ovary

uterus

bladder

pubic symphysis

urethra

clitoris

cervix

rectum

vagina

anus

with penile penetration. Most women learn they have Bartholin's glands only when they become infected, which can cause pain and swelling. Any problems can be taken care of easily by a visit to your health care provider.

Urethra

The urethra (which is not part of the reproductive system) is a short tube that joins the bladder to an opening between the clitoris and vaginal opening. It allows urine to be eliminated from the body.

The urethra can serve as a path for bacteria to enter the bladder, causing cystitis, a general term referring to irritation, inflammation, or infection of the bladder. It is not a

sexually transmitted disease, but its symptoms, which include painful, burning, and frequent urination, may make it very uncomfortable.

There are many ways that bacteria can enter the urethra. The proximity of the urethra to the vagina makes it easy for sex to aggravate an infection. Seeking treatment from a health care provider is important when cystitis first strikes, although women who have had the infection before may feel comfortable treating themselves with over-the-counter medications. If there is any doubt about the cause of the symptoms, it is imperative that a woman see her health care provider immediately and not simply attempt to treat the infection herself.

Vagina

Most people think of the vagina just as an opening within the fleshy folds of the vulva, but it actually is an elastic, muscular tube about 4 inches (10 cm) long that joins the vulva to the cervix. Shaped like a flattened tube—imagine the sleeve of a shirt—it can stretch to receive a penis of almost any size or allow the delivery of a baby. (The vagina is often referred to as the birth canal during childbirth.) The vagina also provides sexual pleasure and a passage for menstrual blood to leave the body.

The vagina responds almost immediately to sexual arousal: within seconds it begins producing lubricating fluid that increases a woman's pleasure and makes

her anatomy

Q+A

Q: What is a "tipped" uterus and a "prolapsed" uterus?
A: Some women are born with their uterus tilted forward or backward of the normal angle the uterus takes in a woman's body. The condition is also known as a "displaced" uterus and does not usually cause any health, reproductive, or fertility problems.

A much more serious condition than a tipped uterus, a prolapsed uterus means the uterus has moved beyond the structures that support it into areas where it does not belong. If the ligaments supporting the uterus are weak, it can drop into the vagina. Such a problem is often found in older women or in a pregnant woman who has had several pregnancies. A prolapsed uterus can be painful and can interfere with conception. It is generally treated with surgery or a device worn in the vagina called a pessary to reposition the uterus and strengthen its natural supports.

penetration easier. Without this fluid, penetration can be painful. It is therefore recommended that lubrication be applied, if necessary, to make penetration easy and pleasurable. Although the upper two-thirds of the vagina are not especially sensitive to touch (it is more sensitive to pressure), the lower third, especially around the vaginal opening, is highly sensitive to touch.

Cervix

The cervix (from the Latin for *neck*) is the narrow part of the uterus that protrudes slightly into the top of the vagina. The cervix has a small opening called the *cervical os*, through which menstrual blood and sperm travel. The cervix also secretes mucus that changes in texture and appearance throughout a woman's monthly ovulation cycle. People using the birth control method known as natural family planning (see page 253) and couples who are trying to get pregnant use the cervical mucus as an indicator of ovulation and fertility.

The cervix is capable of expanding dramatically—just as the uterus and vagina can—to allow for the delivery of a baby. When a woman is pregnant the cervical os is blocked by a plug of mucus, the expulsion of which is an indicator that labor has begun (see page 268).

Uterus

Also called the womb, the uterus is the primary female reproductive organ. This pear-shaped, muscular organ figures largely in three processes: menstruation, pregnancy, and labor. The inner lining of the uterus is called the *endometrium*, which after puberty grows and changes throughout the menstrual cycle to prepare to receive a fertilized egg. If a woman does not become pregnant, the enriched layer of the endometrium is shed during

Q+A

Q: What are Kegel exercises and how can I do them?
A: Developed by Dr. Arnold Kegel in the 1940s, these exercises were designed to help women who had problems with passing urine involuntarily when they sneezed, when they had sex (often most severe at climax), or at other times. The exercises not only helped the women with their urinary incontinence, they had the unexpected result of increasing vaginal sensation. Kegel exercises are now used by women who want to tone their vaginal muscles (especially pregnant women and new mothers) and those with involuntary urination.

The exercises are easy to do. First, become aware of the muscles you use when you need to delay urination. Contract those muscles for a slow count of three (don't use your abdominal muscles), then relax them for the same slow count. Repeat the combination ten times several times a day for eight to ten weeks. To keep track of your progress, insert a finger into your vagina and tighten the muscles around it. As the weeks pass, you should be able to feel a big difference. Once the exercises have restored muscle tone, it can be maintained easily by doing Kegels several times a week. And remember: one of the biggest advantages of Kegels is that you can do them anywhere, at any time, and no one would ever know it.

menstruation. Unless a woman is pregnant or experiencing other problems, this process recurs every four weeks or so from puberty until menopause.

The uterus is normally about 3 to 4 inches (7 $\frac{1}{2}$ to 10 cm) long and about 3 inches (7 $\frac{1}{2}$ cm) wide. During pregnancy, it can grow to four times that size, creating a comfortable home for a developing child. Under the endometrium is a muscular layer called the *myometrium*, which gives the uterus its amazing flexibility. The muscles of the myometrium contract during labor to push a baby out of the uterus, into the birth canal (vagina); and out into the world.

Fallopian Tubes

A pair of slender ducts attached to the upper portion of the uterus, the Fallopian tubes are the route a woman's ova (plural for ovum, or *egg*) take to get from the ovaries (see below) to the uterus. They are named for the sixteenth-century anatomist Gregorio Fallopio, who first described them. The Fallopian tubes are not attached to the ovaries, but their upper ends, which look like the bell of a trumpet (but with a rough edge), cup the ovaries. When an egg is released from one of the ovaries, suction draws it into the opening of the Fallopian tube nearest to it.

The walls of the Fallopian tubes are lined with cilia, hairlike structures that move as the tubes contract slightly. The wavelike action of the cilia moves the ovum slowly toward the uterus, a trip that can take

Q+A

Q: My wife had to have one of her ovaries removed. Will she still be able to get pregnant?
A: Yes. As long as your wife has one healthy ovary (and no other fertility or reproductive problems), she will release an ovum during each cycle, creating the possibility of pregnancy. Because the ovaries work together in a unique way, when one is removed, the other picks up the slack and releases an egg every cycle. When your wife reached puberty, she had around 200,000 ova in each ovary and would only have released a total of 300 to 500 during her fertile years. Just like with a man's sperm, there are plenty of eggs available.

twenty-four to thirty-six hours. The Fallopian tubes present a challenge to sperm trying to make their way to an egg, because the sperm must swim against the current created by the motion of the cilia. This evolutionary safeguard helps ensure that only the healthiest sperm reach an egg to fertilize it, making it more likely that the pregnancy will be a successful one.

If and when fertilization (the joining of sperm and ovum) takes place, it usually occurs in the upper end of a Fallopian tube. The cilia move the zygote (the name for a newly joined egg and sperm) toward the uterus, where it will implant, and pregnancy begins. Sometimes the zygote gets stuck in the Fallopian tube and begins to grow, causing what is called an *ectopic pregnancy* (see page 266). Ectopic pregnancies can be dangerous and need to be treated medically.

Ovaries

A woman has two ovaries that are roughly oval in shape (1 inch thick x 1 inch wide x 1 $\frac{1}{4}$ inches long

[2 $\frac{1}{2}$ cm thick x 2 $\frac{1}{2}$ cm wide x 3 cm long]) and are located above and to either side of the uterus. They are not directly connected to the uterus or the Fallopian tubes. The purpose of the ovaries is to produce eggs. A woman is born with nearly one million eggs; she reaches puberty with approximately 200,000 ova in each ovary and between 300 and 500 of these will be released through a process called *ovulation* during her reproductive years, from puberty to menopause. Each ovum is contained in a follicle, a cavity in which an egg rests until it is mature. When ready, the egg rises through the follicle, which bursts (causing the twinge some women feel at ovulation) and releases the egg into the Fallopian tube near it.

Among the many fascinating aspects of a woman's reproductive system, the functioning of the ovaries stands out. When a woman is healthy, these two organs work in harmony to create a pattern of ovum release that varies from woman to woman but ensures that an egg will be available for fertilization each

her anatomy

Q+A

Q: Is it safe to have intercourse while I'm having my period?
A: The answer to this question varies from culture to culture. Some ancient cultures believed sex during menstruation was not advisable for the woman or the man, and the societies that have grown from those cultures often have maintained the same attitude. Contemporary Western cultures seem to neither advocate nor discourage it, leaving the decision up to individuals.

---

menstrual cycle. One ovary will release an egg for a certain number of cycles (one or more), and then the other ovary takes over to release its egg or eggs. A woman's body has the remarkable ability to adjust to the loss of one ovary, because the remaining ovary automatically begins releasing an egg every cycle.

Menstruation

Menstruation is the cyclical shedding of the lining of the uterus when it is not needed to support a fertilized ovum. Culturally, it is an important sign that a girl is becoming a woman, which could be seen as a powerful and positive personal transformation. But for hundreds of years this natural process has been greeted by men and women around the world with negative attitudes. In many cultures, menstruating women were (and sometimes still are) considered ill or unclean and so were not allowed to participate in a

wide variety of social activities. Young women were told not to run or study while on their periods; other women were not allowed to touch food; still others were isolated by themselves or with other women. If a culture teaches its women that menstruation is a bad thing, they will perceive it that way.

It's important to note the restrictions a woman's monthly bleeding placed on her also allowed her to take a break from daily work and spend time sharing knowledge with other women in her society. This time could be especially enriching for young women, giving them the opportunity to learn not only about sex, pregnancy, and child rearing, but also about medicine, history, and many other subjects.

Menstruation has traditionally been described in terms of "loss"—the loss of the uterine lining, the death of tissue, the deprivation of hormones. However, recent research has led to another interpretation of the process. Because it seems inefficient and costly to a woman's health for her body to build up and then shed the uterine lining every month, these researchers claim there must be a positive evolutionary purpose for menstruation, otherwise it would not occur. Their theory is that menstruation is a cleansing process, one that protects a woman's reproductive system from harmful microbes that may have been introduced into her body through sexual contact. The proof and wide acceptance of such an idea could go a long way toward changing attitudes about menstruation.

Menstruation Facts

The specifics of menstruation vary widely from woman to woman, but what follows are some guidelines that apply to most women. A young woman may experience her first menstruation (referred to as *menarche*) anytime between the ages of nine and eighteen. A menstrual period takes place approximately every twenty-one to forty days and typically lasts from three to seven days. Some women have their periods at regular intervals (for instance, every twenty-eight days), but other women do not. Unless a woman is pregnant, nursing, ill, severely underweight, or has problems with her reproductive system, she will menstruate every month for around forty years. The tapering and termination of menstruation is part of a natural process called *menopause* (see pages 208–209), and it generally occurs between the ages of forty-five and fifty.

The average menstrual cycle lasts about twenty-eight days. Five days after menstruation begins, the pituitary gland sends a signal via hormones to the ova contained within the follicles of the ovaries. Ten or twenty of the follicles start to grow, and the eggs begin to mature. (Usually only one ovum reaches maturity and is released.) The growing follicles release estrogen, which signals the endometrium (see pages 204–205) to thicken with blood and tissue in preparation to receive a fertilized egg. As an ovum reaches maturity, its follicle begins to release progesterone, which prompts the endometrium to produce additional nutrition for a fertilized egg. Around the fourteenth day of the menstrual cycle, one of the eggs matures and is released from its follicle (this is ovulation) and the egg moves into a Fallopian tube (see illustration, page 203). If the egg is not fertilized, it dissolves or passes out of the body along with vaginal fluids.

When no fertilized egg implants in the uterine lining, the process that has been building up the lining stops and, by around the twenty-fourth day, the lining begins to loosen. By the twenty-eighth day, it begins to break away and flow out through the cervix and vagina as menstrual fluid, which is a combination of tissue, mucus, and blood. The first day of the period is the first day of the new menstrual cycle, because the endometrium begins to form a new lining in preparation for the next (possibly fertilized) egg as soon as the old lining begins to separate and flow out.

Side Effects of Menstruation

Most women experience one or more of the following symptoms in response to the approach or arrival of their periods: cramps, headaches, backaches, acne, nausea, breast tenderness, fluid retention, fatigue, irritability, and depression. This is quite an array of unpleasant side effects (the umbrella term *dysmenorrhea* is often applied to these symptoms), and the tension they can create is very real. Some cultures attribute these symptoms to purely psychological or emotional factors, but that is oversimplifying the impact that strong hormonal changes can

have on a woman physically. Cultural attitudes toward menstruation and women can also play a role in how a woman experiences the side effects of having her period.

There are ways a woman can try to reduce the effects of dysmenorrhea, such as eliminating caffeine, reducing salt in the diet, getting more exercise, increasing rest, and reducing stress. If these methods don't work, she should talk to her medical advisor, since menstrual pain can also be a sign of medical problems such as infection, tumor, and endometriosis (see "Q+A," page 202).

Managing Menstruation

A woman born a thousand years ago would most likely recognize and know what to do with a contemporary sanitary napkin (pad) or a tampon. Women throughout history have used some version of these products, whether they were made out of natural sponges, grasses, or cloth.

One problem these women didn't have to worry about was *toxic shock syndrome* (TSS), a serious bacterial disease that primarily affects menstruating women under the age of thirty. Symptoms of TSS include fever (over 102°F/39°C), nausea and vomiting, diarrhea, dizziness, or lightheadedness (TSS can cause a

precipitous drop in blood pressure that may be fatal), and a sunburn-like rash. A woman who experiences any of these symptoms and is using a tampon during menstruation should get medical attention immediately. Also, anyone using tampons should change them regularly and avoid wearing them at night.

The majority of TSS cases have been associated with tampon use, but the cause of the disease is not yet known. One reason for the confusion is that around 5 percent of the TSS cases reported occur in women who don't use tampons and another 5 percent occur in men. The theory most widely accepted today is that the superabsorbent materials used in tampons allow women to use them longer, and they become breeding grounds for the bacteria that cause the disease.

Menstrual Complications

Irregular Menstruation. Many women do not ovulate and menstruate on a regular cycle—one cycle may take twenty-five days, the next thirty-five—but the irregularity itself does not indicate a medical problem. However, if a woman experiences unusually heavy bleeding and a great deal of pain during her menstration, a medical problem may exist and

Q+A

Q: I don't use birth control when I have sex during my period, but lately I've been wondering whether that's wise. Can a woman get pregnant while she is menstruating?
A: Yes. If you do not want to get pregnant, you and your partner should always use birth control, even when you are menstruating.

her anatomy

she should visit her health care provider as soon as she feels something is wrong.

A woman may miss a period completely without it indicating a medical problem. Unusual stress, travel, illness, and weight loss can cause a missed period or two, and a woman's cycle corrects itself when the stressor is gone. A woman who misses her period often—a few times a year—should visit her doctor.

Amenorrhea. The absence of menstruation when it would normally be present is called amenorrhea. A woman who has reached puberty and never had a period is experiencing primary amenorrhea. A woman who has had periods in the past but stops having them has secondary amenorrhea. Either type of the disorder may be caused by hormone imbalance, some diseases of the brain, ovaries, or pituitary gland, extensive drug use, or intense emotional stress. (Pregnancy also causes secondary amenorrhea, but the period's absence is normal in that case.) Either type of amenorrhea needs to be evaluated by a medical professional.

Hysterectomy

A hysterectomy is the surgical removal of the uterus. The procedure gets its name from the Greek word *hystera*. As the removal of one's uterus is an irreversible surgery, it should not be undertaken without serious consideration. The lack of a uterus entails permanent sterilization. Therefore, a hysterectomy should take place only when a woman and her medical advisors

have unmistakable evidence of disease or disorder that can be cured only by the removal of her uterus.

There are life-threatening conditions that require hysterectomy, such as cancer of the uterus or cancer of the cervix, vagina, Fallopian tubes, or ovaries that affect the uterus, severe and uncontrollable infection or bleeding, life-threatening blockage of the bladder or intestines by the uterus or a growth in the uterus, and rare but serious complications that occur during childbirth, such as a ruptured uterus.

Conditions that are not life-threatening but may require hysterectomy are precancerous changes in the endometrium, severe and recurrent pelvic infections, extensive endometriosis, extensive and large fibroid tumors, and uterine prolapse (see "Q+A," page 204). Many of these conditions can be treated nonsurgically, depending on their severity.

Unfortunately, some conditions are treated by hysterectomy unnecessarily, such as fibroids that are not causing problems, abortion, sterilization, cervicitis, mild uterine bleeding, and pelvic congestion.

Note: No woman should agree to a hysterectomy unless she has been shown conclusively by her health care provider that no other option is available.

Menopause

Strictly speaking, menopause occurs when a woman ceases to ovulate, which usually occurs when she is between the ages of forty-five and fifty-five. However, the physical changes that cause ovulation to stop

begin years before a woman's ovary releases its last egg, and can continue for years afterward. The emotional and psychological changes that accompany menopause make this period an important transition in a woman's life. Although a woman at first may feel a sense of loss when she is no longer sexually fertile, she usually discovers a sense of freedom because she no longer has to deal with the complications of menstruation and birth control.

A change in her menstrual cycle is usually the first sign a woman is approaching menopause. Her period may get shorter with lighter bleeding or longer with heavier bleeding. Sometimes, premenstrual symptoms become more intense or change in some other way. Unpredictable menstruation is another sign of menopause. A woman's period may stop for a few months, and then begin again. Some women experience no changes whatsoever in their cycle until menstruation just suddenly stops.

Note: Abnormal bleeding may be caused by an issue unrelated to menopause, such as a problem in the uterus or with its lining. Any woman should contact her doctor if she experiences unusually heavy bleeding, a flow that lasts longer than usual, bleeding that occurs more frequently than every three weeks, or bleeding after intercourse.

Effects of Menopause

The main side effects women experience as a result of menopause are hot flashes and vaginal changes. The hormonal imbalances that occur with menopause cause the blood vessels in the skin to dilate and constrict irregularly. This irregularity may cause the sensation of heat, unusual sweating, and the headaches many women experience during menopause. Hot flashes can be triggered by stress, a hot environment, spicy food, coffee, or alcohol.

The hormonal changes that cause hot flashes may also affect a woman's vagina. Most menopausal and postmenopausal women may experience thinning of the vaginal walls, loss of elasticity, flattening of vaginal ridges, foreshortening or narrowing of the vagina, and dryness and itching. Performing Kegel exercises (see page 204) may improve vaginal muscle tone, and using a personal lubricant can relieve dryness during intercourse. If a woman is still using birth control methods like condoms or a diaphragm, she should use a water-based lubricant.

Coping with Menopause

The two main medical treatments for menopause are estrogen replacement therapy (ERT) and hormone replacement therapy (HRT). Because of recent research showing that these therapies—especially ERT—may increase the risk of certain cancers, such as endometrial and breast cancer, their use has become controversial and some women have stopped treatment. The therapies have been shown to have some benefits, however. Estrogen replacement therapy calls for the supplementation of the lower levels of estrogen produced naturally by a woman's body after menopause. The

supplements, which can be taken orally, in patches, or in cream or vaginal suppository form, relieve the effects of hot flashes and vaginal dryness. Estrogen replacement therapy also provides protection from osteoporosis, heart disease, and stroke.

Hormone replacement therapy, which is the supplementation of a woman's estrogen and progesterone with additional estrogen and an artificial progesterone called progestin, has been shown to reduce the risk of endometrial cancer. If a menopausal or postmenopausal woman who has not had a hysterectomy wants some kind of hormone therapy, HRT is probably the better choice. Hormone replacement therapy in low doses combined with calcium supplements may also help reduce the bone loss that comes with age.

Breasts

A woman's breasts play a number of roles in her life: they can give sexual pleasure; they can shape her self-image and how others see her; and they allow her to feed a baby. Some women find having their breasts caressed highly erotic and arousing, while others don't find it especially stimulating. Whether or not the breasts are a focus of foreplay, it is normal for a woman's nipple to become erect in response to sexual arousal. The subject of how breasts affect the way a woman sees herself and how others see her is worthy of a book of its own—the intensity of focus on women's breasts is astounding. It is no surprise that feelings created by breast-related imagery in media and entertainment and the verbal and nonverbal responses from

Q+A

Q: I've been diagnosed with osteoporosis, and I'm only 38. Will I have to give up my active sex life?

A: Very few medical problems require a person to stop having sex, but some may call for an alteration in sexual activity. Osteoporosis, which causes the structure of the bones to thin and makes them more likely to break, usually occurs only in women who have reached menopause, but can occur in younger women and in men. Your diagnosis may mean you'll have to be more careful about vigorous sex now and to choose positions that are safe for you as you age. Your doctor will be able to offer more guidance, but here are some issues to keep in mind:

- A more leisurely style of lovemaking may be better for your health, and may actually increase your enjoyment of sex.
- Communication is key in a satisfying sex life, but it is especially important as you age or if you have a health problem. Talk to your partner about what is best for you, emotionally and physically.
- Whether you are newly diagnosed or are trying to prevent osteoporosis, take these steps to keep your bones as strong as possible: increase the calcium in your diet; increase the time you spend exercising; and reduce both alcohol intake and cigarette smoking.

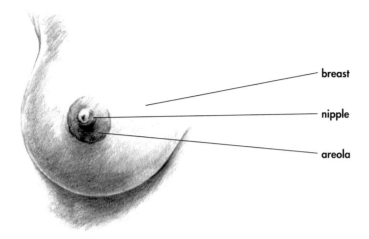

breast

nipple

areola

the people around her are likely to be complex. The opportunity to breast-feed a baby can be an extremely fulfilling experience for some women and incredibly frustrating and uncomfortable for others.

Breast Anatomy

These structures that can play such a complex role in a woman's life are not very complex in themselves. Breasts rest atop the pectoral muscles, and are comprised of a *nipple* and an *areola* on the outside (see illustration, above), and the *milk glands* and the *milk ducts* on the inside. The breast's fatty tissue protects the internal

structures (see illustration, page 211). A woman's nipples may be partially erect at all times, flattened when not aroused, set deeply into the breast, or even inverted (completely recessed into the breast). The nipples are richly supplied with nerve endings, which makes them highly responsive to stimuli, including touch (whether a lover's hand or a baby's mouth). The nipples are erectile tissues that respond to various stimuli, such as cold temperatures, a sneeze, and orgasm by becoming erect. A baby feeds and receives milk from the nipple because the ducts leading from the milk-producing

glands end there. The suction from a baby's mouth or a breast pump pulls the milk from the ducts through the porous nipple.

The areola (plural, areolae) is the pigmented area that rings the nipple. The color varies greatly from woman to woman, as does the size, and some women have hair within or surrounding the area. The small bumps on the areola are oil-producing glands that lubricate the area during breast-feeding. The oil helps protect the mother's tender skin from the abrasion caused by frequent breast-feeding, helping to reduce infections that may be dangerous to the mother and her baby. The areolae darken during pregnancy, then lighten again, but will always remain somewhat darker than before pregnancy.

The milk (mammary) glands are a series of sacs inside the breasts that produce milk and a milk-like fluid called *colostrum* when a woman is pregnant and breast-feeding—and only then. The breasts respond to hormonal changes caused by pregnancy by producing milk. When her baby is born, the first fluid he or she will drink is colostrum—nutritious liquid that contains high levels of protein and important antibodies that help protect newborns from certain diseases. The breasts provide colostrum for the first few days, and then a woman's milk "comes in," which means the breasts have stopped producing colostrum and have begun producing milk.

The milk ducts transport milk from the mammary glands to the nipple. When a baby sucks on the nipple and the area around it, the ducts

Q+A

Q: My husband loves to touch and kiss my breasts, and really focuses on them during foreplay. I'm happy he's enjoying himself, but all that handling doesn't excite me very much. Is that unusual?

A: No. Many women find that their breasts are not the most exciting part of their body and prefer to be caressed elsewhere during sex. If you haven't told your husband where and how you would like to be touched, you should. If you tell him what you want him to do, it's likely you will be as happy and enjoy yourself as much as he does.

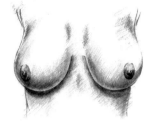
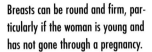
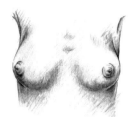
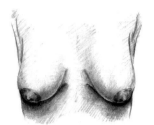

Breasts can be round and firm, particularly if the woman is young and has not gone through a pregnancy.

Divergent breasts are far apart and point away from each other. Nipples can either point out, down, or straight.

Bell-shaped, with large areolae, these breasts have folds extending laterally from the breast bone.

Breasts can also be narrowly gapped. Inverted nipples are common, but they may cause difficulty during nursing.

release the milk. Two hormones—prolactin and oxytocin—stimulate milk production. Prolactin prompts the milk glands to make milk, and as long as the baby nurses, prolactin is released to induce continued milk production. The other hormone, oxytocin, prompts milk to move from the glands into the milk ducts in a process known as "let down."

Breast-feeding seems as though it should be a natural process that a baby and mother know how to follow innately. This is not the case, however, as breast-feeding is a learned skill that can take many days for a baby (and a mother) to acquire. If a baby does not nurse vigorously enough, less prolactin and oxytocin are released, so less milk is produced by the glands and "let down" into the ducts and nipples. As with any acquired ability, breast-feeding takes determination and practice, which bring the desired result: milk for the growing baby.

Breast Size

Most societies place at least some importance on a woman's breast size and shape; in some cultures, such as in countries in the West, the focus

can be extraordinary. The pressure placed on girls and women by this attention can lead to painful anxieties and unnecessary surgery. Culture affects body image, body image affects self-image, so if the message a woman gets from her culture is that there is only one desirable breast size and shape, then she is most likely going to believe her breasts are too small, too large, or the wrong shape.

What women need to understand is that breasts are just as individual as any other part of the body (see illustrations, above). A nose can be wide and point down or be thin and turned up. Lips can be full or flat. Feet can be small or large. In the same way, there is no right breast size or shape. Although women may feel that other areas of their bodies, such as noses and lips, need treatment

internal breast anatomy

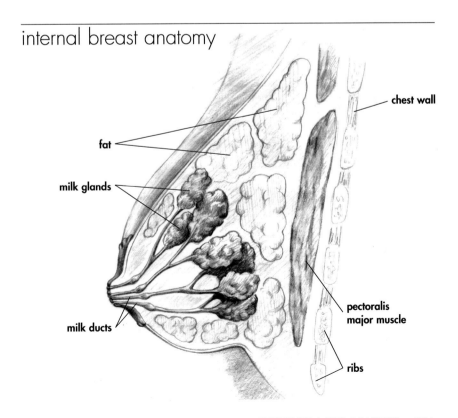

chest wall

fat

milk glands

pectoralis major muscle

milk ducts

ribs

her anatomy

Q: My boyfriend has told me he thinks my breasts get bigger when we have sex. Is that possible?

A: If a woman has never breast-fed a baby and has not reached menopause, it is normal for her breasts to swell during sexual arousal. Certain areas of the body swell with blood when a person is aroused, and, in women, the breasts are one of those areas.

---

to change or enhance them, more women express dissatisfaction with their breasts than other parts of their bodies.

Breast Enlargement

The number of women undergoing breast enlargement surgery has increased tremendously in the past three decades. The procedure is controversial because it is almost always performed for cosmetic reasons, but can pose serious health risks. However, some women find the change improves their self-image and mental health. The surgery requires general anesthesia and hospitalization, and consists of an incision being made in the breast tissue and chest muscle, and the insertion of a saline-filled silicone shell at the base of the breast. Implants have one drawback that is more serious than any other: They make it difficult for a woman or her doctor to detect lumps in the breast tissue. Breast self-exams are critical in the early detection and treatment of breast cancer.

Breast Reduction

The pressure in most cultures tends to push women toward wanting larger, not smaller breasts. However, there are women who feel their breasts are too big and choose to have their size reduced for cosmetic reasons. More often, breast reductions are performed to alleviate chronic back problems, or when the breasts interfere with normal movement.

Breast-Related Complications

The most common health problem women experience related to their breasts is lumps. Although 75 to 80 percent of lumps are benign, a woman who learns she has one is likely to be quite frightened. Fear of finding a lump may be the primary reason so many women do not perform breast self-exams, even though almost all lumps are found by a woman herself and early detection can save her life.

Breast Cancer. This is among the most common cancers in women around the world. In its early stages, breast cancer usually is not painful, but as the cancer grows, it can cause changes in the breast tissue. If a woman discovers any of the following changes, she should seek medical attention immediately:

- a lump or thickening in or around the breast or in the underarm area;
- a change in the size or shape of the breast;
- discharge from a nipple;
- a change in the color or feel of the skin of the breast, areola, or nipple (i.e., dimpled or puckered).

When a woman discovers she has a lump in her breast, her breasts will be examined thoroughly. The primary forms of exam are *mammogram, needle biopsy,* and *surgical biopsy.*

A mammogram is a low-dose X-ray of the breast that allows the doctor to assess the size, shape, and location of the lump. Mammograms are an important diagnostic tool because they can show tissue changes that may become lumps or detect the growth or spreading of abnormal tissue. Recommendations about how frequently women should have mammograms vary from country to country. See your health care provider to determine how early and often to have a mammogram.

A needle biopsy is usually performed with local anesthesia in a doctor's office rather than in a hospital. The test consists of the doctor inserting a needle into the lump and withdrawing fluid. If the lump breaks down or collapses immediately, it was probably a fluid cyst, which is usually benign and will soon disappear. A lump that does not collapse is not necessarily dangerous. Either way, the sample will be sent to a pathologist for examination.

Surgical biopsies are usually performed under general anesthesia in a hospital, although in some cases local anesthesia may also work. The surgeon makes an incision in the breast, then all or part of the lump is removed, and the incision is closed. The procedure usually leaves a scar, but does not change the shape of a woman's breast. The tissue sample is analyzed to determine whether it is cancerous or not. If the lump was benign, a woman will be advised to do self-exams and get frequent mammograms and gynecological exams. If the lump is cancerous, she and her doctors will discuss treatment options.

When a woman is diagnosed with cancer, she may have several treatment options from which to choose. Treatment methods are categorized as local or systemic. Local treatments remove, destroy, or control the cancer cells in a specific area. Surgery and radiation therapy are examples of local treatments. Systemic treatments destroy or control cancer cells throughout the body. Chemotherapy and hormone therapy are systemic treatments. A woman may have one form of treatment, or a combination of treatments, depending on the type of cancer she has.

Surgery is the most common treatment for breast cancer, and three specific procedures are most commonly used. A *lumpectomy* is the removal of the lump and a portion of the tissue around it. The rest of the breast is preserved. A *partial mastectomy* requires the removal of the tumor, some of the normal tissue surrounding it, and the lining over the chest muscles. In this procedure a large portion of the breast may be lost. A *total mastectomy* is the surgical removal of the entire breast—this is generally performed to prevent spreading of the disease.

Radiation therapy is often used after breast surgery. It involves the administration of doses of high-energy rays to kill remaining cancer cells. Sometimes, radioactive materials are implanted in the breast within thin plastic tubes.

Chemotherapy is the use of medications administered intravenously to kill cancer cells, and may be used after surgery. It usually takes place in cycles, with a treatment period followed by a period of recovery, and so on. Chemotherapy drugs tend to be powerful and have many side effects, including nausea and the loss of all body hair.

Hormone therapy prevents cancer cells from receiving the hormones they need to grow. This treatment may include the use of medications that change the way a woman's hormones work, or it may mean the surgical removal of the ovaries, which produce the hormones that support cancer cell growth.

Immunotherapy helps a woman's body fight cancer cells by triggering her immune system with drugs.

All breast cancer treatment methods have advantages and disadvantages. A woman must learn all she can about treatment options to get the best medical care possible.

Noncancerous Lumps. Seventy-five to 80 percent of all breast lumps are noncancerous and are most often caused by two conditions: *fibroadenoma* and *fibrocystic disease*. Fibroadenoma is a tumor comprised of fibrous tissue. It is round, firm, painless, and movable, and is common in women ages fifteen to forty. Some research

suggests that this condition may indicate a higher risk of breast cancer later in life, but the results are not definitive. Fibrocystic disease causes painful cysts that are filled with fluid. The fluid can be drawn off by a doctor if they become too large or too painful. Women with the disease generally experience symptoms more acutely immediately before their periods. As with fibroadenoma, fibrocystic disease may suggest a higher risk of cancer later in a woman's life.

Q+A

Q: I am thirty years old and am worried about breast cancer. Is performing a breast self-exam the most effective way to search for lumps in my breasts?

A: Examining your breasts is an important way to find breast cancer early, when it's most likely to be cured. The more you examine your breasts, the easier it will be for you to tell if something unusual has occurred. The breast self-exam (BSE) is an essential part of taking care of yourself and reducing your risk of cancer.

Try to get in the habit of doing a BSE once a month. Examine yourself several days after your period ends, when your breasts are least likely to be swollen. It is not unusual for lumps to appear at certain times of the month, but then disappear, as your body changes with the menstrual cycle. Only changes that last beyond one full cycle, or seem to get bigger or more prominent in some way, need your doctor's attention.

His Anatomy

A man's sexual anatomy is a complex system of organs and ancillary structures made up of the following components: penis, scrotum, testes (testicles), vas deferens, seminal vesicles, ejaculatory ducts, Cowper's glands, prostate gland, and urethra. Because the penis and, essentially, the testicles are outside the body, they are the most noticeable sexual organs and respond most obviously to their environment and sexual arousal. It is no surprise, then, that these structures receive so much attention. Accordingly, they are discussed first. The following pages describe in detail the male sexual anatomy—both internal and external structures—and discuss issues such as penis size, circumcision, and health problems affecting sexual activity. Erectile dysfunction is described briefly in this section and in more detail on pages 234–235.

The Penis

In addition to providing the route for the elimination of urine, the penis allows for the expulsion of semen—the fluid containing sperm, the male sex cell necessary for the fertilization of a woman's ovum (see page 262). During erection (see pages 216–217), the penis responds to stimuli by growing larger and rigid, unless a man suffers from erectile dysfunction.

The penis consists of three main parts: the root, the body, and the glans. The root of the penis is attached to the abdominal and pelvic walls. The body of the penis is the middle portion, which consists of three cylindrical areas of soft tissue bound together by fibrous tissue and covered by skin. The penis contains no cartilage or bone. The three areas of erectile tissue (the two *corpora cavernosa* and the *corpus spongiosum*) expand in response to sexual stimulation. Sexual excitement causes large amounts of blood to rush into the soft tissue; the blood is then trapped, because the vessels that drain blood from the penis have become compressed. This process—the penis moving from a flaccid state to a rigid one—is called an *erection*. The penis will remain rigid until a man ejaculates (i.e., semen is propelled out of the penis through the urethra) or stimulation ceases. At orgasm, a sphincter at the base of the bladder closes so that urine won't be expelled during ejaculation and semen does not enter the bladder. After ejaculation, the penis returns to its flaccid state.

The head of the penis is called the *glans*. In an uncircumcised man, the glans has a covering called the *foreskin*, or *prepuce* (see illustration, page 216), which shields the sensitive mucosal surface of the glans (see illustration, page 215) and allows it to remain moist. After circumcision, the glans remains smooth and sensitive, but develops a keratin layer. Usually, the foreskin can slide back to expose the glans after a boy has reached age two. In an adult, when the penis is erect, the foreskin retracts. During intercourse, it glides up and down the shaft but leaves the

Q: A strong odor seems to be coming from my penis. What could be the cause of that?

A: If you are uncircumcised, the most likely reason for the odor you are detecting is smegma, a waxy substance secreted by glands in the foreskin. Smegma can contribute to bacteria growth and infection if the area is not properly washed. Good hygiene calls for the foreskin to be retracted whenever you bathe (or at least once a week), and for the glans and foreskin to be rinsed thoroughly with water.

Another source of odor may be urine. Often, a drop or two is left on the tip of the penis after urination, and those drops can end up on your underwear or clothes. If you carefully shake or press those last few drops of urine from your penis and change your undergarments every day, your odor problem should go away.

Strong genital odor may be perfectly normal for you or it could be a sign of serious health problems. If good hygiene does not solve the problem, see a doctor, just to be sure. Sexually transmitted diseases can cause malodorous discharges from the penis or lesions in the genital area. Urethral infection can also cause odor. Whatever the cause, the odor generally disappears after medical treatment begins to take effect.

glans almost completely uncovered. Whether or not a man has been circumcised, the glans is highly sensitive. The concentration of nerves in the foreskin and glans is tremendous, making the structure responsive to pressure and touch. Where the head of the penis meets the shaft is a rim of tissue called the *corona*. When a foreskin is present, it is attached to the underside of the penis body near the corona by a membrane called the *frenulum*. Circumcised men may have only a fragment of the frenulum remaining.

Normally, all boys are born with a foreskin. Parents decide, for religious, cultural, or medical reasons, whether their baby should be circumcised and have this covering of skin removed. Circumcision is a controversial subject, and is discussed in more detail on pages 217–218.

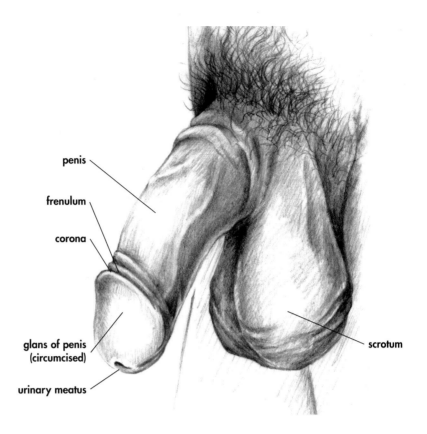

penis
frenulum
corona
glans of penis
(circumcised)
urinary meatus
scrotum

Penis Size

The penis grows in size and length most rapidly during puberty (apparently, so does a young man's anxiety about how large his penis should be). Penis growth is usually complete at the end of puberty—for most boys, around the age of seventeen. Despite this, having a penis that has reached its full growth does not end a man's questions about his sexual adequacy, especially because some cultures so strongly equate sexual success and masculinity with larger size—bigger with better. However, personal experience generally teaches a man that sexual satisfaction depends on many factors, with the size of his penis being merely one of them.

Genetics play the largest role in determining penis size. It is also important to note that flaccid penis size does not indicate the size a man's penis will be when erect. One man's penis may barely change in size when it passes from the flaccid to the erect state, whereas another man's penis may enlarge dramatically. Reliable statistics show that the length of the average adult penis ranges from $2^1/_2$ to $4^1/_2$ inches (6 to 11 cm) when flaccid, and 4 to 8 inches (10 to 20 cm) when erect.

Any man's flaccid penis changes in response to his environment (e.g., cold weather or a warm pool), activity level, and emotional state. However—contrary to popular belief—a man's body type, weight, and height have no bearing on the size of his penis, flaccid or erect.

Penile Complications

The physical damage most men fear at the deepest level is the loss of their penis. Regrettably, penile amputation (also called *penectomy*) is sometimes necessary because of a catastrophic injury or disease, such as cancer of the penis. However, in most cases, partial or total amputation of the penis is rarely necessary, and does not mean that a man cannot enjoy a satisfying sex life.

If, for some reason, a man loses his penis, it can be reconstructed with a surgical procedure called *phalloplasty*. The new penis can be made from tissue taken from the thigh, belly, or arm, and can be formed to allow for the elimination of urine. Because the new tissue cannot become erect, a man may choose to have his surgeon implant

his anatomy

A man's sexual anatomy includes the penis, scrotum, and testicles. A hood of skin, called the foreskin, covers the head (glans) of the penis. During circumcision, the prepuce of the foreskin, which is the skin that covers the tip of the penis, is removed.

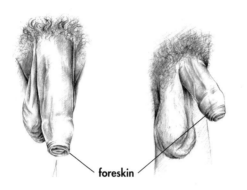

foreskin

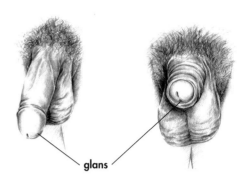

glans

a prosthesis that is rigid enough to allow penetration during intercourse, but is not so rigid as to cause the discomfort and embarrassment of conducting his daily life with a perpetual erection.

As long as injury or disease do not prevent it, ejaculation is physically possible after partial penectomy or phalloplasty. As has been stated before, psychological status has the greatest impact on a man's sex life. If a man believes he is no longer capable of having sex, his psychological state will affect him physically, making his belief a reality. But if he deals with the trauma caused by the loss of his penis, a man's libido can remain powerful, and he can be excited emotionally and physically to the point of orgasm. Also, he

can learn to gratify the needs of his partner in various ways, such as through manual, oral, or mechanical stimulation. The temptation to give up on sex after penectomy may be strong, but a man who, with his partner, puts in the effort needed to reinvigorate his sex life will find gratification is achievable.

Artificial penises that serve for urination and intercourse can be created for female-to-male transsexuals. Although the new penis may look and feel like the real thing, ejaculation is not possible because the transsexual does not have the actual reproductive system of a male. However, orgasm is possible, because the experience of climax actually is separate from ejaculation and can be experienced without it.

Erection

When a man is sexually aroused and his body and mind are healthy and responding normally, his penis becomes erect. Erection relies on a process called *vasocongestion*, in which blood flows into and is trapped in the three areas of spongy tissue in the penis—the two *corpora cavernosa* and *corpus spongiosum*. An erection can take just a few seconds to occur, as is common in adolescent boys, or it may take quite a bit longer. Penile response depends on age and the intensity of sexual stimulation, whether it be seen, felt, smelled, heard, tasted, or simply imagined. The speed with which the erection occurs and whether the penis reaches its maximum possible size do not dictate sexual satisfaction. The penis will remain rigid until a man ejaculates or stimulation stops.

As discussed earlier (see page 215), a man's ability to satisfy his partner has to do with much more than the size of his penis. And worrying excessively about whether his penis is "big enough," or whether he is going to be able to get an erection at all, can cause erectile dysfunction (see pages 234–235). It's important to note that if a man occasionally

Q+A

Q: Can a man ejaculate and urinate at the same time?
A: It is true that both a man's semen and his urine must pass through a tube in his penis called the urethra, but nature makes sure that the two substances don't mix. When a man is about to ejaculate, the prostate gland automatically squeezes shut the duct between the bladder and the urethra, thus preventing urine from mixing with semen. This process is crucial to reproduction, because urine contains much more acid than semen and can damage sperm.

does not get an erection when he expects or wants one, he is not necessarily suffering from erectile dysfunction. The experience can be embarrassing both for a man and his partner, but it is not uncommon—it has happened to almost every sexually active male. Lack of an erection is not a cause for alarm unless it happens with enough frequency to cause psychological damage or stress on his relationship. In such cases, therapy almost always helps.

Circumcision

Circumcision is a surgical procedure to remove the foreskin (see illustration, page 216) from the penis. The practice of circumcision has grown increasingly controversial in the past few decades, and the number of parents choosing to have their male babies circumcised is shrinking. The United States has the highest circumcision rates among Western countries, although the rates vary by region from a low of around 40 percent to as high as 90 percent. Statistics about circumcision rates in other countries vary, but reliable estimates show that in Canada, fewer than half of newborn boys are circumcised, and in the United Kingdom the rate is 25 percent.

Q+A

Q: I've heard that there are men who can maintain an erection for hours and even days. Can that really happen?

A: Yes. And though some men may fantasize about such a thing happening to them, in reality it is extremely painful. The condition, known as priapism, is defined as the occurrence of a persistent erection of more than four hours' duration in the absence of sexual stimulation. Priapism is named after Priapus, the Greek god of fertility, but the condition has nothing to do with reproduction. Priapism is not related to sexual excitement, at least not at first, and if a man suffering from it does become stimulated and ejaculates, the erection does not subside as it would normally. With priapism, blood flows into the penis, but for some reason it is unable to drain as it normally would. When the blood begins to stagnate, the red blood cells stiffen, making it even more difficult for the blood to drain from the penis.

Priapism can occur in all age groups, including newborns, and can be caused by leukemia, sickle-cell disease, and spinal cord disease or injury. Most often, priapism in adults is a side effect of drug therapy—antipsychotic medications and drugs used to treat high-blood pressure can cause it. In rare cases, priapism may be caused by cancer that has infiltrated the penis and prevented the outflow of blood.

The best way to prevent permanent damage from an episode of priapism is to act quickly when it happens. When it occurs, go to an emergency room with a urologist present or request that one be called. Once diagnosed, it is critical to get treatment right away.

One reason circumcision is a divisive cultural issue is that the recognized medical benefits are not always seen as outweighing the potential health risks involved at any age and the alleged loss of sexual sensitivity of the adult from the operation. Also, most circumcisions take place without the patient's consent, because the bulk of the procedures are performed on newborns.

Research confirms that circumcised infants are significantly less likely to develop bladder and kidney

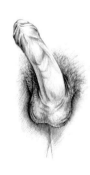

A man's erection may be straight along its length, or it may curve left or right. And, of course, his penis may do two of these things at once. For example, it may lean to the left as well as curve upward.

his anatomy

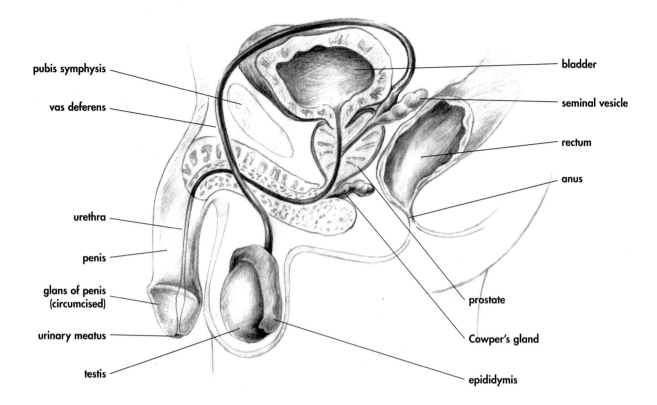

pubis symphysis	bladder
vas deferens	seminal vesicle
	rectum
urethra	anus
penis	
glans of penis (circumcised)	prostate
urinary meatus	Cowper's gland
testis	epididymis

infections. Studies also show that circumcision may reduce the risk of developing penile cancer and a number of sexually transmitted diseases. However, such benefits may not justify recommending circumcision as a routine procedure for all baby boys. Parents should discuss the risks and benefits of the procedure with their child's pediatrician and make an informed decision about what is best for their child.

Many physicians agree that if a circumcision is going to take place, some form of pain relief should be administered. In the past, circumcisions often took place without any anesthetic or analgesic due to a belief that the infant did not feel any pain associated with the procedure. Recent research shows this not to be the case, although the amount of pain is still unknown.

If his parents decide not to circumcise him, it is important that they take proper care of his penis while he is a baby (a pediatrician can provide new parents with the information they need), and teach him how to maintain good hygiene when he is old enough.

Scrotum

The scrotum, or scrotal sac, is a pouch of skin and thin muscle that holds the testes, blood vessels, and part of the spermatic cords. The sac lies behind the penis and, when a man is standing normally, allows one testis to hang on each side of the penis (see next section for details about testes). Sperm are produced in the testes, which need to be a few degrees cooler than normal internal body temperature—98.6°F (37°C)—for the sperm to develop

safely; therefore, the scrotum hangs slightly away from the body. The scrotum functions as a climate-control system and a safety net for the testes. The muscles in the scrotum move the testicles closer to the body in response to outside stimuli (cold temperatures) and internal stimuli (fear and anger). The primary purpose of the scrotum is to keep the testes at the ideal temperature for sperm development. If the testes are too warm for too prolonged a period of time, they can be permanently damaged—resulting in infertility.

Testicles

The testes, or testicles (testis is singular), are two oval organs, each about the size of a walnut, contained in the scrotal sac. The testis of an adult male weighs a little less than an ounce, although one testis may be slightly

The scrotum lies behind the penis and holds the testes. The testes are two oval organs, each about the size of a walnut and weighing less than an ounce. One testis may be slightly larger and hang lower than the other. Also, as a man ages, his scrotum may drop slightly.

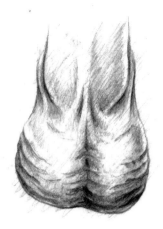 

larger and hang lower in the scrotum than the other. Although the penis may be seen as the organ that makes the man, without the testes, a boy would never become a man.

The testes have two main roles in the sexual system: to produce sperm (short for *spermatozoa*, the male sex cells), and to produce sex hormones called *androgens*, the most important of which is testosterone (see Hormones, page 220). The testes begin producing sperm during puberty and continue to produce them, barring injury or disease, until death. Testosterone production begins *in utero*, increases significantly during puberty (contributing strongly to sexual maturation), and maintains a high level until around age sixty, when production begins slowly to drop.

Testicular Problems

Undescended Testes. The testes develop in the abdominal cavity of a male fetus. Normally, they descend into the scrotum before birth, but in close to 4 percent of male babies, one or both of the testicles do not drop. This condition is called *cryptorchidism*, or undescended testicle. In 65 percent of infants suffering from cryptorchidism, the condition resolves itself before nine months of age. Boys with testicles that do not descend into the scrotum by one

Q+A

Q: My roommate came home from a date recently complaining about having "blue balls." What are blue balls, and why do they happen?

A: The term refers to the sensation caused when a man is aroused but does not ejaculate. Sexual excitement in men and women leads to vasocongestion—the rapid accumulation of blood in the genitals. In a man, vasocongestion causes the penis to become erect and the testes to grow. If he does not reach orgasm and ejaculate (especially after an extended period of arousal), the extra blood in the area does not flow out quickly, as it would if he had ejaculated. The blood that remains can cause the pelvic area to ache, with the testicles feeling especially tender. The extra blood eventually will dissipate, softening a man's erection and alleviating his physical discomfort.

The emotional discomfort that accompanies "blue balls" can increase a man's perception of his physical distress. Because many men see the goal of sex only as orgasm and ejaculation, they can feel frustrated and dissatisfied when they do not achieve that goal. This frustration can lead a man to put pressure on his partner to satisfy him, whether or not his partner is willing or even able to do so. A man who learns that ejaculation is not a requirement in every sexual encounter, and that sex can be meaningful and pleasurable without orgasm, is going to have a more relaxed and satisfying sex life.

By the way, the testicles do not actually turn blue, but the skin of the scrotum may seem to be bluish because the blood that engorges the area has been depleted of oxygen. Newer blood is a bright red, while older blood is darker and appears bluish when seen through the skin. If your blue balls last for several hours or days after arousal has stopped, see a health care professional.

his anatomy

year of age need medical attention in order to evaluate the problem and consider any possible solutions.

Undescended testicles are usually treated with hormone injections (to stimulate movement of the testicle into the scrotum) or surgery. Currently, the trend is to treat the problem early in a boy's life in order to prevent irreversible damage to the testis, which can cause infertility. A man with an untreated undescended testicle is also at increased risk of developing cancer in both testicles, regardless of when the undescended testis was brought into the scrotum.

In about 5 percent of boys with undescended testicles, surgery reveals that they do not have the testicle. This is called a vanished or absent testis, which may be caused by interrupted blood flow in the uterus during development.

Sometimes a descended testicle can move back out of the scrotum due to the strength of the muscular contractions that pull the scrotum toward the body in relation to the small mass of the testicle before puberty. Surgery is not necessary in this situation, because the testicle drops permanently at puberty.

Hormones

Androgens are a group of hormones that stimulate or control the development and maintenance of masculine characteristics in humans; specifically, these are physical development, sexual desire, and behavior. The primary and most well-known androgen is testosterone. Androgens are produced primarily in the testicles, and, to a much lesser degree, by the adrenal glands. Just as a woman's body normally produces small amounts of testosterone, men produce small amounts of the female sex hormone estrogen.

The changes of puberty, caused primarily by testosterone, are triggered by the pituitary gland, which functions under the influence of the hypothalamus gland. Puberty begins once the hypothalamus gland allows the pituitary gland to signal the testes to increase the production of testosterone. The tremendously increased levels of testosterone in turn stimulate the growth and development of the penis, scrotum, and testes, and the secondary sex characteristics, such as pubic and facial hair, muscle growth, and deepening of the voice. Testosterone

production continues at the higher level until much later in life, when there is a gradual decrease. Although many other factors can have a much greater impact on a man's sex drive, low testosterone levels may decrease libido at any age.

Sperm

Male sex cells are the spermatozoa, referred to as sperm. The sperm hold half of the genetic information necessary to reproduce life, the other half being carried by the ovum (egg), the female sex cell. Each sex cell contributes twenty-three pairs of chromosomes, which are dense coils of DNA, and the total forty-six chromosomes determine everything about the child from gender to eye and hair color. Generally, the sperm govern a baby's gender, because they contain two kinds of sex chromosomes (XY), while the ovum carries only one type (XX). In normal development, when an egg is fertilized by a sperm, the sex cells combine as XY, which means the baby will be a boy, or XX, which means a girl will be born.

Spermatogenesis (sperm production), which takes place in the testicles (see pages 218–219), begins around puberty and continues for the remainder of a man's life. The process requires around two-and-a-half months to produce a mature sperm, which develops in stages. A brief description of the stages of spermatogenesis shows that a single sperm cell's life begins in the seminiferous tubules, where elemental germ cells turn into spermatogonia, with forty-six chromosomes each. The spermatogonia divide repeatedly, eventually producing cells called primary spermatocytes, still with forty-six chromosomes. These divide again to produce secondary spermatocytes, now with twenty-three chromosomes each. The next cell division produces spermatids, which then develop into spermatozoa, or individual sperm cells.

A healthy young man will produce more than one hundred million mature sperm daily, with a normal sperm count consisting of twenty million sperm per ejaculate. With sufficient semen (the mixture of fluids that form a man's ejaculate) and forward motility (the capacity to swim), concentrations as low as five to ten million can cause pregnancy. Sperm that are not ejaculated eventually break down and are reabsorbed by the tissue in the testicles. This is normal and does not cause any physical discomfort or damage to a man's reproductive system.

A single sperm, because it is only one cell, cannot be seen with the naked eye. When massed together, all of the many millions of sperm released in one ejaculation would be no larger than a grain of sand.

The sperm consists of three parts: a head, a body, and a tail. The head contains the twenty-three chromosomes contributed by a man to his child's genetic makeup. The body of the sperm provides the "food" converted into energy by the sperm so that it can move on its own after ejaculation. The sperm's tail, the *flagellum*, is a whiplike structure that lashes back and forth, propelling the sperm forward through the liquids

Q+A

Q: What happens if a man loses both of his testicles?

A: In the case of disease or catastrophic accident causing the loss of both testicles, a man is seriously affected, but a boy's future would change drastically. The testes produce sperm, so the loss of both would ensure sterility, whenever it happened in a male's life. More importantly for a boy, however, the testes produce testosterone, an important male sex hormone that triggers the changes in adolescence that physically transform a boy into a man. If he loses his testicles before puberty, the lack of testosterone will prevent his voice from deepening, his facial and pubic hair from growing in completely, his sexual organs from growing to normal adult size, and his body in general from developing to a normal adult size and stature. The adrenal glands also produce testosterone, but only 5 percent of what is needed for normal development. Hormone therapy may help, but young men who have lost their testes rarely have normal sex lives, because they have diminished libidos and only in rare cases can achieve an erection or ejaculate.

Testicle loss in adulthood can be devastating, but, with the exception of sterility, the physical side effects are not as severe as those faced by a prepubescent. Research shows that when a man's testicles are removed, he loses muscle mass, his metabolism and respiration slow, and he loses body fat. His sexual functions may be retained with carefully monitored male hormone treatment.

it encounters during intercourse and fertilization. A sperm must be able to move on its own through the vagina, uterus, and Fallopian tubes to reach an ovum and fertilize it. It takes an hour for sperm to move 5 to 7 inches (about 13 to 18 cm), and, of the millions of sperm ejaculated, only about a hundred ever reach the general vicinity of the female egg.

The Road Sperm Take

Once sperm have been "born" in the testes, they start down a road that can lead them out of the penis as a result of ejaculation. The road is made up of a series of chambers and tubes that are met and fed by various glands. Describing the route may take longer

than the time it takes for the sperm to actually make the trip, since sperm usually start down the course only as a result of sexual excitement. Regardless of timing, what follows is a detailed description of the sites along a sperm's route. Since the prostate is an especially important point on the sperm's road, problems related to it will be discussed at the end of the section.

Epididymis

Newly developed sperm move from the seminiferous tubules (see illustration, page 223) into the *epididymis*, the tightly coiled, crescent-shaped tubes located on the upper surface of each testis. In each epididymis, sperm take on nutrients and

his anatomy

complete their maturation process. Sperm remain in the tubes until ejaculation—whether caused by intercourse, masturbation, or nocturnal emission—or until they naturally break down and are absorbed into the surrounding tissue. During their time in the epididymis, sperm are completely inactive.

Vas Deferens

Also called the *ductus deferens*, the two *vasa deferentia* are thick-walled tubes that transport sperm cells out of the epididymis in each testicle during sexual arousal. The vas deferens is the main transporter of sperm. Its walls contain three layers of muscle and nerves. Stimulation of these nerves during arousal causes the muscles to contract. These contractions propel sperm forward toward organs that secrete the fluids that mix with sperm to become semen, the substance a man ejaculates.

Each vas deferens is around 18 inches long (about 28 cm) and travels out of the scrotum through the spermatic cord and into the abdomen. In the abdomen, the tubes pass behind the bladder and then each expands to form an ampulla— a kind of reservoir—that joins with a seminal vesicle to form an ejaculatory duct inside the prostate gland (see illustration, page 223).

Because the two vasa deferentia are easily accessible structures that carry sperm and nothing else, they are the ideal place for the birth-control method called a vasectomy (see pages 256–257). In this simple surgical procedure (usually performed in the doctor's office), each

vas deferens is cut and sewn shut, preventing sperm from mixing with the other components of semen. A vasectomy prevents fertility, but does not affect sexual functioning in any other way.

Seminal Vesicles

Once sperm have traveled from the epididymis through the vas deferens, they reach the ampulla, the end of the vas deferens that meets the seminal vesicles. The seminal vesicles are pouches that secrete fructose, a sugary fluid that provides nutrients for the sperm and protects them by neutralizing acid, such as remnants of urine in the urethra or the acidic fluids in a woman's vagina and uterus. The mixing of sperm and seminal fluid is the beginning of the fluid called semen.

Ejaculatory Duct

The ends of the vas deferens and the seminal vesicles join to form the ejaculatory ducts, two tubes about 1 inch (about 2 1/2 cm) long that lie inside the prostate gland and lead to the urethra. When sperm and seminal fluid are driven into the ejaculatory ducts by muscular contractions in the vas deferens, they combine with additional fluid secreted by the prostate gland to form semen. (The Cowper's glands secrete a clear, pre-ejaculatoy liquid that lubricates the urethra in preparation for ejaculation. Strictly speaking, this sticky, mucus-rich fluid is not a component of semen.) Semen collects in the ducts just before ejaculation, when reflexive muscle contractions will propel the fluid from the ducts out of the urethra in several quick spurts.

Q+A

Q: I am thirty-five years old and was recently diagnosed with testicular cancer. I need to have radiation therapy; however, because my wife and I want to have another child, I am worried about my fertility. Can sperm banking really keep my sperm frozen and healthy for a few years?

A: Sperm banking (or cryobanking) allows a man in your situation to store his sperm before starting radiation or chemotherapy. Sperm banks freeze sperm specimens and store them in liquid nitrogen-cooled refrigerators for as long as you wish. Before you start your radiation treatments, you will probably be advised to collect specimens over at least two weeks to begin the sperm-banking process. Specimens can be stored because, although freezing does affect the capacity of some sperm to fertilize eggs, it does not affect enough of the sperm in the sample to prevent fertilization.

There are costs associated with sperm banking, which vary among institutions, but some insurance companies cover part of the cost. You and your physician will most likely want to start treatment as soon as possible, so it is important to locate a sperm bank and start the banking process quickly. Talk with your physician about your worries and ask for a referral to a fertility specialist.

An erection is caused by blood flowing into and filling two spongy bodies of tissue that run the length of the penis. The *corpus cavernosum* runs along the top of the penis, and the *corpus spongiosum* runs along the urethra.

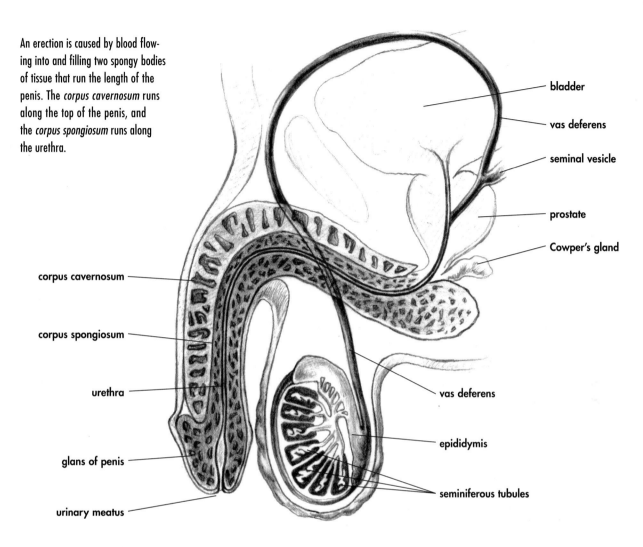

bladder

vas deferens

seminal vesicle

prostate

Cowper's gland

corpus cavernosum

corpus spongiosum

urethra

glans of penis

urinary meatus

vas deferens

epididymis

seminiferous tubules

Prostate Gland

The prostate gland is a doughnut-shaped structure that lies under the bladder (see illustration, above) and is about the size of a walnut in a young man. As men age, the prostate grows, sometimes causing health problems. Made up of a series of concentric zones, it surrounds the bladder's neck and the top section of the urethra—the tube that carries urine from the bladder. The prostate is partly muscular and partly glandular, with ducts opening into the prostatic portion of the urethra. Through these ducts, the prostate gland secretes a slightly alkaline fluid that protects and nourishes the sperm. Prostatic fluid forms roughly 35 percent of the volume of semen, with a larger amount contributed by the seminal vesicles. Only about 1 percent of the total fluid a man ejaculates is sperm. In a healthy man, the sphincters (valves) at the top and bottom of the prostate gland function to stop urine from leaking into semen during intercourse. These sphincters also prevent semen from entering the bladder. (Information about health problems related to the prostate follows.)

Prostate Complications

A young man may know he has a prostate gland, but he probably doesn't know exactly where it is. Some men find out they have the gland the first time they have a physical after they've turned forty. Since the best way for a physician to examine the prostate requires a rectal examination, a man's first introduction to the prostate can be at best a surprise and at worst embarrassing and uncomfortable.

Whenever a man learns about his prostate, he needs to understand how important it is to his sexual health and to his health in general. Prostate disease rates vary widely according to country, region, and ethnicity, but the problems affect a huge percentage of men around the world. Prostate diseases usually occur in men over age fifty (or men with a family history of prostate troubles), but doctors recommend that regular examinations begin at age forty in order to catch potential problems early. A yearly rectal examination frequently allows a man's doctor to detect prostate disease before symptoms develop. At this early stage, even prostate cancer is curable.

Prostatitis. *Prostatitis*, a swelling of the prostate, is often the reason a young or middle-aged man visits his doctor with complaints involving his genital and urinary systems. The symptoms that most often cause the doctor's visit are painful urination or ejaculation. Prostatitis is actually an umbrella term for three different types of the disorder.

Acute infectious prostatitis is the least common type and is usually caused by bacteria. Doctors often recommend treatment with anti-microbial medication or an antibiotic. Acute infectious prostatitis comes on suddenly, and its symptoms—frequent and urgent urination, lower abdominal pain and pressure, burning during urination, and chills and fever—can be severe and life threatening because of the danger of blood infection. A man experiencing these symptoms needs to see his doctor or go to an emergency room immediately. He will most likely need to be hospitalized.

Chronic infectious prostatitis is also caused by bacteria and, therefore, can be treated with antimicrobial medication or antibiotics. Unlike an acute prostate infection, the only symptom of chronic infectious prostatitis may be a recurring bladder infection. Although its symptoms may not be as severe, a chronic prostate infection can be as potentially debilitating as the acute form because of its recurrent nature.

Chronic noninfectious prostatitis is diagnosed when all the possible infectious causes for a man's prostatitis have been eliminated, but the disease persists. This is the most common type of prostatitis and it is difficult to treat successfully. A man of any age may suffer from it, and its symptoms may come and go without warning. Antimicrobial medications or antibiotics do not work for this type of prostatitis. A man diagnosed with chronic noninfectious prostatitis most likely has a urologic problem that leaves him vulnerable to prostatitis. It is essential that he undergo a thorough evaluation to discover the underlying cause of the problem (for example, kidney stones or urethral cancer).

Prostate Cancer. Prostate cancer, a common type of the disease, often grows slowly and begins in the outer prostate. Although early prostate cancer often causes no symptoms, as the cancer develops, it may spread to surrounding areas, such as the bladder and pelvic bones.

The best protection a man has against prostate cancer is early detection. Regular checkups, including a

rectal exam, are crucial to the early treatment of any prostate disease, but especially cancer. Any man who experiences changes in urination, including increased frequency, hesitancy, or dribbling, could be exhibiting symptoms of cancer and should be seen by his health care provider as soon as possible.

Appropriate treatment for prostate cancer is based upon the stage the disease has reached and other factors, such as a man's age and general physical condition. Treatment options include hormone therapy, surgery, radiation, chemotherapy, and observation. Below, each treatment is described: first, the goal of the treatment, and then its impact on a man's body and sex life. It is important for a man with prostate cancer (and his loved ones) to understand all the treatment options, because many doctors will choose to use a combination of therapies to treat this serious disease.

The goal of *hormone therapy* is to reduce the production or block the effects of testosterone (see page 220), a male hormone that can stimulate the growth of certain types of prostate cancer. Hormone therapy is not a cure for prostate cancer, however, it can slow the disease's progress thereby improving the patient's quality of life.

Surgery is an attempt to cure prostate cancer by removing the gland from the body physically. This usually requires the removal of the entire prostate and, depending upon the size of the tumor, some tissue surrounding it. A surgeon will try to remove only the tissue that is necessary to protect a man's health. A noninvasive treatment called *cryosurgery* freezes the prostate through an incision instead of removing it.

Radiation therapy uses high-energy X-rays, either beamed from a machine or emitted by radioactive seeds implanted in the prostate. External radiation calls for the prostate and the area around it, including the pelvis, to receive varying levels of radiation to kill malignant cells and possibly cure the cancer. A man receiving internal radiation therapy has tiny radioactive implants placed directly into or next to the prostate gland.

Chemotherapy uses drugs to target and destroy rapidly dividing cancer cells. However, chemotherapy drugs can also have negative effects on healthy noncancerous cells that divide quickly, such as those in bone marrow, the lining of the gastrointestinal system, and hair follicles.

Because prostate cancer often spreads very slowly, a man who is older or has other serious health problems may never need treatment. Instead, his doctors may suggest observation, or "watchful waiting." This involves the careful monitoring of the cancer without active treatment. It may be an option for a man whose cancer is not causing any symptoms, is expected to grow very slowly, or is small and contained within one area of the prostate. It is less likely to be an option for a younger, healthy man with a fast-growing cancer.

A man who has been diagnosed with prostate cancer and is trying to choose a treatment has to consider

---

Q+A

Q: I am twenty-two years old and not married. I masturbate at least once a day. Can I run out of sperm?
A: No. As long as you are healthy, your sperm production will continue, with a slight decrease in later years, throughout your life. A man who ejaculates frequently and in a short period of time will still have sperm in his semen, but the number of sperm and the amount of semen most likely will decrease with each ejaculation.

---

many factors, including all side effects. A man over seventy may feel that suffering incontinence and impotence for the rest of his life is an unacceptable option, while someone younger may be more concerned with destroying or removing the cancer than with how the treatment will affect him afterward.

Surgery and radiation are the treatments most likely to cause impotence or sterility. It is possible to undergo prostate surgery that spares the nerves and muscles that control erection and ejaculation. However, a surgeon will have to remove any tissue that is affected by the cancer, regardless of its impact on a man's sexual functioning. Chemotherapy, because it is designed to slow the disease, not cure it, causes fewer sexual problems, and "watchful waiting," depending upon how the disease is progressing, may cause none.

Not all prostate cancer risk factors can be controlled, such as family history, age, or race. But some risk factors are controllable. A healthy diet and lifestyle, and regular prostate exams may mean a man never has to make the kind of choices advanced prostate cancer calls for.

Cowper's Glands

The two pea-size glands lying on either side of the urethra, just below the prostate, are called the Cowper's glands (see illustration, page 223). These glands produce an alkaline fluid when a man is aroused. This fluid prepares the urethra for ejaculation by neutralizing the acid of any residual urine, therefore creating a healthy environment for sperm. During arousal, the pre-ejaculatory fluid may form drops at the tip of the penis. Sperm are often present in this fluid, even though ejaculation has not yet occurred. This is why *coitus interruptus*, or "pulling out" (removing the penis from the vagina just prior to ejaculation), is not a reliable method of birth control.

Urethra

Sperm exit a man's body through the urethra, a tube surrounded by the *corpus spongiosum*, one of the cylindrical spaces of soft tissue of the penis (see page 214). This tissue runs from the bottom of the bladder to the opening at the tip of the penis. In men, the urethra serves a dual purpose: it transports urine from the bladder during urination, and carries semen during ejaculation.

Sex Drive

Despite the casual use of the phrase, there's no single standard for determining a "healthy" sex drive. Interest in sexual activity not only varies from person to person—your perception of a "strong" sex drive and "frequent" need for sex might seem quite low to someone else, and vice versa—but it can even fluctuate regularly within individuals. One person's sexual appetite can change from week to week, month to month, or year to year, or from one stage of life to another depending on numerous factors.

Satisfaction with one's own level of interest in sexual activity is a complex and highly personal matter. But some of the more serious problems connected with sex drive involve the repercussions of extreme feelings—the fallout when a man or woman is continuously consumed by the desire for sex or, conversely, loses the urge to be physically intimate. Extended, unexpected, and unwanted changes in levels of sexual interest can cause individual discomfort—and perhaps be symptoms of a larger physical or emotional issue. For couples, differences in sexual desire can strain relationships.

Differences in the level of sexual desire can lead to one person feeling dissatisfied and frustrated, and the other feeling pressured or guilty.

The frequency and intensity of individual sexual desire depends on an intricate web of chemical, psychological, medical, and social factors. At the deepest chemical/anatomical level, sexual urges are rooted in the brain center, and are affected by shifts in hormone levels and other complex cerebral behaviors. Researchers who study brain function, are gaining a better appreciation of the various biological factors that affect a person's sex drive.

But there's much more to sexual desire than brain chemistry. Feelings about oneself, one's partner, or potential partners can influence the intensity of desire for sexual contact at any given time. Certain prescription and recreational drugs, physical health and fitness, and stress levels can affect sex drive. All these factors simultaneously contribute to the frequency and intensity of sexual desire. Although they are interrelated, we discuss each element separately below.

Chemistry

Many chemicals produced by the body and brain play a direct or indirect role in individual sex drive. While our understanding of the processes is getting better, it's still surprising how little we know about how they work. We do know that a chemical imbalance or a nerve circuit or transmitter problem in an area of the brain may result in a host of disorders that affect sexual desire, arousal or the ability to achieve orgasm. Here's a look at a few organic chemicals that are subjects of ongoing investigation in regard to their role in sex drive.

Testosterone and Estrogen

Testosterone (see page 220) is the hormone most directly linked to male desire; when testosterone levels are low, men may experience a reduced sex drive or impotence. (Women produce testosterone as well; the female body converts it to estrogen, which regulates egg production. Low levels of testosterone in women are sometimes associated with reduced sex drive.) The male

---

Q: Do aphrodisiacs like Spanish fly and oysters really enhance sexual performance and desire?

A: Aphrodisiacs (named after the Greek goddess of sexual love, Aphrodite) such as oysters and Spanish fly have been used for thousands of years, yet almost no scientific research exists that proves their effectiveness. That said, oysters are rich in zinc, which may lead to better overall health and subsequently an increased sexual appetite. However, Spanish fly is a toxin that irritates the urogenital tract. Made from dried blister beetles, Spanish fly causes the genitals to swell, burn, and itch. High doses can lead to genitourinary infections, vomiting, and in some extreme cases, death. Although minor symptoms of burning in the genital area may increase one's sexual desire, the fact remains that most aphrodisiacs work on a psychological level with little or no physiological benefits.

body also breaks down some testosterone to create an active form of estrogen called estradiol. Estrogen in both men and women is believed to play a part in triggering the release of dopamine (see below).

Dopamine

Integral to central brain functioning, dopamine is a neurotransmitter—it transmits nerve impulses. High levels of dopamine in the brain are correlated with sexual interest.

Serotonin

High levels of the neurotransmitter serotonin are associated with feelings of pleasure. Many drugs that are prescribed to treat depression and anxiety regulate serotonin levels. But too much serotonin in a person's system sometimes decreases sexual desire because this neurotransmitter can also act as a depressant.

Epinephrine and Norepinephrine

These neurotransmitters are associated with sexual arousal. It is believed that they excite the body by increasing cardiac output, causing both heart rate and blood pressure to rise.

Oxytocin

Produced by the pituitary gland, testes, and ovaries, oxytocin plays an important role in pregnancy and is thought to stimulate emotional bonding between a woman and her newborn baby. The release of oxytocin has been connected to the spasms caused by an orgasm, leading scientists to theorize that it's also released after sex to stimulate emotional bonding between men and women.

Q+A

Q: I was raped when I was in college and I've had problems getting close to men physically since. I have been dating a man who I really like, but I've been putting off having sex because I've always reacted badly to it—I get shaky and weepy and have to stop. I'm afraid if I try having sex with him, the same thing will happen and I will drive him away. What should I do?

A: Most women find they need to talk to a counselor of some kind to get through the emotional repercussions of sexual assault (see pages 286–287), and since it sounds like you have not been able to process the trauma of being raped—which is completely understandable—you need to seek out professional help. If you believe that your relationship with this man has the potential to get serious or become long-term, you need to talk to him about what he expects from the relationship. Based on his level of commitment, you can decide whether to share with him your past experiences and talk about their impact on you now. Follow the advice of your counselor when you find one and he or she will help you deal with your past, your present, and your future.

Nitric Oxide

When a man or woman becomes sexually aroused, nitric oxide is produced in and around the genitals, causing blood cells to dilate and increasing blood flow to that area. Medications such as Viagra and Levitra, which are prescribed to treat erectile dysfunction, often affect nitric oxide levels in the body.

Psychology

Enthusiasm for sex depends a great deal on intellectual and emotional elements, encompassing an individual's past sexual experiences, body image, ideas about intimacy, and overall feeling of self-worth. That's why people seeking to boost a very low sex drive or come to terms with uncontrollable sexual desire often seek psychological counseling. Through therapy, an individual may identify the causes of his or her discomfort and shed light on ways to overcome them.

Sexual Experiences and Ideas

What a person has been taught about sex, how they learned it, and their history of sexual contact can all affect desire. People who have had mostly positive sexual experiences tend to be comfortable with physical and emotional intimacy, and confident about sharing their sexual thoughts and desires with a caring partner. They are also more likely to have healthy sexual relationships as adults. Conversely, many people who have had traumatic sexual experiences have a hard time feeling positive about physical intimacy. Unfortunately, rape and molestation are more common than most of us want to believe. Feelings of shame, embarrassment, or guilt may inhibit individuals who have had negative sexual experiences from seeking treatment that can facilitate recovery.

There are other, more subtle ways in which people can develop psychological discomfort with sex. During our formative years, we hear a lot about sex from our parents, teachers, the media, and friends, some of which is negative or simply false. Those early ideas have a way of lingering into adulthood and causing problems.

Body Image
Sex means sharing intimate parts of your body with another person. Body image (see pages 240–241)

Q+A

Q: I find that I enjoy sex about once a week. My partner enjoys sex two or three times a week. Things are starting to get strained because of this disparity. Should I see a therapist?
A: What, exactly is your goal? You enjoy sex once a week and your partner enjoys it more often. This does not mean you have a problem and your partner is normal. Nor does it indicate that one's preference is better or healthier than the other's. (Of course an extreme in either direction might be unhealthy.) A better idea might be to try to work it out yourselves and negotiate this in the same way you do other issues in your relationship. If this does not work out satisfactorily, a qualified therapist may be able to help.

plays a large role in sexual encounters—the more comfortable you are with your body, the more relaxed and pleasurable sex is likely to be. Many women have difficulty achieving an orgasm because they are too worried about their appearance to truly let go and enjoy the moment. Learning to celebrate the body can increase enjoyment of sex, and in turn, boost desire.

Self-Worth
Low self-esteem leads some people to believe that no one would or should be attracted to them, so they repress their own desire. Some may measure their self-worth based on feelings about their own sexual attractiveness, deciding that infrequent sex is proof of their own undesirability. Others may use sex for self-validation, overcompensating for low self-esteem by seeking out sex more often than is healthy.

Physical Health and Fitness
The better a person's overall health, the more robust his or her sex drive will be. People who exercise and eat well have a higher sex drive than people who don't. Exercise can also lead to a prolonged sex life, as elderly people who stay physically active often retain a stronger sex drive than those who don't. This isn't to say it's impossible to have a satisfying sex life without exercise. But a person who is looking for ways to improve sex drive or safeguard it, exercise and a sound diet are effective strategies.

Many factors affect sex drive. What follows here is a list of specific health issues that affect sex drive.

Stress
It's difficult to focus on physical pleasure while struggling with anxiety. There are many simple relaxation techniques that not only reduce stress, but also increase physical and emotional intimacy with a partner. Some types of stress can be alleviated by a massage, a hot bath, or a long talk. Yoga and exercise can reduce stress, as can a good night's sleep. If stress becomes too much to handle, consider consulting a professional therapist.

Lack of Sleep
Sex requires energy. A tired person is seldom an extremely aroused person. Getting the proper amount of rest can increase energy and overall health, and therefore sex drive.

Medication
Certain prescription medications have sexual side effects. Drugs commonly used to treat high blood pressure, anxiety, psychosis, and depression can reduce desire. A person taking such medications should talk to their doctor if they suspect medication is lowering their sex drive.

Alcohol and Drug Use
People sometimes think using alcohol or drugs will increase their sex drive because those substances lower inhibitions, allowing them to relax. However, alcohol and drug use have proven to reduce or even eliminate sex drive in the long run.

Relationship Issues
How a person feels about their sexual partner (or partners) at any given time is bound to affect how

Q+A

Q: I'm not as interested in having sex with my husband as I used to be. Is there anything I can do to increase my sex drive?

A: Both psychological and physical factors can affect sex drive. Although counseling can address the psychological issues, physical factors can stem from hormonal imbalances. Menopause and aging decrease estrogen levels in a woman's body, which can decrease vaginal lubrication and genital sensation. The male hormone testosterone can also affect the female libido. Researchers are still determining whether testosterone treatments are a viable aid in increasing sexual desire in both men and women. The first step is to discuss the issue with your health care provider.

often he or she wants sex. In the beginning of a relationship, for example, the urge to have sex may occur more frequently than after ten years of marriage (though, of course, the opposite may also be true). During periods of stress or difficulty in a relationship, sexual desire is likely to wane. Yet some people find that stress in a relationship causes them to want sex more. This may be because they are striving to maintain or increase intimacy. Every sexual encounter is unique, and although there are some general patterns that many people experience, there are no hard-and-fast rules. (Sex within and outside of romantic relationships is discussed on pages 258–261.)

Sexual Triggers

Sexual triggers (or turn-ons) are images, odors, textures, flavors, or sounds that cause humans to think about and desire sex. Knowing which sensations trigger thoughts about sex can help an individual boost his or her sex drive. For example, if a woman knows that candlelight sparks her interest in sex, she can use that trigger when she is having difficulty getting in the mood. Similarly, a man who finds the idea of having sex outdoors highly erotic can propose a camping trip with his partner. It's difficult to know what causes one sensation or combination of sensations to be more of a turn-on than others, and why some sensations are only sexy to some. From puberty onward, we each develop our own associations with sexual pleasure, which are largely subconscious.

Sex Drive and Aging

The ability to respond sexually and enjoy sex continues until death. The effect of aging on sexual activity varies enormously from person to person. For many elderly people, the death of a spouse may mean the end of active sexual expression, but this need not be the case. Overall health remains an important factor in sex drive, especially during a person's later years. A number of chronic illnesses are often accompanied by reduced sexual activity, even though the response potential is still functioning. The most important predictor of how people will behave sexually in their later years is often how they behaved when they were younger. If they had an active, fulfilling sex life through their earlier years, they are likely to continue it through middle age and beyond.

Treating Low Sex Drive

Both men and women can suffer from problems of desire. How to treat those problems is not simple. As discussed above, the causes of inhibited sexual desire are still a subject of speculation. Anxiety about sex, fear of intimacy, anger with a partner, and relationship troubles may inhibit a person's sex drive, or they may interact with and aggravate one another. It is also possible that organic problems may be wholly or partly responsible. Certainly anyone who feels his or her level of desire is consistently inadequate would be well-advised to have a thorough checkup.

Treatment for inhibited sexual desire or sex drive is usually multi-dimensional. Both individual and relationship psychosexual therapy is common. Medication to control anxiety or depression may be indicated. Erotic exercises to be performed at home may be proposed by the sexual therapist—touching, undemanding pleasuring activities, and body-image exercises are some of the methods often used to address low sex drive. The treatment approach is flexible and often integrates a variety of psychotherapeutic and pharmaceutical methods, but success rates in treating inhibited sexual desire are apparently lower than with other sexual problems.

Arousal and Orgasm

Arousal occurs when a person becomes more and more sexually excited. The physical and psychological impact of arousal reaches its peak with orgasm—an explosion of pleasurable sensations. As those sensations recede, the body returns to its normal state. Arousal and orgasm are easier to study than sex drive, because the body's physical response can be observed and measured. However, both are greatly affected by one's psychological state. What a person thinks or feels can influence the speed of arousal and the ability to climax. As has been shown in study after study, psychological issues are most often at the root of problems related to arousal and orgasm.

Arousal

Sexual arousal causes several changes in the body. The most obvious in both men and women is *vasocongestion*, or the rapid accumulation of extra blood in the genitals. In a man, vasocongestion causes an erection, because blood flows into the spongy tissue of the penis, causing it to swell. The speed at which the erection occurs, and whether the penis reaches its maximum possible size, depend primarily on two factors: the type and intensity of stimulation, and the man's age. Older men often experience a slower rate of erection (see page 293).

Vasocongestion in a woman causes vaginal lubrication. Increased blood flow creates pressure in the vaginal area, which forces the vagina and cervix to secrete a fluid called modified plasma transudate. As with a man, the speed at which lubrication occurs depends almost completely on the type and intensity of stimulation.

The same activities arouse both sexes: physical stimulus through touch, sight, smell, taste, and sound, and the more intangible stimulus of sexual fantasy (see pages 273–274). Each person responds according to his or her emotional and physical states, as well as the intensity of the stimulus. Both men and women also experience an effect called *myotonia*, a tensing of the muscles that causes tonic spasms throughout the body. After orgasm, the spastic effect fades and then eventually disappears, leaving the person feeling especially relaxed and satisfied.

During arousal, a woman experiences several responses that a man experiences to a lesser degree, or not at all. Arousal can cause nipple erection in both sexes, but it is more common and more apparent in a woman. The areola (the dark area surrounding the nipple) deepens in color, and the whole breast swells and increases in size. The increase is greater in a woman who has never breast-fed a baby.

Sexual tension mounts as arousal continues, causing pulse rate and blood pressure to increase. As a result, a flush may appear in both women and men, but it is more common and apparent in women. This redness first appears on the upper abdomen then spreads to

Q+A

Q: What is a "wet dream?" Can women have them?

A: The term "wet dream" commonly refers to an orgasm that occurs during sleep. While sleeping, both men and women can become aroused without external stimulation. A man may become erect while asleep, and a woman's vagina may become lubricated and her clitoris may swell. Occasionally, a man, especially one in his teens or early twenties, will ejaculate while sleeping (thus, experiencing a "wet dream"). A woman also may experience orgasm during sleep. No medical or scientific explanation for this phenomenon has been confirmed, but some researchers believe it is the body's way of maintaining healthy sexual organs. Sleeping orgasms do not happen to everyone: Research shows that approximately 80 percent of men and 40 percent of women will have one sometime in their lives.

Contrary to what might be supposed, wet dreams are not generally the result of sexual dreaming. Men participating in research to study the phenomenon have been awakened when they are observed to have an erection and questioned about their dreams. Only a small percentage reported dreams with any sexual content.

Q: My boyfriend always wakes up in the morning with an erection. Is it from being sexually excited?
A: Morning erections are quite common, and are believed to be a result of testosterone levels, which are highest at that time of day. His erection is involuntary, like other erections that occur during sleep.

the chest, including the breasts. A woman reacts to arousal with a change in the color of the labia, caused by vasocongestion. In a woman who has given birth, the inner labia change from red to a deep wine color, while the labia of a woman who has not had children change from pink to red. This color change indicates that the woman will experience an orgasm if stimulation continues.

In the final stages of arousal, a woman undergoes two more changes: the vagina lengthens and the clitoris retracts into its hood (see illustration, page 201). These responses to continued stimulus indicate that orgasm is imminent.

When the arousal phase reaches the point at which a man or a woman is filled with sexual tension and feels that just a little more excitement will push them to climax, he or she has come to what's known as the *plateau*.

Orgasm

When a man or woman is about to have an orgasm, his or her blood pressure, pulse, and breathing rate peak; muscle tension is extreme. The spark that causes orgasm has not been identified, but an intricate relationship of physical, emotional,

social, and hormonal factors clearly plays a major role. Other forces may influence climax as well. When orgasm does occur, it is because the brain signals the nervous system, which triggers the muscle movements of orgasm. During orgasm, a woman's uterus and the muscles around her vagina contract from two to fifteen times. The contractions occur less than a second apart.

A man's orgasm occurs in two stages. First, he feels he has reached a "point of no return," which is caused by semen pooling at the entrance to the urethra. A man cannot help coming when he reaches this stage. Next, the man ejaculates: a series of contractions of the ejaculatory ducts and the muscles around the penis force semen out of the urethra (see illustration, page 223). The process lasts just a few seconds and the contractions quickly decrease in strength.

The final stage of orgasm is known as the *resolution*. For both sexes, resolution means a gradual return to normal pulse and breathing rates and a drop in blood pressure. If skin flush and nipple erection occurred, they will disappear. A woman's labia and vagina will resume to their normal color and size, respectively. A man's penis will

return to its flaccid state. If the right circumstances exist, a woman in the early part of resolution may experience another orgasm, or repeated orgasms, if stimulation continues. As a rule, however, men cannot. A man must pass through what's known as a *refractory period*, during which time the penis is unlikely to become erect or remain erect for long. The length of the refractory period may be minutes or hours, but primarily depends on a man's age: the younger he is, the shorter the interval necessary between erections.

Q: When my wife told me that reaching orgasm every time we had sex was not the most important thing for her, I was surprised. Shouldn't I be trying to make sure she always comes? And wouldn't the best thing be for us to have simultaneous orgasms?
A: When partners stop focusing on achieving particular sexual objectives during lovemaking, their sex life can improve dramatically. Worrying about reaching specific goals can cause you to forget who you are with and why you are making love in the first place. Relax. Eliminating the focus on stellar performance and the need to achieve explosive and perfectly timed orgasms can lead to much more intimate and exciting experiences for both of you. When a couple refocuses and appreciates their sexual acts as a whole, orgasm becomes just one of the many wonderful and pleasurable aspects of making love.

Multiple Orgasm

Multiple orgasm refers to a person having more than one orgasm in a brief period of time and in response to continuous stimulation. In theory, only a woman can experience multiple orgasm and, in reality, few women do experience it. However, once a woman discovers that she can have multiple orgasms, it is likely to happen again.

Because men require a refractory period between erections, they are not able to have multiple orgasms.

Simultaneous Orgasm

Simultaneous orgasm is not a typical occurrence for most couples, nor is it necessary for a satisfying sexual experience. Knowing what is going on in your own body, and being sensitive to what your partner is experiencing will help you communicate feelings and desires. That knowledge and communication (not necessarily verbal) can create the stimulation required to make sure both partners experience a complete response.

Q+A

Q: Even though my wife has never said anything, I think I'm too fast when we have sex. Do a lot of men feel this way?

A: This is a very common feeling, and it's important to share this concern with your wife. Tell her what you are worried about and ask her to discuss it with you. You may find that her response alleviates your worries or creates a dialog that will lead to improved communication and increased pleasure for you both.

Many people find it difficult to discuss sex and their feelings about certain aspects of sex with a partner, but overcoming your hesitation is important. Sensitive discussion can lead to a sexual relationship brimming with trust and satisfaction for now and the future.

The Effects of Aging
On Men

To some degree, age affects sexual response in almost everyone. A middle-aged or elderly man needs more time to become erect and may require increased physical stimulation of the penis to maintain the erection. Then again, once his erection is achieved, he may actually be able to maintain it longer than he could when he was younger. When an older man loses an erection, because of ejaculation or otherwise, he experiences a longer refractory period (see page 231), needing a longer time in between erections and orgasms.

Aging is liable to diminish the force of a man's ejaculation and the power of his orgasmic sensations. There also may be less semen ejaculated, which would contain fewer sperm, and the chances of fertilizing an ovum would be diminished. Nevertheless, the number of sperm in the ejaculate is still tremendous, and, because most of the sperm will be healthy, a man can remain fertile at any age. Male hormone (testosterone) levels do not change appreciably until a man has reached his sixties or even his seventies, and the drop is rarely large enough to have a physical effect on desire or potency. Unfortunately, for some men, age causes side effects of another kind.

The most prevalent sexual difficulty aging men encounter is an inability to accept physical changes due to time. Rather than accepting and accommodating himself to slower erection, longer refractory periods, and less powerful ejacula-

Q+A

Q: Can a woman ejaculate like a man does?

A: Not as a general rule, but research has shown that some female study participants did release fluid from the urethra during orgasm. The research claimed the fluid was not urine, and after analysis was found to resemble male semen, but contained no sperm. Debate about the origin and purpose of this substance has been intense, with additional research claiming that the supposed ejaculate is more similar to urine than to semen.

Whatever the fluid's source, very few women experience female ejaculation, and the phenomenon does not mean a woman's genitalia are anything other than normal and healthy. Those who do ejaculate say they enjoy the additional moisture.

tions, a man may choose to shun sex completely. By doing so, he also rejects fulfillment for his partner. The result can be psychologically debilitating and damage a man's relationships. At any age, sexual health and fulfillment rely on the recognition of your needs and abilities, whatever they may be.

On Women

For women, aging brings menopause, with all of its wide-ranging transformations (see pages 208–209). As a woman approaches menopause, her ovaries begin to produce less estrogen. The adrenal glands continue to produce estrogen, but after menopause, the ovaries generate only tiny amounts of the sex hormone. Fortunately, the decrease in total hormone production does not significantly affect orgasmic satisfaction,

the ability to achieve multiple orgasm, or the sensitivity of a woman's clitoris.

Physical changes affecting sexual encounters do accompany menopause. For example, an older woman's vagina may take longer to become moist in response to stimulation. Also, contractions during orgasm decrease and the duration of each orgasm is shortened. Myotonia, a response to sexual excitement (see page 230), also declines, and, after an orgasm, a woman's body returns more rapidly to its normal condition. Because the labia and vagina thin with age, they do not become as swollen in response to stimulation. This, along with decreased natural lubrication, creates the potential for discomfort or even pain during intercourse. The application of saliva or a personal lubricant can eliminate the difficulty.

For a woman, troubling psychological or emotional issues related to sex most often center on menopause. Changes in sexual response, fertility-related self-image, and weight can interfere with a woman's sex life. Many women have difficulty accepting the inability to reproduce. However, if such issues are dealt with through self-nurturing, along with caring discussions with her partner, a woman may pass through this potentially difficult phase of her life with her self-image intact (or improved) and her potential for sexual pleasure and fulfillment as great as, or greater, than before menopause.

Sexual Complications

The sexual difficulties women and men most often encounter have two sources: the physical and the psychological. Problems of physical origin are more easily diagnosed and treated than the nonphysical, but, whatever the source, the results manifest themselves in the body's response during sexual activities. The problems a man will most often experience are premature ejaculation and erectile dysfunction. A woman may encounter difficulty achieving orgasm, pain during intercourse, and vaginismus.

Complications for Men

Premature Ejaculation. An exact definition of premature ejaculation is difficult to establish, because the problem is a subjective one. Ejaculation that occurs before the penis enters the vagina obviously is premature, but how long should an orgasm take after penetration?

Q+A

Q: How can I delay my orgasm if I feel like I'm going to come too soon?
A: Once you are able to identify the approach of premature climax, you can use a variety of techniques to delay orgasm. A simple change may make the difference, or a more involved intervention may be necessary. For example:

- Modify the way you move during intercourse.
- Slow down or stop genital contact and resume kissing and caressing.
- Try the "squeeze" technique: interrupt intercourse (withdraw the penis from the vagina) to apply light pressure on the front and back of the penis just below the head for between four and twenty seconds. This technique can be repeated as often as necessary, but requires some patience and cooperation from your partner. Couples using the squeeze method eventually can get to the point where withdrawing from the vagina is not necessary, because simply squeezing the base of the penis delays orgasm.
- Some men delay orgasm by reducing the stimulation they receive during sex through the use of anesthetizing creams. This technique, however, may diminish the pleasure felt during sex.

arousal and orgasm

Q+A

Q: Is there a difference between premature ejaculation and retarded ejaculation? Is there treatment for either of these?

A: Yes. One is the opposite of the other. Premature ejaculation is when climax occurs too quickly and without a man's control, while retarded ejaculation (also called delayed ejaculation or ejaculatory incompetence) is an inhibition of ejaculation, possibly to the point of inability to climax. Those who experience retarded ejaculation can get an erection, but can't ejaculate easily, so it takes an unusually long time to climax.

A man who suffers from delayed ejaculation may experience it often or only occasionally; he may be able to climax during masturbation or oral sex, but only infrequently. He may rarely, if ever, achieve orgasm during intercourse. The cause of the problem is not completely understood, but it seems most often to have psychological underpinnings. Stress, anger, and traumatic events related to masturbation ("getting caught") may cause retarded ejaculation, or a man may simply be trying too hard to control when he climaxes. Trouble in the relationship between a man and his sex partner is another possible cause. Whatever the problem, it can be diagnosed and treated medically or through psychological counseling.

Two minutes? Five? Fifteen? A commonly accepted definition of premature ejaculation is that a man reaches orgasm and ejaculates without control and before he (or his partner) wishes or expects it to happen.

Health care professionals agree that premature ejaculation is the most common sexual dysfunction in men, and that it can lead to additional problems: feelings of inhibition, guilt, embarrassment, and frustration, damage to self-image and relationships, and erectile dysfunction. Most men experience premature ejaculation at some point in their lives, but if the problem occurs consistently and interferes with the pleasure of a man and his partner, he should seek treatment.

Premature ejaculation is rooted in physical problems only rarely, and can be treated medically when necessary. Most often, the underlying cause is psychological. Relationship trouble, stress, depression, and other mental and emotional health issues can aggravate the situation. Therapy is one possible avenue for treating premature ejaculation. A therapist can help a man become more aware of his physical responses during sex, especially those immediately preceding orgasm. Qualified psychosexual therapists—who work with individuals and couples willing and able to make the necessary effort—can help cure premature ejaculation in as little as a few weeks.

Erectile Dysfunction. Erectile dysfunction can be divided into two categories: primary and secondary. A man who has never achieved or maintained an erection firm enough for intercourse would be diagnosed with primary erectile dysfunction. Less than 10 percent of those experiencing difficulty fall into this category. Secondary erectile dysfunction refers to the experience of a man who has demonstrated an ability to attain an erection and have intercourse in the past, but is not able to do so at the present. Secondary erectile dysfunction is far more common than primary, and responds to treatment more quickly and successfully.

Erectile dysfunction can affect a man of any age, sexual orientation, and marital status, but the possibility of occurrence increases with age. Erection is an involuntary process— a reflex—so a man cannot control it. With erectile dysfunction, the physical responses to arousal (see pages 230–231) do not occur, despite the fact that the man may be sexually excited and stimulated. The list of possible causes for erectile dysfunction is long (see below), but, regardless of its source, dysfunction should not be considered a significant problem unless it happens often enough or for a long enough time to become damaging to a man's psyche or to his relationship with his sexual partner.

Difficulty having an erection can have physical or psychological sources, or a combination of both. The most common causes include:

- Neurological disease or injury;
- Surgery;
- Prescription medication, including antidepressants, opiates, antihypertensives, diuretics, hormones, and non-steroidal anti-inflammatory drugs;

Q: Is it possible for a woman to come too quickly?

A: As with premature ejaculation in men, the answer to this question is somewhat subjective. Premature climax in women is rare, but a woman who is experiencing it can suffer many of the same side effects as a man. In almost every case, a therapist can help a woman who is consistently dissatisfied with the power or timing of her orgasms.

• Diabetes or vascular disease;
• Hormone imbalance;
• Consumption of alcohol or other drugs;
• Anger toward partner or other problems in the relationship (such as incompatibility, boredom, poor communication, or insensitivity);
• Shame, fear, or guilt related to sex in general or to a particular sexual experience in the past;
• Fear of rejection, performance anxiety, lack of trust, or an overly developed sense of competition;
• Physical fatigue, stress, anxiety, or depression;
• Past or present trauma or abuse.

The introduction of drug therapies has created what appears to be a viable option for most men experiencing erectile dysfunction (see "Q+A," right). Such medications may offer a physical solution to the problem, but do not cure any underlying psychological disorder that may be contributing to the problem. Seeking individual counseling or seeing a skilled sex therapist with your partner are both effective routes to dealing with erectile dysfunction. A qualified therapist can offer exercises that help both partners deal with specific issues, while fostering healthful and effective communication between them.

A reduction or complete eradication of erectile dysfunction may take weeks (or even months) of effort, even with the help of a professional therapist. A readiness to talk openly about sex and any problems related to it is the most important factor in the pace of improvement. A man and his partner also need to examine the scope of other issues that may be adversely affecting their relationship and deal with them as well.

Complications for Women

Orgasmic Difficulty. Failure to achieve orgasm is the most common sexual complaint of women. Some women have never had an orgasm through self-stimulation or sex with a partner. Others reach orgasm infrequently. However, most women do have the potential to become orgasmic on a fairly regularly basis.

As with men and erectile dysfunction, an important distinction exists between primary and secondary orgasmic difficulties. Primary orgasmic difficulty indicates that a woman has never experienced an orgasm. Secondary orgasmic difficulty means that a woman might have orgasms under certain conditions and not in others, or that she has experienced orgasms in the past, but is no longer doing so.

Q: Is there a medication that can help with erectile dysfunction? How does such medication work?

A: One medicine widely prescribed to treat erectile dysfunction is Viagra (sildenafil citrate). It is taken orally thirty to sixty minutes before sexual activity. Erection requires the release of nitric oxide, a chemical discharged in response to sexual stimulation, in certain areas of the penis. Nitric oxide activates other substances that allow additional blood to flow into the penis and make it erect. Sildenafil citrate enhances the effect of nitric oxide by inhibiting phosphodiesterase type 5 (PDE5), which is responsible for the penis becoming flaccid. When a man who has taken sildenafil citrate is sexually stimulated and nitric oxide is released, the medication prevents the PDE5 from having its normal effect of creating flaccidity, so a man may become and remain erect.

Medical and government oversight groups recommend that anyone wishing to use medications like sildenafil citrate get a complete physical examination beforehand. Men with heart disease, very high or very low blood pressure, or certain eye conditions must exercise extreme caution. As with any prescription medication, you should discuss any risk factors and the possible side effects with your physician.

arousal and orgasm

Q+A

Q: My husband has not been able to get an erection for almost a year. It makes him feel horrible, and has just about destroyed our sex life, but he refuses to go see a doctor about it. What can I do?

A: Offering loving support and showing a readiness to work with your husband to help solve his erectile dysfunction could help him take the step of getting help. It is important to realize that if the source of his problem is not physical, it is psychological, and may possibly be a sign of problems in your relationship. Your husband may be exhibiting the most obvious symptom, but it is likely there are others—you may be experiencing some, too. Working with a skilled sex therapist could make the difference for you and your husband.

And remember that sexual dysfunction is a difficult issue for anyone to face, at any age and of either sex. Be patient. It may take your husband some time to admit that he needs help.

Generally, a woman's treatment may include any combination of individual, couple, and group therapy, plus behavioral therapy and instruction in a variety of masturbation techniques. The treatment for a woman experiencing primary orgasmic difficulty differs from the treatment for secondary difficulty in that it should begin with a complete physical examination. Once physical or medical problems have been either diagnosed or eliminated as the source of the problem, a woman and her doctor or therapist can decide how to proceed.

Although some women can enjoy sexual activity without reaching orgasm, many others feel unhappy, discouraged, and frustrated. A woman who is not able to reach orgasm during sex either alone or with a partner may believe she is missing out on one of the pleasures of sex, and that she is failing herself and her partner somehow. Most likely, she is feeling unfulfilled. The tension created by these feelings pushes a woman even further from the state that would most easily lead to orgasm.

Orgasmic difficulties can be caused by physical problems, but most often they have a psychological basis. The following psychological factors (alone or in combination) may be the cause of difficulty:

- Ignorance of the genitalia and how the body responds to stimulation;
- Shame, fear, or guilt related to sex in general (due to negative conditioning in childhood or uncomfortable sexual experiences in adolescence);
- Inability to let go (fear of losing control);
- Not participating fully in sex (expecting the partner to bring about orgasm);
- Anger, in general or particularly toward the partner;
- Problems in the relationship (incompatibility, boredom, poor communication, or insensitivity);
- Fear of rejection, performance anxiety, lack of trust, or struggle for power;
- Fatigue, stress, anxiety, or depression;
- Past or present trauma or abuse;
- Alcohol or drug consumption.

Many books and online resources offer help for women suffering from orgasmic difficulty, but seeking guidance from a professional therapist, at least for a time, is a good idea. Treatment for orgasmic problems is as variable as the women who seek it and the therapists who provide it.

Painful Intercourse. Painful sexual intercourse, or *dyspareunia*, has a number of causes. As with other sexual difficulties, the source can be either physical or psychological. Physical causes include inadequate lubrication, pelvic or vaginal infections, abnormal growths (fibroids, ovarian cysts, or endometriosis), allergies to contraceptive products or semen, the configuration of the reproductive and sexual organs, bowel or bladder infections, and any past injuries to the vulva or vagina from childbirth, surgery, rape, or sexual abuse.

Psychological and emotional causes may include the preconditioning that sex is wrong or painful; fear of becoming pregnant; fear of injury to an unborn child during pregnancy; lack of sexual arousal (and therefore vaginal lubrication) caused by insufficient foreplay; fatigue or anxiety; ignorance and lack of sexual experience; past sexual injury or psychological trauma; and a lack of desire for one's partner. The risk of pain occurring during intercourse increases with pregnancy and the postpartum period, stress or a recent illness, alcohol or drug consumption, and menopause.

Identification of the problem's source can lead to effective treatment. Physical causes can be diagnosed and treated by a health care practitioner. Problems that have a psychological or emotional basis can be alleviated through better communication with the partner and the help of a professional therapist.

Vaginismus. An involuntary spasm of the muscles at the opening of the vagina, called *vaginismus*, can tighten, narrow, and even close the vagina, making penetration difficult or impossible. The condition is unusual and arises most often in response to another physical or psychological problem. Treatment requires identification of the condition's source so that an effective therapy can be formulated and applied.

How Sex Therapy Can Help

The decision to see a sex therapist about arousal and orgasm issues— or indeed for any sexual problem— is a difficult one. Most people imagine that they'll find it uncomfortable to talk to a stranger about such personal matters. However, remember that a sex therapist or any other counselor is a trained professional whose goal is to help you.

What follows is an overview of the kind of recommendations you might hear from a therapist.

The Emotional and Intellectual Components

- Allow yourself to be sexual.
- Assume responsibility for your own sexual functioning.
- Learn about sexual anatomy and the physiological responses to sexual excitement.
- Realize that an orgasm cannot be forced.
- Focus on creating an erotically stimulating environment in which there is no "race to the finish line."
- Talk to your partner about what you both find stimulating.
- Identify and deal with any issues interfering with your sexual expression.
- Develop a healthy fantasy element in your sexual activities.

The Physical Component

- Learn how to reach orgasm through masturbation: a sex therapist can offer a progression of sensually stimulating exercises. Also, using a vibrator by yourself or with your partner can help you learn what feels best for you.
- Discover and move in ways that increase your excitement and pleasure during sex. Self-stimulation can help (remember that the clitoris, just above the urethra opening, is the most important physical source of sexual stimulation for women).
- Don't limit yourself to intercourse. Experiment with other sexual practices (oral and manual stimulation or body rubbing).
- Tense the muscles in your legs and thighs. This will increase myotonia (see page 230), which can help trigger orgasm.
- Do Kegel exercises (see "Q+A," page 204). Kegel exercises help maintain good tone in the pelvic muscles, which can improve sensation and, therefore, stimulation and response.
- If necessary, learn methods to prevent premature ejaculation, such as the "squeeze" technique (see "Q+A," page 233).
- Try sexual positions that place the woman on top. There is likely to be more direct clitoral stimulation in these positions.

Q+A

Q: I've been taking an antidepressant for about six months and I've found that it has totally eliminated my sex drive. This side effect has become intolerable for me. What are my options?

A: It sounds like you need to visit your doctor again. Many antidepressants can reduce sex drive, but some of the newer drugs designed to treat depression are less likely to have that side effect. You don't necessarily have to make a choice between depression and a satisfying sex life. Ask your doctor if it makes sense to switch to a different antidepressant and be clear that the side effects you are experiencing are unacceptable— that's important information.

Sexual Attitudes

How a man or woman thinks and feels about sex in general strongly influences how he or she experiences it physically. Sexual attitudes are shaped by many factors, including age, sexual experience, and even the individual's environment. A person's culture, as well as his or her current social, religious, and political environment, all come together to form an idea of what sexual behavior is appropriate and inappropriate. As one or more of the factors change, attitudes are likely to change.

Defining Appropriate Sexual Behavior

Wardell Pomeroy, an early sex researcher who worked at the Kinsey Institute (an American organization that conducts research and scholarship in the fields of human sexuality, gender, and reproduction) formulated a system that attempts to designate "good" and "bad" sexual behavior by describing what is "normal" behavior. The definitions are helpful in some ways, but they succeed most by making clear how difficult it is to designate anything definitively "normal" or "abnormal," especially when sex is the subject.

Pomeroy's system defined sexual behavior based on three values: statistics, a moral or religious code, and psychological or sociological assessment. *Statistical Normality* states that, "If the majority of people engage in the behavior, then it is normal and right." Such a definition seems straightforward, but sexuality and the activities associated with it are rarely agreed upon within a society. For example, there are sexual pursuits that are widely practiced, but rarely accepted as normal and good behavior. Masturbation is a sexual behavior that almost every human being engages in at some point, but it has a stigma, even today, that prevents it from being seen as completely acceptable. Something being statistically normal does not necessarily mean society gives it the stamp of approval.

Moral/Religious Normality states that, "If a behavior is at variance with a widely accepted religious or moral code, it is abnormal and wrong." This definition would seem to offer a strong basis for deciding whether a behavior is "right" or "wrong," but its accuracy is limited by the fact that many people who profess to belong to a religion or live by a particular moral code often deliberately act in ways that defy their accepted religious or moral law. Such behavior may be so widespread that it is not perceived as abnormal at all. For instance, certain religions prohibit most methods of contraception, but many of those religions' adherents use the prohibited contraceptive methods regularly. These people are not seen as abnormal by the bulk of society or even by most members of their religion.

Psychological/Sociological Normality states that, "If a sexual act leads to diminished self-esteem, or if the act is based in anger, hostility, or vengeance, it is abnormal and wrong. If the act harms another person or society in general, it is abnormal and wrong." This characterization may be the one most easily understood today, but it also has weaknesses. What "harming another person" consists of, and whether something "diminishes self-esteem" are matters of opinion that vary by culture, subculture, and individual. Giving a sexual partner the flu through oral contact could be seen as "harming" them, but would not be considered wrong by most people. A less simplistic example is a couple who creates an unwanted pregnancy, which could be seen as harming them and society. Such an instance may be unfortunate, but it would not be considered abnormal in many communities. In general, however, deciding whether a sex act is right or wrong based on whether it causes significant harm or distress is a common-sense approach to the question.

Two other standards for defining normality of sexual conduct are widely used, one based on legal standards and the other based on animal behavior. *Legal Normality*, simply states that, "If a behavior violates the law, it is abnormal and bad." This standard offers another seemingly cut-and-dry method for making decisions about sex acts, but it, too, has flaws. Laws reflect the values of a society in general, but since values may differ from one subculture to the next, the laws may not represent the attitudes of all the people who must live by those laws.

Phylogenetic Normality states that, "If other mammals do it, it is normal and good." This definition removes human morality from the assessment

Q: My boyfriend is much more conservative than I am where sex is concerned, and our ideas of what's okay are so different that we are starting to have problems. What can we do to resolve our difference?

A: First, each of you needs to think about what you like and don't like, what feels comfortable and what doesn't, and figure out why. Next, you need to discuss your findings with each other. Your problems may not be caused so much by what each of you likes and dislikes as by lack of mutual understanding or confusion about the other's preferences. Open communication can lead to better understanding, which in turn can help you and your boyfriend make decisions about your sexual preferences and what compromises may be necessary.

of sexual activity and focuses on whether a behavior occurs naturally in other mammals. Looking at sex from this perspective may work from a scientific viewpoint, but it is hardly a practical system to apply to human society. It may be natural for other mammals to engage in sex with siblings and offspring, to abandon their offspring before they are capable of caring for themselves, and to harm sexual partners during intercourse. For a variety of society-affirming reasons, such behavior in a human being is not considered right.

Formation of Sexual Attitudes

How a person feels about sex in general is strongly influenced by exposure to sexual stimuli from birth and the attitudes of those around them toward sex and the body. Equally important—some would say more so—is the development of identity and body image (see pages 240–241) during adolescence, especially in the context of how a teenager sees sexual behavior being expressed in his or her peer group

and society in general. Ideally, a young person's influences will help create a positive body image, allowing comfortable exploration of sexuality and a balanced approach to the opposite sex.

When a person does not feel comfortable with their body and sexuality, or feels unhappy or unsatisfied with their sexual encounters—especially in terms of committed romantic relationships—he or she is most likely responding to past negative experiences. No matter how troubling or embarrassing feelings about sexuality can seem, it is important that they be dealt with. Talking to a friend, a sexual partner, or a therapist can lead to healthier attitudes toward sex and sexuality.

What We See on Television

The way sex and sexuality are portrayed on television and in the movies has little or nothing to do with real sexual behavior—such depictions are fictionalized and usually highly idealized. Imagine a couple in real life sorting through a problem with the speed and

satisfying resolution with which couples on television do. It's not likely to happen. A character in a film can cheat on a spouse or engage in risky sexual behavior and suffer no negative consequences: no sexually transmitted diseases, no unwanted pregnancy, no discovery of betrayal. Real people, however, get pregnant when they don't use contraception, they contract dangerous diseases, and they hurt loved ones deeply and damage their relationships when they are promiscuous.

As for depictions of first-time sexual encounters, the media would lead one to believe that it's possible and even likely that the first time a couple has sex they will move gracefully together and will know how to please each other without ever speaking about it. Such encounters in real life are often awkward, and the participants can be nervous. Also, the average man or woman does not have perfectly toned muscles. The physique required by actors to be considered sex symbols is difficult (and likely impossible for an average person) to achieve, not only because of genetics, but also because real naked bodies can't be improved in postproduction.

Because of the barrage of unrealistic imagery that today's world presses on people every day, it is wise (and necessary) to remember that fictionalized sex and sexual activity is just that—fiction. It's important for men and women to let real experiences and healthy feelings color their expectations of sex and sexual partners. Doing so will lead to a more satisfying sex life.

Body Image

"You are beautiful." This a comment that anyone would want to inspire, but how many people can believe it when they hear it? Body image can dictate whether a man or woman can understand and accept such a compliment. Body image is made up of a number of psychological factors: perception of physical appearance, feelings about appearance, feelings about the body in general, and ideas about how others perceive the body. All these factors combine to create body image, and, whether the result is a negative or a positive one, a person's sense of identity is deeply affected by the outcome.

With a positive body image, a person has an accurate perception of the size and shape of their body, and feels comfortable with it. A negative body image indicates that a person has a distorted perception of their body's shape and size, compares their body to those of others, and feels shame, awkwardness, and anxiety about their physical appearance. Dissatisfaction with the body affects how people think and feel about themselves. A poor body image can lead to emotional upset, low self-esteem, unhealthy dieting, anxiety, depression, and eating disorders.

An individual's perception of his or her body is subjective, and may have little or nothing to do with how others actually see him or her. Such subjectivity means that a person who has the physical attributes his or her society considers attractive does not necessarily feel attractive. Self-doubt, self-consciousness, and lack of confidence—all problems that accompany poor body image—decrease the chances for a person to experience a satisfying sex life. Acceptance of one's body, no matter what it looks like, and believing that the whole person is what counts the most are the attributes that indicate healthy body image and that are lastingly attractive.

One of the difficulties that arises with body image is that, short of plastic surgery, there is little anyone can do to alter how he or she looks standing nude in front of the mirror. Staying fit and eating a healthy diet have the strongest impact, but even these efforts won't necessarily change a body that lies far outside society's ideal (as promulgated in advertising and entertainment) into what it is not. The lack of control over something that can affect personal identity so strongly can create emotional conflict for anyone, but the problem is especially painful for those whose bodies change as a result of disease, disability, or necessary medical treatments, such as surgery.

Since it is possible to change the body's form only to a certain extent, and those changes are not guaranteed to alter a person's self-perception, improving body image depends upon changing the emotional response to body perception. It takes work, but the tremendous number of stories about people who have recovered from serious eating disorders, who are happy with themselves in the face of terrible disfigurement, and who can learn to love their bodies after years of sexual abuse, prove that the creation or recovery of positive body image is possible. And a positive self-image is the key to a healthy, happy sex life. They may not have been referring to sex at the time, but what psychologists, teachers, pastors, and parents have said is true: it's who you are on the inside that counts.

How Body Image Develops

The formation of body image begins at birth. How babies are touched, looked at, and spoken to teaches them either that they are loved, which leads to positive self-image, or that they are somehow deficient, which leads to poor self-image. Some children are fortunate in that their parents and siblings show them love and teach them early on that they are valuable. Such positive early learning can influence a child's development, even into adulthood. Children who are shown that they are loved, body and soul, just for who they are, will love and accept themselves (which subsequently will have a positive impact on their sex lives), and they will be able to show love to others throughout their lives (another sign of healthy intimacy). They also will be less likely to succumb to self-destructive activities, such as eating disorders, smoking, and drug use, or become abusive or exploitative toward others.

Young children are curious about their bodies and the bodies they see around them. Exploration of the genitals is normal in toddlers, and needs to be limited only by what the family feels is socially acceptable. Questions about sexuality are typical of young and older children alike, and giving accurate (though not too detailed) and unembarrassed answers is the best way to help form healthy ideas about body image.

Parents may be surprised to see changes in their children, especially girls, at a younger age than they experienced themselves. Exposure to advertising and entertainment has had an impact on the children in some cultures, causing them to become highly attuned to body image issues well before the onset of puberty. Adolescence, because it brings rapid and substantial physical and emotional changes, is the time when body image tends to emerge most strongly as a crucial element of a person's self-image. Teenagers examine and interpret the changes they are experiencing in the light of what their culture tells them is important. Many adolescents discover (to their dismay or empowerment) that how a person looks can dictate, to a large extent, how society perceives and treats them. Self-esteem is especially fragile in teenagers, and feeling that they do not meet with the approval of their peers can have a huge impact. The peer group expresses what is considered ideal for everything from physical stature to breast and genital development, from hair color and style to sexual conduct. Not being able to keep in step, physically or socially, can damage a young person's sense of identity.

As with other aspects of puberty, body image may become and remain a preoccupation into adulthood. Many adults also struggle to keep up with changing social standards, deciding to undergo whatever procedure (breast augmentation, face-lifts, hair implants) that they believe will make them meet society's accepted standard. Body image becomes the focus of self-image, leaving a person vulnerable as the natural changes of age occur, which are beyond our control. Poor body image not only damages an adult's self-image, it can create a vicious circle by teaching children that their value lies in how they look, not who they are. Children who hear negative comments about body size and shape will learn that such attributes affect how they are seen and treated by others. Teaching children to take care of their bodies for the sake of their health can create an invaluable foundation for positive body image and self-care habits, which will carry on into adulthood.

Improving Body Image

Once a negative body image has developed, it is difficult to alter. Therefore, it is important to foster a positive self-image in children. An adult who tries to improve his or her body image will find the efforts rewarding. Also, others will react positively to this new self-esteem, which can lead to an enhanced sex life. However, the most effective method for dealing with poor body image is the help found in individual or group therapy. A therapist can help identify how inaccurate ideas about the body have formed, and teach a person to see themselves differently, replacing distorted views with accurate and positive ones.

Q+A

Q: I'm a 36-year-old married woman who has gained almost 15 pounds over the last seven or eight years. I just don't feel attractive anymore, and so I don't feel comfortable taking my clothes off in front of my husband or having sex with the lights on. This is beginning to cause problems between my husband and myself. What can I do?

A: Your problem may stem more from a negative body image than excess weight. Did you notice a change in your husband's sexual response to you as you started gaining the weight, or was it your idea to turn off the lights in the bedroom because you felt uncomfortable with your husband seeing you naked? Chances are your husband still finds you very attractive. Ask him what he loves about your body and tell him to be specific. Then—and this is the difficult part—trust him and believe what he says. It's a big step toward improving your self-image and accepting who you are. Also, reassess your wardrobe: How do your clothes fit you since you gained the weight? Sometimes treating yourself to a new outfit or some sexy new lingerie can help change how you feel about your body both clothed and naked.

Birth Control

Before a man and woman have sexual intercourse, they both need to consider the possibility that a pregnancy may result. If parenthood is not their goal, they should become familiar with and practice a method of birth control, an umbrella term for the numerous strategies to prevent an unwanted pregnancy.

Male condoms are sheaths of either thin latex, plastic, sheep or lambskin worn on the erect penis during intercourse. They usually come rolled into a ring shape.

Total abstinence from sex is one form of birth control, and it's the only strategy that is 100 percent effective. Abstinence is strongly advocated in many cultures (especially among parents of teenagers), but most people, whatever their age, find abstinence difficult. People who are going to have sex owe it to themselves—and to a child who may be born from an unplanned pregnancy—to examine their feelings about birth control and the available options before they act.

A form of birth control that works well for one person or couple may be wrong for another. When selecting a birth control method, variables such as age, access to medical care, finances, frequency of sexual activity, and number of partners all factor into the equation.

Be aware that every option other than total abstinence leaves open some chance, however small, of fertilization. Before having sex, both partners should respect that chance, and think about what they would do if their chosen method were to fail.

This section discusses the various birth control options available today, including how they work and the pros and cons of their use, to help anyone who is sexually active make an informed decision about the method that's right for them.

Birth Control Methods for Men
Condoms
Condoms are sheaths that cover the entire erect penis, acting as a barrier that prevents any semen a man ejaculates from entering the vagina.

The ejaculate remains in the sheath, which is then carefully discarded. A condom should be used only once. Used properly, condoms for men offer a significant degree of protection against not only fertilization and pregnancy, but also sexually transmitted diseases (see pages 282–285).

Even when used properly (see basic instructions and illustrations, below), condoms for men have a failure rate of 11 percent—which means out of every hundred women (and their partners) who rely on

Putting on a condom: place the rolled condom over the tip of the hard penis, leaving a half-inch space at the tip to collect semen. Pinch the air out of the tip with one hand while placing it on the penis. Unroll the condom over the penis with the other hand, smoothing out any air bubbles. (Friction caused by air bubbles can cause the condom to break.)

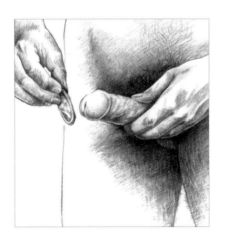

them as their main form of birth control, 11 are expected to get pregnant. Using a spermicide with a condom makes it a much more effective form of birth control.

There are no medical risks associated with using condoms. Condoms made of latex (rubber) or polyurethane (plastic) are inexpensive, easy to use, and require no medical examination or prescription. Some people report skin sensitivities to latex, a problem that is easily solved by switching to polyurethane condoms. Women who suffer from vaginal irritation after exposure to latex condoms usually find relief by placing a water-based lubricant either in the vagina or on the condom.

Some condoms are made of sheep or lambskin (see page 245); be aware that sheepskin condoms do not provide protection against STDs such as HIV/AIDS.

Unless otherwise marked, condoms are all the same size and will fit any erect penis. (Some manufacturers have made extra-large condoms available, though they are seldom necessary.) In the United States and

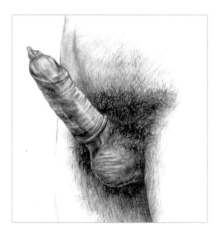

Q+A

Q: Is it true that you can't catch an STD if you use a condom?
A: No, though a condom will greatly reduce the risk. If you have sex with a partner who is infected, a condom is not a 100 percent defense. If you know that you or your partner has a curable STD, there is only one way to guarantee it will not be passed along: no sex at all until the disease is cured. If your partner has an incurable STD such as herpes, you must decide whether or not you are willing to accept a degree of risk by continuing to have sex using a condom. For each incurable disease, there are specific recommendations for couples who continue to have sex. Speak to your doctor about your specific situation, and he or she will be able to advise you on the risks involved and any preventative measures.

in most European countries, condoms sold to the public must meet government standards regarding elasticity, strength, and leakage prevention. Some condoms have textures described as ribbed or meshed. Texture should have nothing to do with a condom's effectiveness—all approved condoms must meet the same government quality standards. Couples may find that the texturing or ribbing provides pleasurable sensations during intercourse.

Ultra-thin condoms are designed to offer increased sensitivity, or more of a "natural" flesh-to-flesh feeling, which appeals to some men, though others prefer thicker condoms that reduce sensitivity and, therefore, help prolong sex. Different brands of ultra-thin condoms offer varying degrees of thinness.

Using a Condom. Some men prefer to place condoms on themselves, while others enjoy having their partner do it. Whoever will be fitting the condom should open the condom

wrapper before any genital contact. Don't use scissors or any sharp object to open the wrapper, because the condom may be damaged accidentally. Place the rolled-up condom on the tip of the erect penis, and unroll it over the penis's entire length. Remember, pre-ejaculate fluid can cause pregnancy and transmit STDs, so always put on a condom before letting the penis come in any sort of contact with the vagina or anus.

Condoms unroll in one direction only. If the person fitting the condom begins to unroll it the wrong way, throw it away and replace it with a new one, as some pre-ejaculate may have made contact with the outside portion of the condom.

Some condoms have a reservoir tip to collect ejaculated semen. If a condom does not have a reservoir tip, do not roll or stretch the condom tightly against the head of the penis; leave about half an inch of space to allow room for the ejaculate by pinching the tip of the condom with one hand as the other hand unrolls it.

birth control

Q+A

Q: I sometimes have a problem with premature ejaculation. Do condoms prevent a man from ejaculating quickly?

A: "Quickly" is a matter of opinion. Condoms don't cure what is considered medically as premature ejaculation. They do sometimes make intercourse last a little longer because they reduce sensitivity, which can delay the approach of ejaculation and prolong a session of lovemaking.

After ejaculation, but before the erection is lost, hold the base of the condom against the penis shaft while withdrawing the penis from the vagina. Remove the condom promptly. Waiting until the penis becomes flaccid before withdrawing could cause the condom to slip off and accidentally allow semen to enter the vagina.

Before discarding a used condom after sex, check it thoroughly to be certain it has not broken or developed any tiny holes.

If a condom tears or bursts during sex but before ejaculation, discontinue sex immediately and remove the condom. If and when the couple resumes intercourse, they should do so only with a fresh condom in place. Keep in mind that because some pre-ejaculation may have occurred, even a small tear in the condom puts a woman at risk of becoming pregnant.

If a condom breaks during or after ejaculation, a woman is at a much greater risk of pregnancy. One way to respond to a burst condom is for a woman to fill her vagina immediately with a spermicidal foam, jelly, or cream and leave it in place until it dissolves. She may also choose to use an emergency contraceptive pill (see page 252). Another option is to consult a doctor and have an IUD (see pages 248–251) inserted, which can help prevent or terminate pregnancy. In all cases, the woman should see her doctor if her next period is at all late.

Lubricating a Condom. Many couples prefer to use lubricated condoms or to add lubricant to an unlubricated condom. It is essential that only non-oil-based lubricants be used. Never use petroleum jelly (which removes the natural lubrication from the vagina), massage oils, or moisturizers as lubricants; all of these ointments weaken condoms.

Adding a few drops of a non-oil-based lubricant to the inside of the condom before rolling it onto the erect penis can increase the man's sensitivity. Women who usually produce adequate wetness to enjoy sex may find that they need more lubricant when a condom is used. Non-oil-based lubrication should always be used during anal sex to prevent condom breakage.

Condom-safe spermicidal (sperm-killing) foam or cream inserted by the woman into her vagina prior to intercourse can be an effective lubricant, but be aware that spermicides, whether included in a prepackaged lubricated condom or added independently, can cause allergies, and should not be used by those who find them irritating. One final note to keep in mind about lubricant: overdoing it can actually inhibit sensitivity because there will be too great a reduction in friction. It's best to add lubricant a little at a time, as needed.

Maximizing Condom Effectiveness. Always store sealed condoms away from heat—high temperatures break down the rubber and cause tearing. Keeping a condom or two in a wallet or back pocket, although convenient, is a bad idea—body heat over an extended period of time weakens the rubber too much for it to remain reliable.

Most condoms carry expiration dates; do not use a condom that has expired. If there is no expiration date on the wrapper, check for a manufacturer's date. Throw away any condom that is more than two years old. Before using a condom, check the wrapper for tears or holes that may indicate that the condom has been damaged. If there are signs of damage, throw away the condom.

Never wear two condoms at once. Far from doubling your safety, it actually reduces it severely. The friction created by the two layers of latex often causes one or both of them to tear.

Complaints about Condoms. Condoms are the best defense against sexually transmitted diseases, and in combination with spermicide, a highly effective form of birth control.

Nevertheless, some men stubbornly refuse to wear condoms— even when asked by their partner— because they claim it diminishes their sexual pleasure. While this may be true, slightly less sensitivity (in an extremely sensitive area) is a far less serious problem than an unwanted pregnancy or STD. Here are some of the most common reasons given for discontinuing condom use:

- Using condoms can make sex feel less spontaneous and intimate. One response: Turn the application of the condom into a pleasurable experience. Many couples find it quite erotic when the woman slowly puts the condom on her partner's penis.
- A condom reduces the sensation of the penis moving within the vagina (a complaint of both men and women).
- After ejaculation, the man must stop all movement and withdraw his penis, or risk having the condom slip off and cause semen to come in contact with the vagina. (Both men and women regard this interruption as a disadvantage of using condoms.)
- Some people report being constantly distracted by the concern that the condom may slip off or break if intercourse is too vigorous.
- Some men find putting on a condom difficult, and therefore embarrassing. With a little practice, however, this problem can be easily overcome.

Regardless of a couple's feelings about the disadvantages of using condoms, the message bears repeating that condoms are the best defense against sexually transmitted diseases, and in combination with spermicide, a highly effective form of birth control. It is to be hoped that anyone mature enough to have sex is also mature enough to understand that the disadvantages of condom use are minor compared with the overwhelming difficulties of an unwanted pregnancy or STD.

Note: A man should always wear a condom if his partner requests it. If he does not agree, no intercourse should take place.

Skin Condoms. Skin condoms are made from sheep intestines. They look much the same and are used in exactly the same way as latex condoms. Most people use latex condoms because they cost less and provide crucial protection against many sexually transmitted diseases. Animal skin condoms do not provide effective protection against STDs.

Some men and women prefer animal skin condoms to latex ones because they say they can feel more during intercourse. This is probably because skin condoms are often thinner and conduct heat better than those made from rubber. For this reason, monogamous couples who have been tested and are clear of sexually transmitted diseases may prefer to use animal skin condoms.

Birth Control Methods for Women

Women have many more birth control methods from which to choose than men, possibly because women are often the ones making the decision about whether birth control will be used. Most of the methods for women require more thought and preparation than a condom, and some present health risks. However, the variety does provide some freedom and the opportunity for a woman to find a method that works well for her and her partner.

Condoms

Condoms for women are polyurethane (plastic) sheaths shaped similarly to condoms made for men, but with a flexible ring at each end; one end of the sheath is closed, the other is open. The ring at the closed end is pushed deep inside the vagina; the ring at the open end remains outside and lies flush against the outer labia (see illustrations, page 246). The sheath remains in place during intercourse, preventing semen from entering the cervix. After sex, and before standing or sitting up, the woman twists the open end of the sheath closed and pulls it out so that the ejaculatory fluid never comes in contact with the vagina.

With a 21 percent failure rate, the female condom is a less effective birth control method than the male condom. It is also not as effective as the male condom in protecting against STDs, though it does create a barrier against direct genital contact.

Female condoms are available without a prescription at pharmacies and clinics. As with condoms for men, they should be used once and then discarded. Unlike condoms for men, a female condom may be inserted hours before sex, for a smoother transition between foreplay

birth control

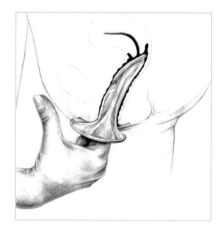

Using a female condom: Holding the inner ring of the female condom through the wall of the pouch, pinch it into an oval shape.

Keeping the ring pinched, insert it into the vagina, and with one finger, push it up behind the pubic bone.

The outer ring of the condom will remain outside the vaginal opening, with its edges covering part of the vulva.

and intercourse. Female condoms are prelubricated, but a woman can also add her own lubrication. Because they are made from plastic (rather than latex), oil-based lubricants will not cause them to deteriorate.

Complaints about the female condom include interference with manual and oral stimulation, its cost, and awkwardness for first-time users. Some women also report that the noises made by the wet plastic moving inside the vagina are a turn-off.

Spermicides

Spermicides, commonly available as creams, jellies, tablets, and suppositories, contain chemicals meant to destroy sperm on contact. When used alone, spermicides are not very effective at preventing pregnancy (tests show failure rates between 20 and 50 percent), nor do they provide protection against sexually transmitted diseases such as herpes, gonorrhea, syphilis, or HIV. But they are highly recommended for use in conjunction

with other forms of birth control such as condoms and diaphragms. Spermicide must be reapplied each time you have sex, because its potency fades quickly. Spermicide is available without a prescription at most pharmacies and clinics.

Spermicides often have an unpleasant flavor or odor, so they are not typically used during oral sex. Also, some people have reported allergic reactions to certain spermicides such as nonoxynol-9, which also has been found to increase the frequency of urinary tract infections in women. Therefore, it is important for couples to try different brands until they find a spermicide that is appealing and does not cause an allergic reaction.

Although couples may decide to engage in oral sex before using spermicide, it is crucial that the spermicide be inserted into the woman's vagina before genital intercourse in order to avoid pregnancy. Some spermicides come with an applicator to assist in this step.

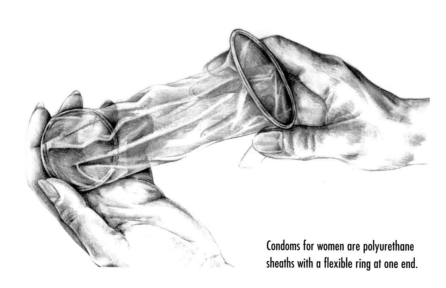

Condoms for women are polyurethane sheaths with a flexible ring at one end.

Diaphragms

A diaphragm is a barrier method of birth control. It is a rubber shield that is inserted into the vagina behind the pubic bone to block sperm from reaching the uterus. The diaphragm comes in different sizes and must be fitted to each individual woman's anatomy so that it completely covers her cervical opening.

For this barrier to be effective, a woman must be examined and fitted for the diaphragm by her doctor or a nurse practitioner. After her examination, a woman will be given a prescription for the precise size of diaphragm she needs, which can be filled at a pharmacy. A woman can insert and remove the diaphragm herself as necessary.

Diaphragms must be used with a spermicidal jelly or cream to kill any sperm that come in contact with the diaphragm. Spermicide can be bought without a prescription at a pharmacy or supermarket. A diaphragm that fits perfectly and properly used in conjunction with spermicide has a 17 percent failure rate.

Using a Diaphragm. Common mistakes that women make when using their diaphragms are failing to use spermicidal jelly or cream and removing the diaphragm too soon after intercourse.

Diaphragms can develop tiny holes or tears, and should be examined regularly for damage.

It is vital that the health care provider shows a woman exactly how to use the diaphragm effectively for maximum protection. Spermicidal jelly needs to be applied inside, and around the diaphragm's edges. The diaphragm is then folded and inserted into the vagina. When it is released, it expands to cover the cervix.

The diaphragm must be placed in the vagina not more than two hours before intercourse, and left in place six to eight hours afterward. If it is inserted or removed too soon, the spermicide will not be effective. Additionally, when intercourse occurs several times in a short period, more spermicidal jelly or cream must be placed in the vagina each time—without disturbing the diaphragm. This is easily done with the applicator that comes with the spermicidal jelly or cream.

It takes some practice to get the diaphragm in place, and also to remove it. Each woman will discover which method works best for her. Some women prefer using plastic applicators, available at pharmacies, others find it easier to use their fingers. For some, a squatting position works well, for others, standing with

A diaphragm is a soft latex or silicone barrier that covers the cervix. It is shallow and dome-shaped, with a flexible rim, and sits in the vagina behind the pubic bone.

one foot up on a chair or the toilet is easier. It's a good idea to insert and remove it a number of times in the presence of a health care provider to get familiar with the process and to make sure it feels comfortable and is correctly positioned every time. Until the insertion of the diaphragm becomes second nature, the couple should use a second form of birth control. Some men learn how to insert a diaphragm and make it a part of

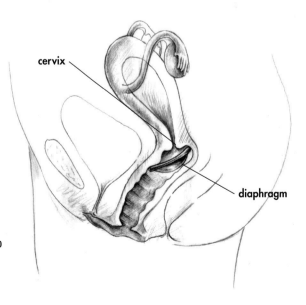

A diaphragm fits over the cervix and is held in place by vaginal muscles. It retains spermicide over the opening to the uterus, preventing sperm from entering.

cervix

diaphragm

birth control

Q+A

Q: My partner says he can feel my diaphragm during intercourse and that it's uncomfortable. What should I do?

A: A diaphragm that is fitted and inserted properly will not come in contact with your partner's penis. If it does, there may be a problem. Consult your health care provider to make sure you have the right size and that you are inserting it correctly.

foreplay. If a couple usually has intercourse before going to sleep, it's a good idea for the woman to routinely insert the diaphragm each night. Remember that spermicide loses its effectiveness after a couple of hours, and must be reapplied if you get the urge to have intercourse in the middle of the night, or upon waking.

Although a rare occurrence, during intercourse, even a properly placed diaphragm may shift. When a woman feels her diaphragm shift, she should stop and readjust it. It is rare that a diaphragm causes pain, but it can irritate the vaginal wall, or press uncomfortably against a full bladder or a full bowel. If using her diaphragm causes a woman pain, she should visit her doctor or a family planning clinic immediately, and use another method of birth control until the problem has been corrected.

It is perfectly safe to use a diaphragm for birth control during menstruation. Though ovulation is unlikely at this time, there is a slight possibility of pregnancy. If that chance makes a couple uncomfortable, they should always use birth control during menstruation. An additional benefit of the diaphragm is that it blocks menstrual blood from reaching the vagina during sex.

After the diaphragm has been removed, it should be washed with mild soap in warm water, dried, and returned to its container. When washing the diaphragm, check it for tiny holes, tears, or cracks by holding it up to the light. It is always wise to have a spare diaphragm of the proper size on hand in case you discover any damage. If a diaphragm is properly cared for, it should last about two years.

Diaphragms have no side effects or medical risks, though allergies to the spermicide are possible. Unless there is a specific medical problem (such as an abnormally shaped or prolapsed uterus), all women should be able to use a diaphragm without problem. Men should not feel the diaphragm at all during intercourse if it is the correct size, and is properly inserted.

Women who choose the diaphragm method of birth control should have their diaphragm size reevaluated at their yearly or biannual medical exam. Any woman who uses a diaphragm needs to visit her health care provider to check her diaphragm size if she gains or loses a significant amount of weight (10 pounds [4 1/2 kilograms] or so), or has any reproductive issues such as a birth, a miscarriage, or an abortion.

Cervical Caps

Cervical caps are small, flexible latex cups that fit directly over the cervix. Like diaphragms, they come in several sizes. Capping the cervix (rather than blocking it, as the diaphragm does) prevents sperm from traveling into the uterus and Fallopian tubes, and fertilizing an egg. The failure rate for cervical caps when used with spermicide is 17 percent.

Like a diaphragm, a cervical cap must be sized and fitted correctly, and the woman must be taught how to place the cap securely by her doctor or a nurse practitioner. One benefit of cervical caps is that they can remain in place for forty-eight hours without requiring a reapplication of spermicide, which is convenient for repeated intercourse. But cervical caps are more difficult to insert than diaphragms.

Women who are allergic to latex should not use cervical caps. When a cervical cap is left in place for longer than recommended, there is also a risk of toxic shock syndrome (TSS), a rare but serious infection.

Intrauterine Devices (IUD)

Intrauterine devices, or IUDs, have several advantages as a birth control method. Inserted into the uterus by a doctor or nurse practitioner, IUDs have a failure rate of less than 1 percent, don't interfere with sexual activity and are fairly inexpensive. Additionally, IUDs are easily removable should a woman decide to try to have a child at a later time. One major disadvantage of IUDs is that they provide no protection against STDs. Another is that sometimes the uterus will reject an IUD, and it will be expelled shortly after insertion or with the first menstrual flow after insertion. Between 5 and 10 percent of women expel their IUDs (they tend to be women who have never had a child). There is a very slight increased risk of a Fallopian tube (ectopic) pregnancy when using an IUD, so women with a previous diagnosis of pelvic inflammatory disease, a previous ectopic pregnancy, abdominal or Fallopian tube surgery, or fertility treatment—which also increases the risk of ectopic pregnancy—are advised not to use an IUD.

Another disadvantage is the risk of infection to the uterus, Fallopian tubes, and ovaries. In addition, an IUD can migrate through the uterine wall. A woman considering an IUD should discuss all these risk factors with her doctor.

A note of caution: Although IUDs work well for most women, there are some medical conditions that make it unsafe for a woman to use one. These include: an infection of the cervix or vagina, or a history of cervical infection; uterine abnormalities, including the uterus being tipped forward or backward; being at risk for STDs, or having contracted an STD; problems with blood clotting; ovarian cancer or the presence of large noncancerous fibroid tumors in the uterus; and anemia. Also, women who have had trouble getting pregnant and who want to get pregnant in the future are advised against using an IUD. If there is any chance a woman might be pregnant, she should not have an IUD fitted, as it will almost definitely cause a miscarriage. (see "Q+A," page 250).

Normally, physicians and nurse practitioners will check for these high-risk conditions. A woman should never attempt to put in or take out an IUD herself—an IUD must be fitted and removed by a physician or another qualified health care professional only.

Different IUDs work in different ways, but all are structured the same. A string attached to the end of the T-shaped IUD hangs down through the cervix and into the vagina. Doctors use the string to remove the IUD. (Women with

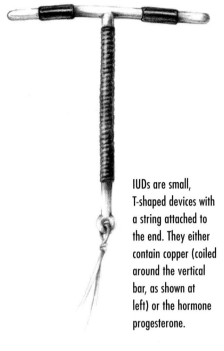

IUDs are small, T-shaped devices with a string attached to the end. They either contain copper (coiled around the vertical bar, as shown at left) or the hormone progesterone.

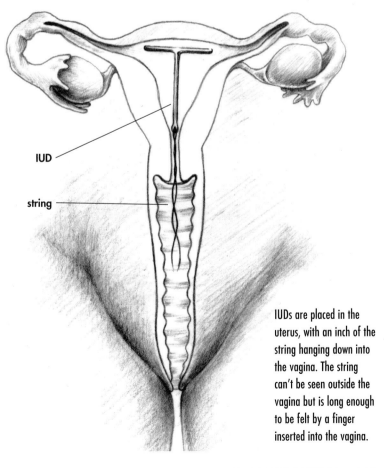

IUD

string

IUDs are placed in the uterus, with an inch of the string hanging down into the vagina. The string can't be seen outside the vagina but is long enough to be felt by a finger inserted into the vagina.

birth control

IUDs should feel for this string after every menstrual period to check that it is still in place.)

After examining a woman and evaluating her medical history, the clinician will suggest the type of IUD that is right for her. Any possible allergy to copper will be an important factor in this decision (see "Types of IUDs" below).

To insert the IUD, a practitioner introduces the IUD gently through the vagina and cervix into the uterus using an inserter tube. The IUD is flattened during insertion, and opens once it is released inside the uterus. Local anesthetic is an option to prevent any pain during the procedure.

After the IUD is placed in position and the tube removed, threads attached to the IUD are trimmed to hang at the back of the vagina. A woman should regularly feel for these threads; as long as they can be found in the same place, the IUD is still in its proper position. A noticeable change in the threads—whether they cannot be found, or they seem longer than they used to—requires a call to the health care provider without delay, as it may indicate that the IUD has shifted position.

Some women experience cramps or bleeding for a few days or even two weeks after getting an IUD. In the event of serious pain or bleeding, she should contact her health care provider immediately. As a doctor will inform any woman getting an IUD, the risk of infection is greatest in the first month after the IUD is inserted (if an STD is present in the vagina, it can be carried up into the uterus during the insertion of the IUD).

An IUD can be inserted at any time during a woman's monthly menstrual cycle, but most clinicians prefer to insert it during menstruation, taking advantage of an expanded cervix that makes placement easier and less painful.

After the removal of the IUD—a simple and safe procedure that can be done at any time by a doctor or clinician—a woman can become pregnant right away, though some physicians advise women to wait a month or two, to give the uterine lining (endometrium) time to return to its usual thickness and to resume functioning as it did before the insertion of the IUD.

Q+A

Q: Is it possible to get pregnant with an IUD in place?
A: Yes. In rare cases, a pregnancy can occur despite the presence of an IUD. The typical result is a miscarriage within weeks, signaled by severe cramps and bleeding. However, healthy babies have been safely delivered with no harm to the mother with an IUD in place. If you think you are pregnant with an IUD in place, it is crucial to contact your health care provider as quickly as possible.

In addition to the significant risk of miscarriage, pregnancy with an IUD in place presents the possibility of uterine infection. If an infection is detected, the IUD must be removed through a procedure called a dilation and suction curettage (D&C), which gently opens the uterus and cleans the lining, ending the pregnancy.

If a pregnancy is discovered before a miscarriage occurs and no infection is detected, a health care provider may attempt the delicate procedure of removing the IUD without threatening the pregnancy. If this can't be done, the risk of eventual miscarriage and infection may lead the provider to advise ending the pregnancy. But if he or she feels the risk is manageable, they may allow the IUD to stay in the uterus, maintaining close medical scrutiny of the mother and pregnancy. Under these conditions, the pregnancy may extend to term.

Types of IUDs. Currently, two types of IUDs have been proven safe and effective—the copper IUD and the progesterone IUD. The first releases minute amounts of copper—less than would be stored in the body as a result of eating a normal diet—to inflame the lining of the uterus, rendering it unable to accept a fertilized egg. Although it may seem unsafe, there is no evidence that this extremely small addition of copper is harmful; it doesn't even show up in blood samples.

Copper IUDs can remain in place for up to ten years, depending on when the device's supply of copper runs out. They are also an effective form of emergency birth control if inserted into the uterus within a few days after having unprotected sex. However, a side effect of copper IUDs is that they can cause heavier bleeding and/or increased cramping during menstruation. Ten to 15 percent of women have copper IUDs removed due to one or both discomforts.

Progesterone IUDs release a hormone that causes the mucus in the cervix to become sticky, which prevents sperm from passing through and into the uterus. Some types of progesterone, such as levonorgestrel, reduce menstrual bleeding and cramps, and actually decrease the risk of pelvic inflammatory disease (PID). Depending on the type of progesterone it uses, the IUD can remain effective for approximately five years.

Oral Contraceptives (The Pill)

The Pill, an oral contraceptive available by prescription only, is the single most popular form of birth control because it is easy to use, does not interfere with sex in any way, and has a failure rate of only 1 percent.

A woman on the Pill takes it every day for the first twenty-one days of her menstrual cycle, which changes her hormonal balance. Normally, her body produces hormones that send a signal to the reproductive system each month, triggering the ovaries to release an egg. The hormones in the Pill mimic those created by her body when a woman is pregnant, fooling the ovary into not releasing an egg. If no egg is released, a woman cannot get pregnant. However, menstruation continues because the uterus "knows" that there is no pregnancy and so it continues to shed its lining.

There are around twenty varieties of the Pill on the market, of varying chemical strengths, and with different benefits and drawbacks. Negative side effects can include blood clots, dizziness, and nausea, as well as changes in menstruation, mood, and weight. In rare cases, there is the risk of cardiovascular disease. But according to some studies, certain types of the Pill can help reduce the risk of ovarian cancer. One primary disadvantage to using the Pill is that it offers no protection against STDs.

Women who take the Pill may have lighter, less painful periods. Some types of the Pill can help alleviate acne. Each woman must decide, with her health care provider's help, which type of Pill is best for her. Before prescribing the Pill, a health care provider takes a personal and

The Pill comes in monthly packs, for either 21- or 28-day cycles. Both types have 21 active pills containing hormones to prevent pregnancy. The last seven pills in 28-day packs of combination pills are called "reminder" pills and do not contain hormones. They are taken during the fourth week. In 21-day packs, the pills are taken for three weeks.

Q+A

Q: Can you get pregnant if you miss taking one or more pills?
A: Yes. For most types of oral contraceptives, the following guidelines are appropriate regarding missed pills, but your pills may be different so you should always ask your doctor for advice based on the specific type that you are using. Ask about the procedure for missed pills as soon as your oral contraceptive is prescribed; don't wait until it happens.

Generally, if you miss a pill one day, take two pills the next day—the one you missed and the one for that day, and then continue your regular one-pill-a-day schedule. If you miss taking pills two days in a row, take two pills each day until you catch up. Then, continue your regular schedule of one pill a day. When you do miss two pills in succession, be sure to use another method of birth control along with the regular pills until your next period. If you miss taking pills three or more days in a row, stop using your pills and use another method of birth control until you have your next menstrual flow. Then, begin using your new pack of pills regularly and continue to use your backup birth control method for at least two weeks. And if you miss your period, visit your clinic or physician right away; do not wait to see if the next one is on time.

birth control

family history, and performs a Pap smear, an STD check, breast and pelvic examination, complete blood and urine analysis, and a blood pressure and weight check.

Some Pill packs come with twenty-one pills, while others come with twenty-eight. Each pill in the twenty-one-day pack contains hormones. In the twenty-eight-day pack, only the first twenty-one pills contain hormones, and the remaining seven pills contain iron, or a mixture of sugar and iron. Regardless of the type of pill used, menstruation usually occurs during the seven non-hormone days, and usually begins two to three days after the last hormone pill has been taken.

The Pill provides immediate protection against pregnancy if a woman begins taking it as soon as her period ends. If she begins any time after that in her cycle, protection will not be immediate, and she must use a backup birth-control method until she starts her second pack of pills.

The Mini-Pill
The Mini-Pill contains only low amounts of progestin and no estrogen. Progestin is a manufactured hormone resembling the natural hormone progesterone, which is produced by the ovaries after ovulation.

The advantage of the Mini-Pill is that it contains lower doses of hormone, and thus offers less interference with the total system. The Mini-Pill does not always prevent an ovum from being released—in fact, it does so less than 50 percent of the time. The Mini-Pill induces other changes. It alters the consistency of cervical mucus, helping to impede the sperm that are attempting to reach the Fallopian tubes. It also disturbs proper development of the uterine lining, making it more difficult for a fertilized egg to implant in the lining. And some researchers believe that the Mini-Pill may hasten Fallopian tube contractions, impeding the movement of the egg. The Mini-Pill has a 98-percent effectiveness rate, but only when it is taken on a strict daily schedule. If even one dose is skipped, effectiveness plummets and medical professionals recommend that a second form of birth control be used.

Mini-Pill users seem to have less breast tenderness, but can have irregular periods and spotting; they also tend to have less nausea, headache, and leg pain than users of other oral contraceptives.

A complete medical evaluation and prescription must be obtained before using the Mini-Pill.

Emergency Contraception Pills
Emergency contraception pills (ECPs) are either prescribed by a doctor or sold over-the-counter, depending on where you live. The pills must be acquired and used within three days of unprotected sex, as a form of after-the-fact birth control. The pills contain a very strong dose of progestin (or a combination of progestin and estrogen) that disrupts the lining of the uterus and makes it difficult for a fertilized egg to become implanted.

The first dose is taken as soon as possible after unprotected sex; the second is taken twelve hours after the first dose. A second doctor's visit and continued medical supervision are necessary. Emergency contraceptive pills are about 75 percent effective; side effects include dizziness, headache, breast tenderness, and nausea. If a woman vomits soon after taking ECPs, it may be necessary to repeat the dosage. A woman's supervising physician will determine whether this is the case.

Taking an ECP is not the same as having an abortion. For a woman to be considered pregnant, the egg must be successfully implanted in the lining of the uterus. ECPs prevent implantation, thus preventing pregnancy from occurring altogether.

The Patch
The Patch, a prescription-only option that became available in 2001, prevents pregnancy in the same way as the Pill, except that the Patch releases its hormones into the bloodstream through the skin.

The patch resembles a small adhesive bandage—it's just as thin and only measures about 2 square inches (about 5 square cm). It's applied onto a woman's lower abdomen, a buttock, or upper body, where it releases a steady flow of the hormones progestin and estrogen through the skin and into the bloodstream. This influx of hormones convinces the woman's body that it is pregnant, and thus prevents the monthly release of an egg.

The one benefit of the Patch over oral contraceptives is that instead of taking a pill every day, a woman need only replace it once a week for three weeks. On the fourth week she has her menstrual period and no patch is required. This might be appealing to women who have trouble remembering to take a pill. The Patch has a 1 percent failure rate, though it tends to be less effective for women who weigh more than 198 pounds. Because it contains the same hormones as the Pill, the Patch has the same benefits and some additional negative side effects. In clinical trials, 5 percent of women using the Patch found it would not adhere to their skin and 2 percent experienced some skin irritation. The Patch does not protect against STDs, and although it is designed to stay on during activities like showering, vigorous friction—like that caused by using a towel to dry—can loosen it. If that happens, a woman should try to replace it in the same spot. If the patch will not stick, a woman should place a new patch on the same spot. If the patch has been off her body for more than twenty-four hours, she should use an additional method of birth control for the remainder of that cycle.

Vaginal Contraceptive Rings

Like oral contraceptives, the recently developed Vaginal Contraceptive Ring delivers estrogen and progestin to the bloodstream, convincing a woman's body that it is pregnant and thereby preventing the monthly release of an egg.

The flexible ring, which is 2 inches (about 5 cm) in diameter, is placed inside the vagina for three weeks. It is removed for the fourth week, when menstruation occurs. The muscles of the vagina keep the ring in place and it does not interfere in any way with intercourse. The failure rate of the Ring is low, at just 1 percent.

The main benefit of the Ring over oral contraceptives is that there is no need to remember to take a pill every day. The risks and side effects of the Ring are the same as those of the Pill. Additional side effects may include vaginal discharge, vaginitis (see page 285), and irritation. Like the Pill, the Ring offers no protection against STDs and requires a prescription from a physician.

If the ring is expelled and remains outside of the vagina for longer than three hours, another form of birth control must be used until the ring has been back in place for seven continuous days.

Injections

Rather than taking a daily pill or using a patch or ring to deliver pregnancy-preventing hormones to the bloodstream, a woman may choose to have injections of progestin or a combination of progestin and estrogen. These shots require a prescription and must be administered by a health care provider on a monthly basis, or once every three months. The failure rate of hormonal injections is 1 percent. They offer no protection against STDs.

The Sponge

The soft, disk-shaped, polyurethane foam Sponge acts as a barrier preventing sperm from entering the cervix, and it contains spermicide that kills sperm on contact. Once removed from the market due to

manufacturing problems, it is being retested and experts predict that it will be made available again in the near future.

The sponge is inserted into the vagina up to twenty-four hours before intercourse. It must be left in place for at least six hours after sex, and for no longer than thirty hours after insertion. There is a slight risk of toxic shock syndrome if the sponge is left in longer than recommended. Other risks include irritation and allergic reactions to the spermicide on the sponge. Many women report difficulty inserting and removing the sponge.

Natural Methods of Birth Control

Natural family planning is a general term used to describe several methods of birth control that do not depend on chemicals (as does the Pill) or mechanical barriers (such as condoms or cervical caps), but instead behavioral methods. *Rhythm* is the best-known natural birth control method, but the cervical mucus method (also known as the Billings method for its originator, Dr. J. Billings) is gaining in popularity.

The concept of natural family planning relies on a solid understanding of how a woman's reproductive system works, how it affects her body, and how to read its signals. Proper interpretation of those signals can tell a couple when it is safe to have intercourse without a risk of pregnancy or when fertility is at a peak to maximize the odds of conceiving a baby. Natural family planning may also require abstaining during fertile periods or using an alternate form of birth control.

Before choosing any natural family planning method, it is crucial for both partners to get advice and instruction from a qualified health care professional. Natural family planning programs are available across the United States and Canada and in most European countries. Family planning centers, clinics, and many physicians can also offer valuable advice in addition to quality health care.

From an effectiveness standpoint, the temperature or BBT (for basal body temperature) method, with intercourse occurring only after ovulation, is generally considered the best natural birth control method. It shows success rates of 98 to 99 percent—similar to those of oral contraceptives. Effectiveness rates for the calendar method alone have not been widely tested, but are likely to be around 70 percent. Rates reported for the cervical mucus method vary from 70 percent to the high 90s. Ultimately, not enough research has been conducted to get an accurate picture of the effectiveness of any particular natural birth control method.

The Rhythm Method. The Rhythm Method prevents pregnancy as the couple limits intercourse to the time of each month when they have predicted the woman is not ovulating. For the method to be successful, the couple must totally abstain from intercourse during the period of the month in which the woman is most likely to ovulate.

To determine when ovulation is likely, and therefore when intercourse should be avoided, couples have two options. Each method may be used on its own, or the two may be used in tandem: the calendar method and the basal body temperature method.

The calendar method requires a woman to track her menstrual cycles for eight to 12 months before putting it into practice. The idea is that with careful observation, the woman can learn to predict her entire monthly menstrual cycle with a high degree of accuracy. Applying simple arithmetic, the couple can, in theory, predict when it is safe to have intercourse without risking pregnancy: In a typical 28-day menstrual cycle, ovulation usually occurs 14 days prior to the beginning of the woman's next menstrual period; the couple can plan on abstaining from intercourse from three days before the predicted date of ovulation (because sperm can live in the woman's body for up to three days) until two days after that date (because an egg may remain viable for up to a day and a half).

Although cycle patterns can be discerned, predictions are far from foolproof. Most women's cycles fluctuate in length over the course of a year, and any number of factors can change the ovulation cycles: illness, weight loss, stress, or any changes in a woman's environment. Also, some couples feel constrained by rigidly scheduled windows of opportunity during which to have intercourse.

With the basal body temperature method, or BBT, a woman uses a BBT thermometer (available at phar-

---

Q+A

Q: Why use natural birth control methods when other methods appear to be much easier to use and much more reliable?

A: For some people, it is a religious matter—Catholicism and Orthodox Judaism, for example, allow only natural methods of birth control, forbidding adherents to employ medication or physical barriers to conception. Medical reasons, which can include allergies, a history of infections, or anatomical abnormalities, may limit some couples' options. In additon, many couples simply feel good about using natural methods, even if they happen to be more complicated than other options, because they have less impact on the body.

macies and clinics) to take her body temperature for several months each morning before she gets out of bed. Based on the information she gathers, she creates a chart on graph paper, sold with the BBT thermometer. This chart will show a fairly steady daily temperature until her time of ovulation, when her temperature will decrease slightly then increase slightly for about three days. The rise in temperature is caused by an increase in the production of progesterone, the hormone that prepares the endometrium for egg implantation. Detecting the slight rise in temperature on the graph requires careful attention, but it is vital to the success of the method, because fertility is high at this time. Couples who want to avoid pregnancy abstain until these three days pass. Knowing when those days occur requires months of recording and analyzing the temperature chart. To further complicate matters, the pattern can be distorted by various situations, such as a fever or other illness, or by not taking the temperature at consistent times.

The most reliable application of the BBT method is for a couple to abstain from intercourse until after ovulation has occurred. Putting this into practice means a couple is limited to about two weeks per month when they can have intercourse.

Cervical Mucus Method. The cervix undergoes changes between the last day of one menstrual period and the first day of the next; this method teaches that the type of mucus discharged by the cervix indicates the current phase of ovulation.

Q+A

Q: Is a tubal ligation the same as a hysterectomy?
A: No. During a tubal ligation, a section of each Fallopian tube is removed. During a hysterectomy, the uterus is completely removed (see page 208). Menstruation and ovulation continue after a tubal ligation; they do not after a hysterectomy.

Once a woman can correlate each phase of ovulation with the type of cervical mucus evident, she can safely engage in intercourse without getting pregnant. Since it is impossible under ordinary circumstances to detect the nature of the cervical mucus during her period, menstruation is considered a time when a woman is potentially fertile. Adequate instruction is absolutely necessary in learning how to use this method effectively.

For a few days after menstruation ends, the cervix's mucus production is extremely limited; the probability of conception during this period is low, and intercourse is generally considered safe. When rising levels of estrogen cause the cervix to begin producing clear mucus that looks like raw egg white—ovulation is imminent. This fertile period lasts for several days, and dictates abstinence for couples seeking to avoid conception. When a thicker, sticky, cloudy mucus appears, the fertile period is over and a couple may resume safe intercourse.

Using the cervical mucus method is labor-intensive—it means blotting cervical mucus on tissue paper or toilet paper several times a day to monitor the cervical discharge for color and consistency, and intensively charting the result. (Using a chart as a reference tool is important if one is to easily discern a recognizable pattern.) Some couples find the process somewhat tedious. And it takes some time to gather enough data to establish a reliable, predictable schedule: It can take up to two months before a couple has enough of a reading to put it into practice.

This method must be practiced for a month or two before it is used as a reliable form of birth control. Keep in mind that stress may affect ovulation and therefore change usual patterns, as may infections and some medications. Those using the cervical mucus method must also learn to distinguish semen remaining in the vagina from cervical mucus.

Sterilization
Sterilization is a surgical procedure that is designed to prevent either a man from fathering a child or a woman from becoming pregnant.

Tubal Ligation
Sterilization for women is called *tubal ligation*. During this procedure, commonly known as getting your "tubes tied," a surgeon cuts and seals the Fallopian tubes. After this operation, eggs cannot travel to the uterus, nor can sperm reach them.

birth control

Tubal ligation does not interfere with sexual interest, pleasure, or performance, nor does it interfere with menstruation or cause menopause. There are several ways of cutting or sealing the Fallopian tubes that do not require major surgery. These methods are virtually 100 percent effective. They do not, however, protect against reproductive tract infections and STDs.

Reversing tubal ligation is possible, but requires long and difficult surgery (see "Q+A," page 257). It is not advisable for a woman to have tubal ligation when she is pregnant or may be pregnant, when she has a serious medical problem such as heart disease, when she is obese, or when she has an active infection of the uterus or Fallopian tubes.

Vasectomy

In the sterilization procedure for men, called vasectomy, a surgeon cuts and seals the two tubes (the vasa deferentia) that transport sperm from the testicles to the penis. After a vasectomy, sperm is still produced by the testis, but it cannot pass the barrier created by the surgery. Therefore, the sperm cannot leave the man's body, come into contact

In a vasectomy, the physician cuts and seals the two tubes— the vasa deferentia— that transport sperm from the testicles to the penis.

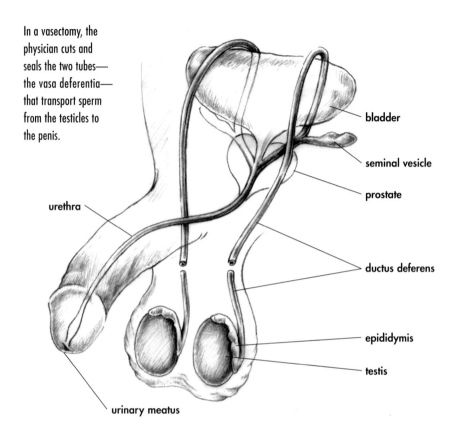

- bladder
- seminal vesicle
- prostate
- ductus deferens
- epididymis
- testis

urethra

urinary meatus

with the egg, and cause a pregnancy. Vasectomy does not interfere with a man's sexual interest, erection, ejaculation, pleasure, or performance and is considered 100-percent safe.

Most vasectomies are performed on an outpatient basis in a health care practitioner's office under a local anesthetic, administered to each

side of the scrotum. Only in cases of unusual medical problems do vasectomies require hospitalization.

During the procedure, a small incision is made in the side of the scrotum; the vas is lifted out and cut by up to 1 inch (2.5 cm). The ends of the vas must then be tied together or cauterized, and put back in the scrotum. That procedure is performed on each side of the scrotum. The entire procedure generally takes no more than 30 minutes. Some pain may be experienced after vasectomy, and the application of an ice pack to the sore area is often prescribed. Performed properly, a vasectomy is an almost fail-safe method of sterilization. Also, the procedure does not produce visible scar tissue: Because

Q+A

Q: Can I use a sperm bank before a vasectomy?
A: Yes. Sperm banks offer the opportunity to store your sperm in a medical freezing unit before your vasectomy. Afterward, if you wish to have another child, the sperm can be artificially inseminated in your partner. However, there can be problems. Some freezing techniques can destroy sperm. Additionally, some cases have revealed that sperm seem to lose their motility after being stored for a long period of time.

Q+A

Q: Is tubal ligation reversible?

A: Yes, it is possible to reverse a tubal ligation, but the procedure is complicated and carries more risk than the original ligation surgery. About 60 to 80 percent of women who have the reversal surgery are eventually able to become pregnant, but the risk of having a tubal (ectopic) pregnancy—one that develops in the Fallopian tube rather than in the uterus—increases. Therefore, before you undergo sterilization, consider the procedure permanent and irreversible. Be absolutely certain that you will never want to become pregnant.

A common dilemma many women face if they've previously had a tubal ligation is whether they should undergo a tubal ligation reversal versus an IVF (in vitro fertilization) procedure. A tubal reversal requires one operation to restore fertility, enabling the patient to have as many children as she wants, whereas an IVF procedure offers a lower, 20 to 35 percent chance of success for each try and can be much more costly in that it could take several attempts before she becomes pregnant. IVF involves taking mature eggs from your ovary, fertilizing them with your partner's sperm in a laboratory and implanting them into your uterus. However, after a successful IVF, a woman will have the child she wanted without needing to repeat the tubal ligation.

---

the skin of the scrotum is textured, the two small incisions will not be noticeable once they have healed.

After a vasectomy, a man can resume having sex as soon as he feels comfortable. Although the surgery is minor, the tissue on the scrotum has been cut and bruised and needs to heal. Vigorous intercourse or masturbation may need to be delayed. It's also important to remember that a vasectomy does not provide immediate protection. Sperm are alive and present in all structures beyond the point of the surgery, such as the seminal vesicles and the ejaculatory ducts. All of this sperm must be expelled before the entire reproductive system can be considered free from sperm. Therefore, another method of birth control must be used until the ejaculate is purged of sperm. A man's doctor will require a test for sperm count after he has resumed sexual activity. The sperm count will reveal the presence or absence of sperm in a

man's semen and will indicate whether additional birth control needs to be continued. It is important to remember that what matters is not how long a man waits after a vasectomy to have unprotected intercourse, but how many times he has ejaculated.

There are circumstances under which it is unwise to have a vasectomy. A hernia or an undescended testicle may make it undesirable, though sometimes the procedure can be performed after such a condition has been corrected. Men who suffer from abnormal blood clotting, very high blood pressure, or heart disease will probably be advised by their doctor that they should not have a vasectomy, as any kind of surgery could be harmful in these instances. The reversal of vasectomy is possible, but requires a long and difficult surgery.

In some cases a vasectomy can be reversed, by a surgical procedure called a vasovasostomy in which the

surgeon stitches the vasa deferentia back together. Unfortunately, the success rate of the vasovasostomy is rather low unless it is performed within three years of the original vasectomy procedure.

Q+A

Q: How can a man who has had a vasectomy still ejaculate if he is no longer producing sperm?

A: Sperm actually makes up a very small part (about 1 percent) of ejaculate. The other 99 percent is fluids secreted primarily by the seminal vesicles and prostate gland, which are unaffected by the vasectomy. These fluids are what compose the postvasectomy ejaculate. Incidentally, only examination of semen under a microscope would reveal that a man has had a vasectomy. The color, amount, and consistency remain unchanged. No one can tell from a man's ejaculate whether he has had a vasectomy.

Casual Sex

Teenagers, college students, and single adults are more likely than other groups to engage in casual sex. A recent survey of teenagers between the ages of fifteen and seventeen showed that almost a third have had intercourse in a casual context.

Some people use casual sex to meet their sexual needs when they don't have (or don't want) a committed romantic relationship. However, most of the consequences associated with casual sex can be serious. One of these is the contraction (or transmission) of sexually transmitted diseases (STDs, see pages 282–285), such as herpes or HIV. Also, people frequently underestimate or disregard the risk that physical intimacy poses to their emotional state, until it is too late and they are hurt.

Women may risk more than hurt feelings when they enter into sexual relationships with a casual attitude. A woman who does not know her partner well may choose someone who does not respect her physically or emotionally, even to the point of possible sexual assault. Women are more frequently victims of this kind of crime than are men.

Protecting Yourself
Condoms

Casual sex and condoms go together, regardless of how urgent the desire is to proceed without interruption. The only form of contraception that offers more protection than a condom is abstinence. If a man refuses to wear a condom when asked, or his partner demands that he not wear one, sexual activity should stop.

Phone a Friend

No matter how tempting it is to let the natural flow of a "hook-up" continue uninterrupted, it is always wise to let someone know where you are going and with whom. It may seem exciting to sneak away for a sexual adventure, but you may be putting yourself in the position to be mugged, kidnapped, raped, or murdered. A quick conversation with, or a phone call to, a friend should never be considered too much trouble. Anyone who tries to prevent such a conversation from taking place is not someone to go anywhere with for any reason.

Be Honest

A person about to engage in casual sex needs to be honest. Just as a man or woman needs to be prepared to be protected from STDs, a person needs to be prepared psychologically and emotionally for the challenges of "no-strings-attached" sex. Nothing can completely protect a person physically during and after casual sex, but an honest self-assessment of desires and expectations in advance can offer mental protection. Anyone who wants a committed romantic relationship, but is trying to be satisfied with casual sex, is going to end up unhappy or unsatisfied. A person also needs to consider the social consequences of treating sex casually, such as criticism and stereotyping.

Being honest with a partner from the outset reduces the risk of that person reacting in undesirable ways. Openly stating expectations can help prevent misunderstandings. If the experience is supposed to be just fun and enjoyable, then say so before sex has taken place so that no one gets the wrong impression. It can be difficult to explain to a person with opposite notions that a recently completed sexual encounter is not the beginning of a romantic relationship. A person who feels deceived or rejected is more likely to feel angry or depressed, which may lead to problems for both people in the long run.

Q+A

Q: I am thirty-one years old and not married. I'm happy with the few relationships I've developed that meet my sexual needs. However, my family has begun to criticize me and accuse me of having commitment problems. I like the way I live. Is my lifestyle unhealthy?

A: As long as you are honest with your sexual partners and protect yourself physically, emotionally, and psychologically, your lifestyle is not unhealthy. If you feel that your needs are being met, then don't change. If, however, you have serious doubts about your lifestyle choices, reassess your needs and decide how best to get them met.

Relationship Sex

Conventional wisdom teaches—and research confirms—that the best sex occurs between two people who care deeply for one another, and who have made a commitment to be monogamous (having sex only with each other). Meaningful relationships are based on trust, which engenders an emotionally safe atmosphere. This safety gives men and women an opportunity to let go of inhibitions and anxieties related to sexual behavior and to express (and explore) their desires. People in committed relationships also tend to be able to communicate effectively with one another, a skill that can be applied to feelings and inclinations related to sex. Choosing to be monogamous expresses the deep level of affection and devotion that can exist between two people.

A significant number of people do not agree with conventional wisdom, saying that other relationship structures, besides monogamous ones, can be just as healthy and fulfilling—sexually and otherwise—and that more scientific research needs to be done to prove it. Most of these non-traditional relationship structures fit under the umbrella term *polyamory*, which will be discussed at the end of this section. However, because current accepted medical and scientific research supports the concept that monogamy is the healthiest relationship choice for most people, the issues in this section will be discussed based on that premise.

Making a Commitment

Committed relationships don't just mean good sex; they are good for you, too. As long as both partners are healthy at the start of the relationship, monogamy eliminates exposure to sexually transmitted diseases (see pages 282–285). Also, studies have shown that people in long-term relationships tend to live longer and have a greater sense of well-being. When it comes to sex and relationships, commitment means happiness.

When a relationship becomes serious, the couple needs to discuss openly whether or not they will become monogamous. No one should just assume that his or her partner is monogamous: the fact needs to be stated clearly and absolutely. And, if monogamy is something a man or woman desires with their sexual partner, he or she needs to clearly express that desire.

Sometimes, the fear of angering or losing their partner will lead someone to accept the idea (and fact) of their partner having sex with someone else, when what they really want is an exclusive commitment—monogamy. Ultimately, such a belief collapses under the weight of the emotions brought up by repeated proof of the lack of commitment in the relationship. When the change comes, it can be extremely painful for everyone involved. That's why it is important for people to be honest with themselves and each other about what they really want from a relationship. No one should ever settle for something less than what they know would make them happy, whether that is monogamy or not.

Cheating

If a person has sex with someone besides the person they have agreed to be monogamous with, they are cheating on that person. Such behavior is viewed by psychologists, not to mention sexual partners, as betrayal, and is usually damaging to a relationship, whether or not the person cheating gets caught. Cheating compromises any commitment a person has made, and undermines the significance of that commitment within the context of the whole relationship. Everyone deals differently with emotions brought up by betrayal: the person who cheated might feel tremendous guilt and regret, or could brush off the episode as meaningless. The person who has been cheated on may respond with understanding and a desire to heal any wounds, or they may be furious and unable to reconcile themselves to the betrayal. Psychologists view cheating as a sign of individual emotional problems or of a conflict within a relationship. If these issues are not dealt with, the person who cheats is likely to do so again. Once the trust in a relationship is lost, it is tough to recapture.

Sex and Divorce

Divorce rates vary widely around the world, the lowest being around 5 percent in Turkey and Macedonia, and the highest around 65 percent in Belarus, Sweden, and Latvia. In

relationship sex

countries such as the United States, the United Kingdom, and Canada, approximately half of marriages end in divorce, while the rate in France, Germany, and Switzerland is closer to 40 percent. Men and women going through divorces must adjust to many lifestyle changes, one very likely being the loss of a committed sexual partner. Although many divorced people wait until their emotions are somewhat settled before they initiate new intimate relationships, they often begin dating again (in spite of the initial awkwardness and discomfort) and develop satisfying romantic and sexual connections. Becoming sexually active too soon is usually a mistake for the recently divorced. Although, on the surface, it may seem healthy, and may even be suggested by friends as a way to feel better, resuming sex too soon can seriously interfere with real emotional recovery.

A common misapprehension about divorce is that it can be caused by "bad sex." Because a healthy sexual relationship is based on a healthy relationship in general, the bedroom may be the first place that trouble makes itself strongly felt. Sex is such an intimate form of communication that uncovers feelings of anger or hostility that one may be feeling toward their partner. Relationship problems that initially reveal themselves during sexual encounters can mislead one into believing that the problem is the sex itself. Divorces are usually the result of some subtle and some obvious factors that combine to drive people away from each other. Sexual difficulties are a symptom of the problems in a marriage, not the cause.

Communication

Long-term relationships require good communication. Where sex is concerned, frequent discussions can help a couple voice concerns, express desires, or suggest creative experiments. The purpose of a discussion may just be to express satisfaction with one's sex life. Most people find that discussing sex immediately before or after the act itself is not as productive as waiting for another time (a comment immediately after an activity has taken place may be taken as a criticism). Making the time for intimate, relaxing conversations can be beneficial in many ways, not just in the bedroom.

One reason to keep the lines of communication wide open is that people change—what they wanted in bed when they were twenty-five will differ from what they want at forty-five or sixty-five. Also, people respond to sex differently depending on what else is going on in their lives. Some people like to have sex as a way to relieve stress, so they may need increased sexual contact during difficult times. For other people, the reverse is true. Stress reduces their desire for sex, and they may need to wait until their lives are running more smoothly before they want to resume having sex.

Q+A

Q: My husband hasn't been interested in sex lately, and I'm worried something serious is the matter. What can I do?

A: Your husband's desire for sex can be affected by many things: his general health and fitness level, whether he has been getting enough sleep, problems at work, hormonal changes, a changing body image, and whether the two of you have been spending enough quality time together. The most important thing you can do is talk to your husband about how you feel and ask him to do the same with you. If necessary, you can enlist the help of a sex therapist. Discussing how you each feel will lead to a better understanding of what you want and need, which in turn can lead to a compromise that satisfies you both.

Frequency of Sex

Most couples wonder at some point whether they are having sex often enough. Even if they are having sex twice a day, they might believe other, "more normal," couples are making love morning, noon, and night. The fact is that no such thing as a "normal" amount of sex exists, and certainly no exact number of times per week that applies to every couple. Normal is different for every couple: some have sex every night, some twice a week, some twice a month and are perfectly satisfied. A couple may go for months or even a year without making love due to extreme stress of some kind, but when the stress eases, they have sex more frequently. Decreased interest in sex may be a sign of a problem with one partner or with the couple's relationship, but more often the source is the natural ebb and flow of life and its pressures. How much two people love each other is neither indicated nor dictated by the frequency with which they engage in intercourse.

Sex Therapy

When a couple decides to seek professional help for their sexual relationship, they may turn to a sex therapist, a highly qualified counselor trained to help with sexual problems and relationship troubles. Sex therapists are not always psychologists. Social workers, nurses, and members of the clergy often have the training and credentials necessary to provide insightful and principled sex therapy. Most sex therapists are affiliated with a medical center or physician's practice so that patients can be examined for physical causes of sexual problems and then treated correctly based on the diagnosis.

Sex therapy offers a safe environment for the discussion of sex, a topic that many people find difficult to approach without embarrassment. Men and women often have different reasons for the difficulty. A man may have been socialized to believe that admitting to doubts and fears about his sexuality makes him seem weak, not just to his partner, but to himself. Most cultures teach that men should be comfortable with sex and in control of sexual encounters. Such messages leave little room for a man to discuss his feelings, as much as he may want to. Women may face other obstacles to a free and open discussion of sexuality. Many cultures stress, whether overtly or not, that a woman is not supposed to be as interested in sex as a man and therefore should not have much to say about it. Also, many women may hesitate to make comments about their sex life to their partner because they are afraid of hurting them.

Many people, both men and women, who are comfortable and capable in all other areas of their lives find themselves feeling too shy and ashamed to talk about how they feel and what they want during sexual situations. They may be afraid that their partner will reject them somehow because they do not understand or approve of their desires. A therapist can help a couple learn to communicate more effectively about sex; that in turn eases anxiety and allows them to open themselves more fully to each other.

A sex therapist not only offers the opportunity for a couple to talk about sex, he or she can provide a couple with the information, methods, and training they need to conquer sexual problems, whether the source is physical or psychological. Usually, the duration of sex therapy is brief, because most couples begin to make changes and see improvements quickly. A good way to find a reputable sex therapist is to ask your general practitioner for a recommendation or referral.

Pregnancy

Having sex can be a wonderful way to spend your time. And it is the only way (outside of a laboratory) that two people can create a new life. Whether intentionally or not, sex can lead to pregnancy. This section explores issues relating to pregnancy, such as the mechanism of conception, the stages of pregnancy, sex during and after pregnancy, labor and birth, plus potential complications such as infertility and miscarriage.

Conception

When a sperm penetrates an ovum, or egg, conception has occurred and the genetic formula that makes each person unique is set. Also called *fertilization*, the process requires all the sperm that reach an ovum (100 to 200) to work together to try to penetrate the egg's outer surface. Once one sperm (or more, but only absolutely simultaneously) has succeeded, the ovum becomes impregnable, so to speak. Remarkably, the chemical composition of the ovum wall changes rapidly, making it impossible for sperm—even ones that have almost penetrated the wall—to make it through.

Conception typically takes place in one of a woman's Fallopian tubes (see page 203), usually within twenty-four hours of ovulation. Healthy sperm can live in the vagina, uterus, and Fallopian tubes for several days and fertilize a viable ovum wherever they encounter it. Because an egg is viable (able to be fertilized) only for twenty-four to thirty-six hours—the window in a woman's monthly cycle for becoming pregnant is a small one. Knowing when ovulation occurs, then, can be just as important for planning as for avoiding pregnancy, especially when you are using a birth control method that depends on the body's natural cycles.

To fertilize an ovum, a sperm must first pass through the outer layer, the *corona radiata* (see illustration, page 263). It must then digest its way through another layer, the *zona pellucida*. Although millions of sperm begin the journey, out of which several may penetrate the outer layers of the ovum, usually only one sperm enters the ovum and fertilizes it.

Once a sperm fertilizes an egg, a single cell, called a *zygote*, is created. Within a few hours of fertilization, that zygote begins to divide and multiply, splitting first into two cells, then four, then eight, doubling quickly as it continues its three-to-five-day journey down the Fallopian tube. In the meantime, the lining of the uterus—the endometrium—has been thickening since ovulation, creating a safe nesting place and immediate source of nutrition for the growing cell cluster when it arrives in the uterus. By day eight or nine, that minute building block of life, now called a *blastocyst*, will have multiplied into 30 to 150 cells, each one destined to become a part of either the embryo or the placenta (the organ through which a baby is provided with nourishment and oxygen until birth). The blastocyst implants itself into the endometrium, and at that point a woman is officially pregnant.

After the blastocyst is fully implanted in the womb, the body begins to secrete hormones such as human chorionic gonadotropin (hCG), which halts the menstrual cycle, typically the first sign that a woman may be pregnant. But it is by no means the only signal.

Signs of Pregnancy

Every woman has a different way of knowing she's pregnant. She may instinctively "feel" pregnant before missing a period, or she may suspect she's pregnant after her body undergoes a few distinct changes. The following are some of the possible signs of pregnancy:

Q+A

Q: Is it true you can be pregnant but still get your period?
A: Some women may experience light bleeding after conception, which they may mistake as their period. The bleeding actually results from the implantation of the blastocyst in the endometrium, which occurs roughly eight to twelve days after conception—just two to six days before your period would normally come. An implantation bleed is typically lighter and shorter than a normal period.

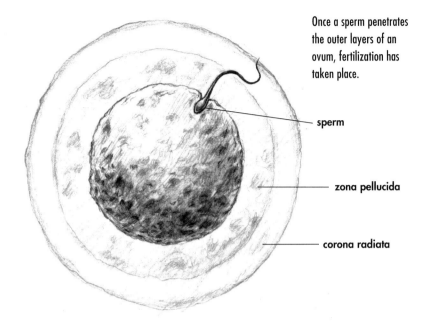

Once a sperm penetrates the outer layers of an ovum, fertilization has taken place.

— sperm

— zona pellucida

— corona radiata

Q: Can you get pregnant if you have sex during your period?
A: Yes, but the chances are very slim. Since sperm can live in your body for up to five days, it's possible that they can be viable (able to fertilize an egg) and in the right place when you ovulate, especially if you have a short menstrual cycle.

- a missed period
- a shorter or lighter period than usual
- enlarged or tender breasts and nipples
- nausea and vomiting (also known as morning sickness, though it can occur anytime)
- frequent urination
- moodiness
- bloating
- change in appetite
- fatigue

If a woman suspects she's pregnant, she should make arrangements to have a pregnancy test as soon as possible. Whether the pregnancy is planned or not, knowing early allows a woman the most options to take care of herself.

Pregnancy Tests

Store-bought pregnancy tests work by detecting the presence of human chorionic gonadotropin (hCG), a hormone released by the developing placenta, in the urine. They provide an easy way to determine, with 95 to 98 percent accuracy, whether a woman is pregnant as early as the first day of a missed period. To use the test, a woman urinates on an absorbent strip and waits for a marking that indicates whether or not she is pregnant (each brand's marking differs). It helps to perform the test first thing in the morning, when hCG levels are at their highest. If a woman isn't satisfied with the results, she should take the test again or schedule a pelvic exam with a physician, which will confirm a pregnancy with certainty.

Detecting a Baby's Sex

An *ultrasound* (or sonogram), typically performed around twenty weeks into the pregnancy to check that the baby

Q: Is it possible to choose the sex of your baby?
A: Some people believe that having sex in certain positions or at a certain point before ovulation can influence the sex of their baby, but this simply isn't true. For couples who want to try to determine their child's sex or rule out a specific sex-related disease, there is one method currently in clinical trials called sperm sorting. It works by separating the X– and Y–bearing sperm in a sample from the father, then reinserting the "chosen" sperm—X sperm cells for a girl, Y sperm cells for a boy—into the mother via in vitro fertilization.

Another method, called preimplantation genetic diagnosis, is normally used to detect genetic defects in the embryo after in vitro fertilization, but it can also be used to determine a child's gender. Keep in mind that neither process is foolproof or without its own set of ethical concerns.

pregnancy

Q+A

Q: I am thirty-five years old and pregnant for the first time. How can I find out if my baby will have health problems?

A: A number of tests such as amniocentesis, ultrasound, and quad marker screen (a test performed on a sample of the mother's blood) can detect blood diseases and birth defects in the developing fetus. Ask your physician or health care provider which ones are right for you, as some tests have risks associated with them.

is growing normally, can detect the child's gender with an 80 to 90 percent rate of accuracy. It uses high-frequency sound waves to produce images of the fetus, from which a physician or technician can visually identify the reproductive organs and gender of the fetus. A more accurate method, but one that poses a slight risk to the mother and child, is called *amniocentesis*, also referred to as an amnio, in which a doctor inserts a needle through the abdomen into the uterus to extract a small amount of amniotic fluid. The cells in the fluid provide information on the baby's sex and the presence of blood disorders and birth defects. An amnio is rarely used, however, for the sole purpose of determining a baby's sex.

Age and Pregnancy

A woman's fertility usually extends from her early teens to her mid-forties, although special considerations exist for mothers at either end of that spectrum. A particularly young mother may face challenges such as raising her baby in a culture that frowns upon teenage pregnancy. Although an older mother is likely to be more emotionally mature (and more secure in other ways, too) than

a teenager, she may be led to believe that her age will compromise her baby's health. The fact is, births to parents over age thirty-five more than doubled during the last two decades of the twentieth century. Millions of first pregnancies have been normal and healthy for women in their late thirties and early forties. Risks of harm to the baby do increase as the woman nears menopause, but if the mother is healthy and her pregnancy is monitored carefully, the chances of a successful pregnancy and birth are high.

Infertility

If a man and a woman hoping for pregnancy have had unprotected sex for more than a year (or six months if the woman is over thirty-five) and still have not conceived, it's time to seek treatment. Luckily, the odds of eventually becoming pregnant are in favor of would-be parents, as doctors can now pinpoint nearly 90 percent of fertility problems, and can treat the vast majority of them.

Treating Infertility

There are many treatment options available for infertility, from artificial insemination to in vitro fertilization,

fertility pills to lifestyle changes. But before you get treatment, you may want to set limits on how long you're going to try to become pregnant and how much you're willing to spend on the different procedures, which can be costly. Although it may be difficult to put a price on human life, stay positive and seek out a support network to help you through a process that can be emotionally trying.

Stages of Pregnancy

Once pregnancy has been confirmed by a visit to the primary physician, a couple generally wants to know approximately when the child will arrive, and what to expect each step of the way. Normal gestation ranges anywhere from thirty-seven to forty-three weeks, though most births occur between the thirty-ninth and forty-first week. To calculate an approximate birth date, count forty weeks from the first day of the last menstrual period.

Pregnancy is divided into three three-month periods (despite the fact that pregnancy usually lasts a little longer than nine months) called trimesters. The first trimester is the first, second, and third months of pregnancy; the second trimester is the fourth, fifth, and sixth months; and the third trimester is the seventh, eighth, and ninth months. Significant changes occur to both mother and child during each stage of gestation.

The First Trimester

Just one week after conception, the fertilized egg, now called the blastocyst, attaches itself to the nourishing wall of the uterus, or endometrium

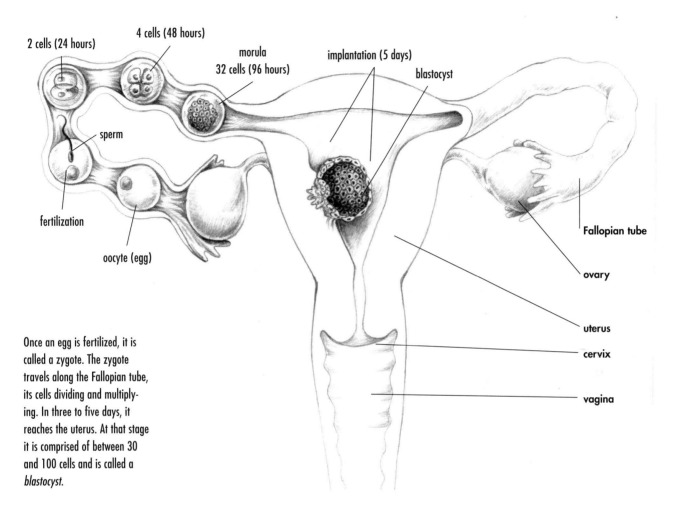

2 cells (24 hours)

4 cells (48 hours)

morula
32 cells (96 hours)

implantation (5 days)

blastocyst

sperm

fertilization

oocyte (egg)

Fallopian tube

ovary

uterus

cervix

vagina

Once an egg is fertilized, it is called a zygote. The zygote travels along the Fallopian tube, its cells dividing and multiplying. In three to five days, it reaches the uterus. At that stage it is comprised of between 30 and 100 cells and is called a *blastocyst*.

(see illustration, above). There, the umbilical cord and a round, flat mass of tissue called the placenta begin to develop, and what starts out as a tiny ball of cells begins to grow into an embryo. Oxygen and nourishment from the mother's blood are filtered through the placenta to the developing embryo, and waste products from the embryo are returned through the placenta to the mother for disposal. During gestation, the placenta also produces hormones necessary to maintain a healthy pregnancy, such as human chorionic gonadotropin (hCG), estrogen, and progesterone.

In addition to the placenta, a transparent sheath called the *amniotic sac* forms around the embryo and fills with fluid. As the embryo grows into a fetus—a process taking just eight weeks—the fluid-filled sac expands around it, acting as a cushion to keep the developing baby safe from outside bounces and shocks. All of these physiological changes

Q+A

Q: Is it okay to have sex while you're pregnant?
A: Pregnancy can be a wonderful time to have sex and to experiment with different ways of lovemaking. No harm can come to the baby or mother from any kind of sex during pregnancy unless your doctor has advised otherwise. One note of caution: If a pregnant woman's partner performs oral sex on her, he must be careful not to blow air into the vagina. A hard blast of air in the vagina can cause an air embolism, which obstructs a blood vessel and poses a serious threat to mother and baby.

pregnancy

Q+A

Q: Can you have a baby after you've had a miscarriage?
A: Yes. Most doctors advise waiting a month or two before trying for another pregnancy, to give the lining of the uterus time to repair itself and to give a couple's emotions time to settle.

may make a woman urinate more, feel nauseous, even cause vaginal changes, such as yeast infections. To counteract these changes, a pregnant woman should get plenty of rest, drink lots of juice and water, and eat high-fiber, highly nutritious meals. She and her baby will need the energy, because the growth of the fetus during this stage of pregnancy is astounding.

By the end of the first month the baby will be a quarter-inch long—smaller than a grain of rice. It has the beginnings of a head, a spinal cord, and a circulatory system. During the second and third months the fetus continues to develop major organs, including the heart, which begins beating by week five or six. Features such as bone cells, nose, eyes, ears, fingers, feet, and toes begin to form—and then function. Though a mother may not be able to feel it, her baby can move its hands, legs, and head and open and close its mouth by the end of the third month. The budding of the clitoris and the developing of the penis and scrotum become refined enough to distinguish the fetus as female or male in the third month as well. By the end of the first trimester, the fetal body structure—only 2 to 4 inches (5 to 10 cm) long and weighing less than an ounce—is fully formed.

The Second Trimester

The finishing touches to a baby's body systems and organs continue during the second trimester, as a woman may begin to feel the new life inside her. The muscles of the fetus have developed enough to allow it to move its arms and legs, a motion called *quickening* that can mark a new, joyful stage in the pregnancy. A woman will probably have more energy in the second trimester than she had during the first trimester. The second trimester is generally considered the most comfortable phase of gestation (morning sickness often has subsided by then). The womb begins to swell, the waistline expands, and blood volume increases so the placenta can function more efficiently. Meanwhile, hair (*lanugo*) begins to grow not only on the baby's head but also all over its body—a fine, protective covering that will be shed within the first week of birth. Eyebrows and eyelashes begin to appear and the eyelids of the fetus begin to open and close. The veins are visible through its thin, transparent skin and its heartbeat can be heard with a stethoscope. By the end of the sixth month, the baby, now 12 inches (30 cm) tall and $1^1/_3$ pounds (a little more than half a kilogram), can hear its mother's heartbeat, too.

The Third Trimester

In the final three months of pregnancy the fetus is strong—and he or she will make this well known. It can kick, somersault, and change position now with increased frequency. A woman's belly becomes large as her baby fills out, taking on weight until it reaches, on average, seven or so pounds. The average length for a fetus is nearly 20 inches (51 cm). A woman may feel more discomfort now, and experience shortness of breath, indigestion, and swelling of the hands and feet. The muscles of her womb will contract more frequently during the third trimester in preparation for labor. In the final month of pregnancy, the fetus, which has been in an upright position, gradually (or suddenly, to a mom's great surprise) turns over completely until the head settles into the pelvis (when this does not happen, the baby is said to be in the breech position; see page 270). This is called *lightening*, an apt description of the way a woman may begin to feel as the ligaments in her uterus relax and she has more room to eat and breathe. Now the baby is ready to enter the world.

Complications in Pregnancy
Ectopic Pregnancy

An ectopic pregnancy, also called a tubal pregnancy, is the growth of a fertilized egg outside the uterus, often in a Fallopian tube. They occur within the first trimester in about one out of every sixty pregnancies. Women who have used an intrauterine device or IUD (see

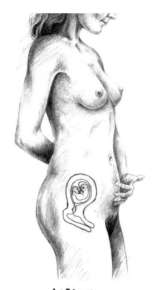
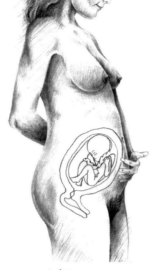
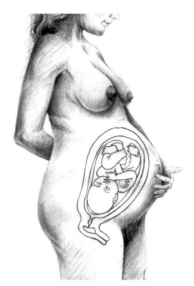

1st Trimester **2nd Trimester** **3rd Trimester**

Pregnancy is divided into trimesters. During the first trimester, the embryo develops into a fetus. Hair and facial features grow during the second trimester. By the end of the third trimester, the fetus is fully developed and ready to sustain life on its own.

"Birth Control," pages 248–251) may be at greater risk for ectopic pregnancy, as are women who have had pelvic inflammatory disease. In the event of an ectopic pregnancy, a woman may experience all the signs of a normal pregnancy and her health care provider may not see any early signs of difficulty during preliminary exams. Typical signs of ectopic pregnancy are pain and cramping on the lower right or left side of the abdomen, abnormal

Q+A

Q: Will I be able to have another baby if I have an abortion?
A: Yes. Your chances of having a healthy baby in the future are in no way compromised by having an abortion. Some evidence suggests that multiple abortions may slightly increase the risk of miscarriage or premature birth, but the research is not conclusive.

vaginal bleeding, weakness, and fainting or dizziness (signs of internal bleeding). If it proceeds undetected, an ectopic pregnancy may cause sudden bursting of the Fallopian tube, massive internal bleeding, or even death, though this is rare.

Miscarriage

A miscarriage is the spontaneous separation and discharge of a developing fetus in the first twenty weeks of pregnancy. A miscarriage seems to be the natural way the body terminates a pregnancy that is not developing properly. It occurs in about 15 percent of all pregnancies. Most miscarriages are triggered by chromosomal abnormalities that do not allow the fertilized egg to develop properly. Some women are also at an especially high risk of miscarriage. Among those in the high-risk category are women with an autoimmune disorder, such as lupus, or an abnormally shaped cervix or uterus.

Miscarriages early in the pregnancy are usually not painful, but they can become severe if they occur in the second trimester. The chief signs are cramping and bleeding, rather like a heavy menstrual flow. Medical care is required for a miscarriage because all the fetal tissue must pass out of or be removed from the body, or else infection will occur.

Symptoms of Miscarriage. Slight bleeding or cramping early in a pregnancy may be a sign of an approaching miscarriage. Your doctor or health care provider may advise you to stay in bed and wait to see what develops. If the bleeding and cramping increases, and you expel some tissue and blood clots, a miscarriage has occurred. You may be asked to collect this tissue if possible, since it can be tested to determine the cause of your miscarriage. That information may help prevent the same problem from occurring in a future pregnancy.

Preeclampsia

Preeclampsia (also known as toxemia, or pregnancy-induced hypertension) is a high blood pressure condition that occurs in some women during pregnancy. By constricting the vessels in the uterus, it disrupts the flow of oxygen and nutrients to the fetus, and slows the baby's growth. Preeclampsia can also increase the risk of placental abruption, in which the placenta separates from the uterine wall before delivery. Though its exact cause is unknown, many doctors believe poor nutrition is largely to blame. Signs include weight gain, rising blood pressure, swelling of the hands and ankles (due to water retention), abdominal pain, and poor vision. Treatment for preeclampsia consists of blood pressure medication, rest, and a properly balanced diet, particularly when it comes to sodium intake. If a mother's blood pressure continues to rise, labor may have to be induced (see "Q+A," below).

The best way to prevent preeclampsia is to eat high-quality protein every day, and make sure to get enough rest, particularly during the last three months of pregnancy.

Labor and Delivery

As a baby grows inside its mother for nine-plus months, her uterine muscles train for the baby's day of delivery. Tightening and loosening, they prepare to embark upon the last phase of pregnancy: labor. Though we still don't know its precise cause, a variety of factors, such as the baby's maturity and size, the mother's hormonal levels, even her emotional state, all seem to play a role in announcing to the body that she is ready to push the baby through the cervix and vagina and out into the world. Though each birth, like each pregnancy, is different, the following are some of the basic first signs and stages of labor.

Early Signs

As labor approaches, a woman's contractions will become more frequent and intense. Her body may empty itself in preparation for birth, bringing on a bout of diarrhea. And as the cervix softens and dilates in response to natural chemicals, such as prostaglandins and oxytocin, the pink, bloodstained mucus that sealed the cervix may begin to discharge, also called the "bloody show."

The waters of the amniotic sac may also begin to leak or pour out, though this should not be of concern in itself, as it is replenished every few hours. For women planning a hospital delivery, many health care providers advise a woman whose water has broken to go to the hospital immediately, because of the increased risk of infection once the amniotic sac has opened. If a woman's practitioner has approved her staying home after her water has broken, she should refrain from baths or anything else that may cause infection, and alert her health care provider if she sees changes in the color of the clear fluid; brown or green staining means the baby has emptied its bowels, and could be a sign of fetal distress. In that case, a woman should go to the hospital immediately.

Stages of Labor

Stage 1. Labor starts with the first uterine muscle contractions, called labor pains, which dilate (open) and efface (thin) the cervix, or mouth, of the uterus. Dilation is measured in centimeters or the width of a finger. In the early phase of labor, a woman may be only three centimeters dilated. In the active phase of labor, which is when hospitals typically admit a pregnant woman, dilation is five centimeters, and when dilation approaches eight to ten centimeters (four to five fingers), she is ready for birth.

Early contractions last roughly thirty seconds each, and can occur like clockwork—ten minutes apart—or more intermittently. They can begin during the day or at night, and last as long as twelve to fifteen hours if it is

Q+A

Q: What is induced labor?
A: Induced labor is a labor that has been started artificially. Typically a synthetic form of oxytocin is dripped intravenously to augment labor and cause the uterus to contract. Labor should be induced only when waiting for natural labor to begin constitutes a health risk to the baby or the mother, as it often results in more painful contractions and possible fetal distress. In some cases, a Caesarean section (see page 271) may be preferable to the use of induction drugs. Be sure to discuss these options with your physician or health care provider before you go into labor.

As the baby descends into the birth canal (1, 2, 3), his or her head is usually the first to emerge. The baby then turns his or her head as the shoulders come out one at a time (4). After the baby is delivered, the umbilical cord is severed and removed along with the placenta (5).

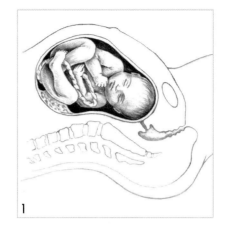

1

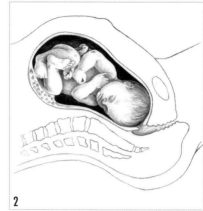

2

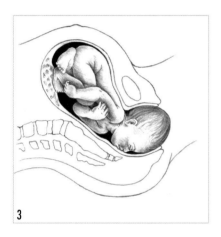

3

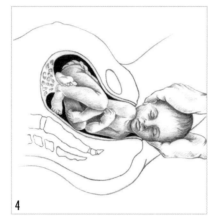

4

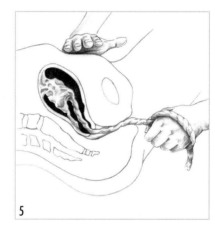

5

a woman's first pregnancy. (Women who have already had a child do not experience these contractions for as long.) When labor pains become more intense and occur closer together— as often as every five to six minutes, for more than an hour—it's time to call the doctor or midwife, as active labor has begun.

At the hospital, or in your home, you may want to walk around or take a bath (if your water hasn't broken), to help relax your body. Women in labor are urged to urinate every hour, because a full bladder can impede the baby's descent. Breathing, massage, and encouragement from a labor coach all help to relax a woman's body as the contractions

become harder and more frequent, from two to three minutes apart. This is the most intense part of labor, and if a woman hasn't had any medication, she may want it now, though her partner can probably coach her through the pain. (An epidural—a spinal anesthetic—needs to be administered earlier in the labor, as a woman will be advised by the hospital staff.) By the end of this stage the cervix is fully dilated at 10 centimeters, and the baby has descended to the pelvic area.

Stage 2. In this stage, a woman pushes her baby through the now fully opened cervix and the vagina (now referred to as the birth canal;

see illustration, above). For women having their first baby this stage usually lasts an hour or two. For women whose birth canals have already been stretched from previous births, labor may last anywhere from twenty minutes to an hour.

As her uterus contracts and a woman uses her abdominal muscles to push, the combined force exerts pressure on the baby and moves him or her down through the birth canal. Women are often coached, however, to let their uterus do the work until they feel the urge to push. If a woman has had an epidural injection, depending on its strength, she may need explicit coaching to help her to push effectively.

At the end of a contraction, when the uterus is relaxed, the baby will recede slightly. As the pushing process proceeds, the baby's head will gradually become visible through the vaginal opening and will remain there, allowing a mother to reach down and touch her baby before it is born. As more and more of the baby's head becomes visible, the pressure on a woman's perineum, the skin between the birth canal and the anus, becomes very intense, and she may feel a burning sensation as the tissue there begins to stretch. To prevent the skin from tearing, a woman must try to control—or even stop—her pushing, and allow the baby's head to gradually stretch out her vagina and perineum instead. It used to be routine for some doctors to perform an incision, called an *episiotomy,* between the bottom of the vagina and the anus, but it is becoming less common. Research has shown that women whose perineum tears heal more quickly than those who receive an episiotomy. An episiotomy is necessary only if the baby must come out more quickly than the mother can control.

Once the baby's scalp "crowns," or becomes visible, the baby is on the verge of birth: the whole head usually emerges in one quick movement. The baby's mouth and nose are immediately suctioned to remove any mucus and make it easier for the baby to begin breathing on its own. A few more contractions push the shoulders out, usually one at a time, and then the entire body. The umbilical cord, which is attached to the placenta at one end and to the baby at the other (where the belly button eventually will be), is clamped or tied and then cut, sometimes by the father, sometimes by the person who delivered the baby. Finally, a couple can see and hold their baby and begin the important bonding between parent and child.

Stage 3. Three to five minutes after the arrival of her baby, a woman will begin to experience mild contractions, and the third stage of labor begins. In this final stage of labor the placenta—now roughly a pound in weight—separates from the uterine wall and passes out of the body as afterbirth, usually within twenty to thirty minutes following the baby's birth. Once it's out, the uterus should contract and firm, preventing bleeding from the place where the placenta was attached. Nursing (breast-feeding) a newborn also helps stop this bleeding, as it triggers the release of oxytocin, which helps keep the uterus contracted.

Birth Complications

Late in the pregnancy, many health care practitioners and clinics will check for possible delivery complications. Some of these complications can be treated before a woman even begins labor; others must be attended to during childbirth. The following are some of the possible complications a woman may encounter and descriptions of how they are treated.

Premature Birth

A baby is premature when it is born approximately four weeks earlier than expected, before the thirty-seventh week of pregnancy. Premature babies, or *preemies* as they are called, have increased health risks because they have missed the final weeks of development in the womb.

Premature births can be caused by any number of reasons, from severe infection in the mother, to a multiple pregnancy, or the early separation of the placenta. In nearly half of all premature births, however, the cause is unknown.

Health care providers may try to halt premature labor by using drugs and ordering complete bed rest. As long as the amniotic sac does not burst, the pregnancy can continue normally. More often, however, a mother and her health care provider will not be able to stop the baby from coming into the world a little earlier than scheduled.

If a baby is delivered prematurely, it is vital for parents to maintain as much contact as possible with the baby. Even the smallest preemies thrive on skin-to-skin contact.

Premature births can have a powerful psychological effect on the parents. The suddenness and unexpectedness of the birth, coupled with the anxiety about the baby's future, make coping with a premature birth difficult. Maintaining close involvement with the baby and with the health care providers as well as talking openly with each other about any feelings of frustration or guilt will help offset these difficulties.

Breech Birth

When a baby is turned around in the womb and his or her buttocks or feet attempt to come out first, it is called a *breech birth.* Although a vaginal delivery is sometimes possible, most doctors will want to deliver a breech baby by Caesarean section (see below).

The health care provider typically discovers the baby's unusual position during an examination in the last month of pregnancy and may be able to rotate the baby into the proper position by applying appropriate pressure on the mother's abdomen. Mothers can also work to get their baby in the right position by performing exercises at home.

Why babies settle into breech position is not known, but too little or too much amniotic fluid, previous premature or multiple births, or uterine fibroids are among the possible reasons.

Forceps Delivery

Forceps are used when it becomes urgent to ease a baby out of the birth canal quickly, though only in certain circumstances. If a baby shows a faint or irregular heartbeat, for instance, forceps may be inserted gently into the vagina to grip either side of the baby's head—a bit like salad tongs—so that the baby can then be carefully eased out. Forceps usually leave temporary marks on the side of the baby's head or on its cheeks.

Caesarean Section

A *Caesarean section*, also known as *C-section*, is an operation for women who experience extreme problems leading up to or during labor. A Caesarean is performed in such cases as when the baby's head is too large to safely travel through the mother's pelvis; in the presence of fetal stress; when the placenta begins to precede

the baby (*placenta previa*); when the baby is in reverse or breech position (see above); when the baby fails to descend; or when the mother has severe diabetes.

If a C-section is required, the doctor will typically make a small horizontal incision in the skin above a woman's pubic bone (called a bikini cut), and then a second cut in the lower section of her uterus. A regional anesthetic is typically given before a Caesarean, so that it will affect the baby less and allow a new mother to see her baby once it is lifted from her uterus. Within thirty minutes the new mom should be stitched up, and can then hold and breast-feed her baby.

Not all Caesareans can be prevented, but some evidence suggests that C-sections may be performed more often than necessary. When possible, discuss the problem and the solutions before having this surgery.

Pregnancy Termination

If a woman is not prepared to have a baby for any reason, or if pregnancy poses a threat to her health, abortion is one option that may be available to her. It can be a difficult decision to make, and it is helpful to involve others in it, but it is equally important that a course of action be taken quickly—the longer the delay, the greater the risk of medical complications. If abortion is the route a woman chooses to take, it should be completed within the first twelve weeks of the pregnancy. It can also be performed as late as after the twenty-fourth week, but only if the mother's health is at risk.

Abortion Methods

There are a number of methods available for terminating a pregnancy. The two most commonly employed include *vacuum aspiration* and *drug-induced abortion*.

Vacuum aspiration, in which the contents of the uterus are removed through a tube, is the quickest, safest method, and is best suited to first trimester terminations. In a drug-induced abortion, a woman receives either an oral dose of mifepristone, or an injection of methotrexate (more commonly known as RU-486, see "Q+A, "page 253), both of which halt a pregnancy's progress, and cause the lining of the uterus and the fertilized egg to be expelled, often in the privacy of the woman's own home.

Clinicians performing abortions after twelve weeks generally use a method called *dilation and evacuation*, in which the cervix is artificially dilated and the fetal tissue removed with vacuum aspiration techniques and forceps. Second trimester abortions require a higher level of medical care and pose greater health risks to the mother.

Abortion law and practice varies widely from country to country. In some countries it may be difficult to receive an abortion of any kind. In other countries it may be difficult to find clinics that are willing to perform second trimester abortions, and unless a woman's life is in danger, it may be illegal to get a third-trimester abortion (see Stages of Pregnancy, pages 264–266). Still other countries legally permit abortions up to the time of birth.

Masturbation

Masturbation—the self-stimulation of one's genitals—is an activity that nearly everyone engages in at some point in their lives. Whether most adults would admit it or not, it is an integral and regular component of their sexual experience from early adolescence through old age. Sex therapists have long considered masturbation an important tool in exploring one's sexuality, particularly in helping women understand and achieve orgasm.

The convenience and pleasure associated with masturbation make it one of the most prevalent (if not commonly discussed) leisure activities in the world, and an effective stress reducer. Although it's popular, most adults consider masturbation their second choice for sexual satisfaction, preferring the intimacy and fulfillment of having sex with a partner.

Masturbation is a healthy activity that becomes a behavioral problem only when it reflects a rejection of other possible sexual relationships. Although there is no "normal" frequency rate for masturbation, problems can arise if one is masturbating often enough to irritate the genitals; if masturbation is used as an excuse to put off other, more productive, activities; or if masturbation becomes an obsession or a compulsive activity.

Masturbation may be popular, but it is not practiced universally. Like other sexual activities, some people engage in it seldom or not at all. If the reason for not masturbating is embarrassment or shame, similar emotions can color other aspects of sexuality, which can cause problems in intimate relationships. If an adult finds that their feelings about masturbation are creating barriers to sexual health, a counselor or sex therapist can help them adjust their attitudes and do away with shame.

For women, masturbation can be an effective way to achieve orgasm. Because stimulation of the clitoris doesn't always happen during intercourse, masturbation is a way for a woman to literally take sexual satisfaction into her own hands. Sex therapists encourage women to explore the mechanics of stimulation and orgasm through masturbation so that they can better understand and communicate their sexual needs to their partners.

Masturbation can play an important role in exploring sexual fantasies (see pages 273–274). Fantasy is a means of working out thoughts and feelings—a kind of mental role-playing—that generally is safe and doesn't hurt anyone. Some people use erotic literature or pornographic material as an aid to masturbation. If pornography doesn't pose a moral or ethical dilemma to an individual, and as long as it is legal (i.e., it does not depict children in a sexual context), it can continue to be a guilt-free element in masturbation fantasies.

Masturbating with Toys

Vibrators are popular aids to sexual stimulation, whether used alone or with a partner. They are electric, usually battery-powered, and vibrate at a variety of speeds and pulses depending on the model. Some vibrators attach directly to a woman's hand and create a vibration through the fingers; others come with a variety of attachments; still others are shaped like a penis. Vibrators—and other sex toys—which are available for both men and women, are available at sex-toy shops and through mail order (for more about sex toys, see Sexy Extras, which starts on page 136).

Q: I am a twenty-four-year-old man and I think I may be dependent on using a vibrator. I use one several times per week. It's been several weeks now, and I now find that I cannot masturbate without vibration. In fact, reaching orgasm with a partner is now almost impossible. Can I have permanently lost sensitivity, or is it something that will return if I were to stop using vibration for a while?
A: Perhaps you should reduce your use of the vibrator for a while, especially if having sex with a partner is important to you. Overuse of a vibrator can actually temporarily or permanently desensitize the penis. (Permanent desensitization is unlikely unless you've been using a particularly powerful vibrator for a long period of time.)

Fantasy

From the first time a girl imagines being kissed by the boy sitting next to her in class and that boy imagines touching the girl's hair or budding breasts, they are engaging in erotic fantasy. Imagining potential sexual scenarios usually begins at puberty, regardless of gender. As long as fantasies don't become more important than, or interfere with reality, they can help keep a person's sex drive strong and their sex life vibrant, even into their later years.

Most people learn to fantasize about sex as they learn to masturbate. Their first forays into the genre are likely to be fairly simple, gaining complexity or intensity with experience. When people's sex lives become more involved, they may continue to engage in simple fantasies. Sometimes, their fantasies may be more elaborate, involving acts and people their social situations would not readily permit them to explore in reality. These imaginings may take place when they are alone or with a partner. Since many cultures teach that certain sexual acts or situations are taboo (especially for women), fantasy becomes an avenue that allows exploration and, to a certain extent, satisfaction for natural human curiosity.

An important distinction needs to be emphasized here: imagining a sexual scenario—of any kind—is not the same as acting it out. Fantasy is not reality. Therefore, the imagination is a place where any and every person has the right to explore their sexuality to whatever extent they wish. Many people report that they often fantasize about people and acts that they would not want to encounter in real life, under any circumstances.

Keeping a proper perspective (and a sense of humor) about what the mind invents will prevent feelings of shame and embarrassment from damaging self-image. Remember that the imagination is the perfect place to push boundaries, because it is safe and completely private.

With the freedom to explore sex through fantasy comes a responsibility: each person needs to understand the difference between fantasy and reality, policing his or her own mental processes to make sure imbalances are not developing. Having only disturbing fantasies and fantasizing frequently (to the point that the fantasies interfere with one's social, work, or sex life) are signs that it's time to seek professional help. A dependence on fantasy—whether when alone or during sex with a partner—is usually an indication of a problem in some aspect of a person's life, one that a therapist could help examine and eradicate.

A healthy sex life can incorporate fantasy. However, since the most important aspect of sex is the connection with a partner, it is critical that fantasy does not prevent a man or woman from being fully present when they are sharing themselves with another person.

Misconceptions about Sexual Fantasies

Sometimes people fantasize about having sex with a member of the same sex and wonder whether that necessarily means that they're homosexual. The answer is no. This

---

Q+A

Q: Some of the time when I fantasize, I imagine pretty specific activities with people other than my boyfriend, sometimes famous people, sometimes people I know. I've always hesitated to tell my boyfriend because I figured he wouldn't like it. Would it improve our sex life if I did tell him?

A: The only way to know whether your boyfriend wants to discuss your fantasies (and his) is to ask him. If you decide you both feel comfortable sharing your erotic imaginings, you should try it. However, keep a few things in mind. First of all, you don't have to discuss your fantasies with anyone unless you want to. Secondly, if you do share them (especially the ones that include people you both know), realize that your boyfriend might feel threatened, even if you have a happy, stable relationship. Lastly, you need to be prepared to listen to his fantasies—whatever they are—if he decides to share them. You never know. Sharing your sexy fantasies with each other may help a fantasy become reality.

fantasy

kind of fantasy is very common; it's a normal method for exploring one's own sexuality. Incidentally, research has suggested that women are more likely to have same-sex fantasies than men because they tend to get less caught up in homophobic fears than their male counterparts. Same-sex fantasies are fairly typical and they are often more reflective of a desire for the type of affection and connection that close female friends tend to share with each other. Rather than suggesting that a woman is gay, these very common fantasies show that she is open to being touched in a more intimate way.

Homosexuality, however, involves more than just the occasional sexual fantasy. It means a person has a preference to and is seriously interested in developing routine and long-term romantic and sexual relationships with members of the same sex and may involve action.

Some feel like they are cheating on their partner when they fantasize about other people during sexual intercourse. Is it cheating? Legally, no. And only the strictest interpretation of some religious doctrines would describe it as cheating, in an ethical, moral, or spiritual sense. But, fantasizing about someone other than one's partner is normal for many people. It could, however, damage the relationship if a person becomes too dependent on the fantasies, since such dependence may interfere with daily life and prevent that person from being fully present when he or she is making love to their partner.

Acting Out Fantasies

Some couples enjoy talking about their fantasies by telling each other what really excites them, before, during, or after sex. Other couples like to share their fantasies and even act out some of them. The range of creative and exciting possibilities is of course, endless—from the controlling schoolteacher, to the innocent maiden, to the lusty first date. These are all ways to fulfill unexpressed sexual wishes.

The choice of whether to discuss sexual fantasies and bring them to life depends completely on the repercussions created by doing so. It would not be a responsible or wise decision to reveal or act out a fantasy that would hurt others psychologically, emotionally, or physically. It may even be criminal to do so. On the other hand, if the fantasy is harmless and your partner is willing to try it, then acting it out would be a great tool for sexual expression.

It can be easy—and electrifying—to carry out a simple fantasy, such as being blindfolded while making love or having sex in an unusual location. What should be acted out and what should be left to the imagination is a matter of common sense and personal beliefs. If a person feels confused or troubled by his or her sexual fantasies, then it would be beneficial to talk with a sex therapist or a psychologist about any underlying issues related to their sexual fantasies. It is also necessary to ensure that your partner is comfortable with engaging in the fantasy.

Q+A

Q: My wife told me that she gets aroused when she imagines being forced to have sex with someone. This seems kind of violent to me. Why would something that would horrify her in reality excite her sexually in her imagination?

A: Humans seem to have a few common fantasies, and being forced to have sex is one of them. A psychologist might explain the fantasy in this way: imagining you are being forced to have sex alleviates any guilt or embarrassment a person may feel about having sex. Depending on your wife's upbringing and sexual experiences, she may harbor anxiety about making love that prevents her from feeling free to enjoy the experience fully. Being forced means you are in someone else's power, therefore you are not responsible for what you feel, so (minus the guilt) you are free to enjoy yourself.

Having a fantasy that involves physical force or even rape does not mean a person wishes for anything remotely like that to happen to them. If your wife's fantasies focus almost exclusively on physical or verbal abuse, she may be having some problems that would justify discussion with a professional, whether a psychologist or a sex therapist. Helping her deal with whatever comes up could strengthen your relationship, deepen intimacy, and improve your sex life.

Fetishism

Medically, fetishism is considered to be a type of mental disorder known as paraphilia. This term has been used since the 1950s to indicate sexual arousal in response to objects (shoes, underwear), an objectified person or animal (children, sheep), or specific acts or situations (inflicting pain, exposing oneself in public) that do not fit within a society's normal sexual arousal or activity patterns. It is important to understand that this term doesn't apply to a person who experiments periodically with *kinky sex*. Instead, fetishism applies to someone who cannot experience sexual arousal or climax without the contexts of unusual behavior.

About Fetishes

The most common signs of fetishism, or paraphilia, include a complete inability to resist the urge to perform the abnormal sexual act, the requirement of participation by nonconsenting or underage individuals, and dysfunction in normal sexual and social relationships. Even when a paraphiliac engages in sex with a consenting partner, that partner becomes depersonalized and objectified. Some activities that are considered paraphilias by certain members of a society may be seen as innocuous diversions by other members of that society, or even by members of a different society, as perfectly acceptable activities. Nonconsensual paraphilias, such as *pedophilia* (sex with children), *exhibitionism* (exposing one's genitals in public), and *telephone scatologia* (obscene phone calling), are considered criminal by nearly all societies.

However, what constitutes a *perversion* or *deviation* is a controversial question, because what is treated as a crime in some places and called a sin by some religions may be accepted behavior in another place or not noticed by another religion. Also, a society's perception of what is perverted can change: homosexuality used to be considered by the medical community (and almost everyone else) to be deviant behavior. General and medical opinion has changed, however, and such a view of homosexuality is no longer the norm. And because, historically, a person identified as a sexual deviant may be shunned, prosecuted as a criminal, or even put to death—all treatment homosexuals have encountered, and to a certain extent, may still encounter—an attempt to discuss what is currently viewed as abnormal sexual behavior with some objectivity could lead to a deeper and broader understanding of the sexual impulse.

In fact, there are those who oppose defining certain sexual practices as paraphilias, stating that, aside from those activities with a criminal component, these sexual activities are not actually pathological. These advocates for change believe that the stigma attached by the medical label "paraphilia" should be removed, just as the stigma attached to homosexuality has been largely removed. For the purposes of this discussion, however, currently accepted medical definitions will be used throughout this section.

Mental health statistics show that paraphilias are more often exhibited by men than by women, and the focal point of their behavior is quite particular. For example, a man who becomes aroused from exposing his genitals in public would not find sexual satisfaction in spanking a partner. Because a paraphiliac is dependent on a particular object or behavior for sexual gratification, such a person finds that sexual activity outside the context of his paraphilia loses the power to arouse or satisfy (unless the object or behavior is present through fantasy).

There are many types of paraphilia; some are seen more often than others. For example, *urolagnia*

Q+A

Q: I consider myself to be a normal man, which means it's a struggle for me to keep my eyes off a woman's breasts when I'm talking to her. Does that mean I have a breast fetish?
A: No. Your actions and feelings would be described medically as a fetish only if a woman's breasts were the exclusive focus of your sexual desire. Also, your sexual activities would have to be centered on the breasts to the point where you were unable to become aroused by any other aspect of a woman's body or being.

fetishism

Q: My husband and I live in an apartment building where we can see into the apartments opposite us. There is a couple across the courtyard who sometimes doesn't close their curtains when they make love, and my husband and I have watched them a few times. I have to admit I find it incredibly exciting, and have begun to want sex only when I can first watch that couple doing it. My husband has noticed this change in me, and I am feeling very strange about the whole thing. What should I do?

A: Whether or not the couple you have been watching are consciously "putting on a show," your response to what you have seen (and chosen to watch) indicates that you are somehow vulnerable to voyeurism. You should find a qualified counselor (or possibly visit a sex therapist with your husband), and work with that professional to deal with your underlying problems. It is important to understand your weaknesses and seek the help you need to overcome them before they damage your relationship or lead you into increasingly unhealthy and antisocial behavior.

(sexual arousal by urine) is more commonly diagnosed than *frotteurism* (rubbing oneself against a stranger or fully clothed person in public). This section focuses on those disorders that are most common and frequently diagnosed in adults.

Many of the paraphilias listed below may seem outlandish or extreme to the point where the thought of such behavior being sexually arousing is unimaginable to most people. However, the extremity is what classifies them as paraphilias. Considering these behaviors in a less extreme version may make them easier to comprehend. For example, during a sexual encounter, some people think it's sexy to "talk dirty;" some enjoy a little spanking, biting, or scratching; and some ask a partner to undress slowly. But imagining each of these acts magnified to the point of psychological dependence may bring a person closer to understanding paraphilia.

A discussion of possible causes and treatment for paraphilia is presented at the end of this section.

Common Fetishes

Sexual fetishism was first described in 1887 by Austrian physician Sigmund Freud. But the concept and certainly the activity is quite ancient. It is a form of paraphilia where the object of affection is a specific inanimate object or part of a person's body. The term arose from fetishism, the general concept of an object having supernatural powers, or an object created by humans that has power over other humans. Freud had discovered a critical aspect of human sexuality: the relationship between human orgasms and conditioning. This is the basis of the theory that claims that fetishism derives from behavioral imprinting in early childhood.

Although the word "fetishism" has been used to indicate many of the behaviors that fall under the term paraphilia, a true fetish is the passion for an object or body part that is not principally sexual in nature, and the uncontrollable need for its presence in order to achieve sexual gratification. A fetish object is almost always physically present during sexual activity, whether the fetishist is alone or with a partner. Fetishists usually collect examples of their desired object, with some of the more common fetish items being women's undergarments and shoes; specific fabrics, such as silk or spandex; or materials such as rubber, leather, or fur.

Some people have a fetish for particular body parts such as feet, hair, or legs, which means that their sexual encounters are focused on these body parts, possibly to the exclusion of their partner as a whole. Most fetishes are not physically harmful. Many people with fetishes pose no danger to others and pursue the use of a fetish object in private, usually through masturbation.

Transvestism

A heterosexual who consistently becomes aroused by dressing in women's clothing is exhibiting the paraphilia transvestism. Someone who dresses in the clothing of the other sex periodically for fun or for effect is not a transvestite; neither is a female impersonator, nor a drag queen (a male homosexual who wears women's clothing). These people are acting out a part within society, not communicating how they want to interact sexually. A true transvestite cannot attain sexual satisfaction without cross-dressing.

Q: When my boyfriend and I have sex, we sometimes bite and scratch each other and pull each other's hair. This isn't sado-masochism, is it?

A: No. Unless your biting, scratching, and hair pulling were specifically intended to inflict pain or humiliation on each other, you and your boyfriend just have a slightly rough style to your love-making. The difference between expressing your sexual excitement and deliberately trying to inflict pain to produce sexual arousal and climax is the difference between some "roughhousing" and a mental disorder.

Voyeurism

To achieve sexual gratification, a voyeur (from the French *to see*) watches other people without their knowledge or consent while those people are undressing, nude, or engaging in sexual activity. A voyeuristic paraphiliac is usually an unmarried male who watches women he does not know, and may become most sexually excited when he is at the highest risk of being caught. As with some other paraphilias, voyeurism means a person cannot reach climax unless he is acting in a socially unacceptable manner. Most voyeurs restrict their sexual activity to masturbation while watching their victims or while fantasizing about previous episodes of voyeurism, but there have been cases in which the voyeur moved beyond watching to stalking, assault, or rape. Advances in technology (such as the creation of miniature cameras) have changed the way some voyeurs do their watching, but the paraphiliac's psychological problem is the same.

Sadism

A paraphiliac who intentionally inflicts pain on another person (or threatens to do so) for sexual excitement is called a sadist. Sadistic sexual behavior covers a wide spectrum. At one end could be the thoroughly controlled role-playing games and activities performed with a consenting companion, during which the response to mild spankings and bites is more of pleasure than of pain. At the other end of the spectrum would be the rare cases of truly sadistic behavior that can be termed assault, because they include torture, rape, or even murder. Such extreme sadists may require a nonconsenting victim in order to feel any sexual pleasure, while others may need to watch their victims suffer before becoming aroused or reaching orgasm.

Masochism

The other side of the sadism coin is masochism. A masochist is someone who gets sexual satisfaction from being subjected to, or threatened with, pain. Mild forms of this paraphilia include bondage (being tied up), being spanked, or being physically overpowered. Often, this behavior is largely symbolic and is carefully choreographed with a partner. More extreme forms include indisputably painful activities such as whippings, partial strangulation, being beaten or trampled, and self-mutilation. Although both the specific mild and extreme activities of masochism may be agreed upon by the participants in advance, the complete reliance on the infliction of pain for the achievement of sexual gratification qualifies a masochist as a paraphiliac.

Sadomasochism

The paraphilia that mingles the sadistic and masochistic roles during sexual interactions is, not surprisingly, called sadomasochism (technically

Q: I heard a joke I didn't understand on the radio about B&D. What does that stand for?

A: The joke you heard was about bondage and discipline, a specific kind of sadomasochistic "pain play" wherein a person is bound or restricted ("bondage") and either threatened with violence or actually beaten ("discipline"). A masochist would need to be bound and beaten (to be caused pain) to achieve sexual gratification, while a sadist would need to do the binding and beating (to cause pain) to climax. Such "play" may be carefully staged, and often calls for the wearing of special clothing such as leather apparel and spiked collars and the use of equipment such as whips, hoods, harnesses, and chains.

fetishism

referred to as *algolagnia*). A sado-masochist is a paraphiliac who is able to experience sexual pleasure in either role, the inflicter of pain —physical or emotional—or the victim of it. Sadomasochism, or S&M as it is commonly called, is also an umbrella term for any or all of the activities practiced by sadists and masochists together.

Exhibitionism

People who feel compelled to expose their sex organs to unsuspecting strangers for sexual stimulation and satisfaction suffer from the paraphilia known as *exhibitionism*. Also called *indecent exposure* and *flashing*, exhibitionism is more commonly performed by men. For some, the purpose of their antisocial behavior is not exclusively sexual, because they are more interested in shocking or frightening their victims than they are in achieving an erection or climaxing. Their primary source of pleasure is the visible response of their victims, whether that reaction is one of shock or fear.

Usually, an exhibitionist does not rape or assault his victims, but there have been exceptions, most often when an exhibitionist is unsatisfied by his victim's reaction.

Exhibitionists are the paraphiliacs who are most often apprehended by the police. Because the risk of being caught seems to be an important factor in an exhibitionist's abnormal behavior, he almost always acts out in public places and in ways that are likely to lead to arrest, such as repeatedly exposing himself at the same street corner.

Q+A

Q: When I was around eight years old, a friend's father saw me walking home from the grocery store and offered to give me a ride home. We stopped to get an ice cream cone, and he asked me to sit on his lap while I ate my ice cream. He kept making weird noises (or so I thought then), and I told him I didn't like the way he was moving me around on his lap, but he wouldn't let go of me. When he put me back on the seat, he said I was a bad girl for making him mad. He said I shouldn't tell anyone he had taken me for ice cream because I would make his daughter and my brother and sister feel really bad, and my parents would be mad at me for eating ice cream in the middle of the day. I never told anyone, but I have had recurring nightmares of him ever since. When I do have a boyfriend, I have a hard time getting close to him. What can I do?
A: Unfortunately, you were the victim of a child molester. Such predators can wreak havoc with a young person's psyche, especially because children often feel that it is their fault when something bad happens. Such treatment at the hands of a formerly trusted adult creates wounds that do not heal easily. The best thing you can do for yourself is to seek professional help. See a counselor, and don't let this man's actions in the past prevent you from having a happy and healthy sex life.

Telephone Scatologia

Repeatedly making obscene telephone calls in order to become sexually aroused is considered another type of paraphilia. The safety and anonymity of the telephone provides the paraphiliac—in most cases male—with an ideal situation for engaging in fantasy and masturbation. Most obscene phone calls fall into three categories. In the first, the caller describes in detail how he is masturbating. The second kind of obscene call includes a threat, such as, "I know where you live, and I'm going to get to you." In the third category, the caller tries to get the victim to talk about herself and reveal intimate aspects of her life.

An obscene phone caller may call the same victim repeatedly, especially if she stays on the phone long enough to satisfy him. But if one victim doesn't give him what he wants, he most likely will try others instead of focusing on her.

Pedophilia

The paraphilia in which an adult's favored or sole method of sexual excitement and gratification is fantasizing about or engaging in sexual activity with children who have not reached puberty is pedophilia. The most likely target of a pedophile is a girl between the ages of eight and eleven. And, unlike the stereotype of a child molester— a stranger waiting near schoolyards, luring a lone child to his car or home with promises of candy and toys—a pedophile is much more likely to be a relative, neighbor, or acquaintance of the child victim.

Pedophilia occurs in men more than women, but there have been documented (and highly publicized) cases of women who have had repeated sexual contact with children. Pedophiles commonly fall into three distinct age groups: over fifty, mid-to-late thirties, and teenagers. Most are heterosexual, and many are married. From the medical point of view, a person who has only isolated sexual contact with children is not a pedophile. A physician or other specialist, when called upon, may describe that person's behavior as inappropriately expressing sexual frustration, loneliness, or personal conflict. Although no single pattern of sexual behavior describes all pedophiles, their activities are almost universally considered criminal.

Causes and Treatments

The causes of paraphilia are not clearly understood. Because humans are, to a certain extent, sexual from birth, some theories about the roots of abnormal sexual behavior focus on early childhood, others on later childhood and adolescence (when masturbation begins). Ultrasounds have shown that boys can experience erections before they are born, and simple observation shows that both baby girls and boys enjoy exploring and stimulating their genitals through rhythmic movement and with their fingers as soon as they can reach their pubic area. Therefore, psychoanalysts theorize that paraphilia may be a response to events associated with unusual—whether pleasurable or traumatic—early sexual experience. Behavioral psychol-

ogists suggest that conditioning is responsible for paraphilia: nonsexual objects that become associated with sexual pleasure through repeated use, especially during masturbation, can become arousing in themselves. Also, experimentation with activities such as voyeurism and exhibitionism may provide a troubled person with especially intense sexual pleasure, which would condition him or her to prefer those activities to others. Recent research shows that paraphiliacs often are extremely isolated individuals who have poor social skills and a limited capacity for developing intimacy of any sort with another person. Some experts hypothesize that this is a cause of the behavior, and others theorize that it is a symptom of their problems.

Whether or not the cause is understood, paraphilias can be damaging to the person performing them and potentially dangerous for anyone drawn, knowingly or not, into the paraphiliac's activities. A person suffering from such a disorder rarely seeks treatment, because the pleasure they derive from the activity is so enormous, especially in comparison to other areas of their life, that they are not able to stop themselves without intervention. Being found out by a family member or being arrested, tried and convicted are usually the only events that will push a paraphiliac into treatment.

Treatment for the disorder may include psychotherapy, cognitive behavioral therapy, behavior modification, hypnosis, antidepressant medications, and a class of medica-

tions known as antiandrogens, which alter hormone levels in a man's body, particularly those of testosterone, thereby lowering sex drive. Antidepressants and antiandrogens reduce the functional underpinnings of the behavior ("I just don't care anymore" or "I'm not able to stop thinking about sex"), and allow a patient to focus on counseling without the distraction of paraphiliac urges.

Outcome statistics on therapeutic treatments for paraphiliacs are incomplete, but they do indicate that treatment is rarely 100 percent effective. That is most likely because the causes of paraphilias are so poorly understood. The treatment that offers the highest success rate combines drug therapy with cognitive behavior therapy, an approach that encourages patients to challenge and confront their distorted thinking patterns about sex.

In addition to those who advocate a change in the definition of paraphilia mentioned above, many professionals would prefer not to identify someone who participates in sexual behavior with other consenting adults as mentally ill, even if the activity might be considered deviant by mainstream society. Most professionals would recommend that an individual seek help only if his or her sexual behavior is criminal, therefore bringing them into conflict with the law, or if that behavior hurts themselves or others. In cases where the behavior is potentially criminal, as in pedophilia, treatment usually ends up taking place within the penal system.

Sexual Orientation

A person's sexual orientation focuses the direction of sexual desire, whether it is toward the opposite sex (heterosexuality), the same sex (homosexuality), or both sexes (bisexuality). The term has replaced *sexual preference* in academic and everyday usage because current research indicates that a person's sexual orientation is biologically determined, and therefore not a question of *preference* or choice.

It's Not Either/Or

When Dr. Alfred C. Kinsey published his report on male sexuality in 1948 (and a subsequent one on female sexuality in 1953), he revolutionized the way Western society viewed sexual orientation. His report has been famous—and controversial—ever since. Kinsey's most fundamental discovery (which has been widely translated and reported around the world) was that significant percentages of the population had sexual attractions, desires, and experiences with both sexes. He determined that a given person's sexual orientation falls along a continuum, often called the Kinsey Scale, of seven different levels, rather than falling into two extremes: exclusive heterosexuality or exclusive homosexuality. Kinsey also observed that an individual's place on the scale could change throughout life, suggesting a potential fluidity in human sexuality. The following are the seven points on his scale, numbered 0–6, are:

0 = entirely heterosexual;
1 = largely heterosexual but with an incidental homosexual history;
2 = largely heterosexual but with a distinct homosexual history;
3 = equally heterosexual and homosexual;
4 = largely homosexual but with a distinct heterosexual history;
5 = largely homosexual but with an incidental heterosexual history;
6 = entirely homosexual.

Although Kinsey's work and that of subsequent sex researchers has helped to educate and open minds about human sexuality (thereby changing culture), most people continue to identify themselves socially, politically, and emotionally as one of three sexual orientations: homosexual, heterosexual, or bisexual.

Kinsey's landmark 1948 report determined that 37 percent of the white males studied had been involved in "at least some homosexual acts to orgasm between adolescence and old age." Thirteen percent of women were found to be in the same category in a later report. Kinsey also found that 10 percent of the men studied were exclusively homosexual. More recent studies have found results ranging from 2 to 8 percent, but the Kinsey percentage is still considered by many to be the benchmark.

Homosexuality

Homosexuality is a sexual orientation that directs a person to seek sexual fulfillment with people of the same sex. Although homosexual activity has been acknowledged in cultures throughout history—including ancient Greece and Rome—the term *homosexual* wasn't used until 1869, when Hungarian-born physician and journalist Karoly Maria Benkert coined the word. Today's homosexual advocacy organizations prefer the terms "gay" and "lesbian" because

Q+A

Q: A friend I've known since high school recently came out to me. Does this mean he was attracted to me when we were in school, or did he suddenly make a choice to be gay?

A: Sexual orientation is a deep-seated and profound aspect of our identity that many researchers believe to be genetic. The American Psychiatric Association states, "Human beings cannot choose to be either gay or straight. Sexual orientation emerges for most people in early adolescence without any prior sexual experience. Although we can choose whether to act on our feelings, psychologists do not consider sexual orientation to be a conscious choice that can be voluntarily changed." And, as far as your friend's attraction to you, it is entirely possible. On the other hand, do you find yourself sexually attracted to every woman you see? Sexual attraction to any one person is no less mysterious, individual, and unpredictable for homosexuals than it is for heterosexuals.

Q: I am a young man and I have been dating a woman for a few weeks. She just told me she considers herself bisexual. Does this mean she will need to sleep with women while we are going out?
A: Many bisexual individuals maintain one monogamous relationship at a time. It is a mistake to assume that all bisexuals need to be enjoying multiple sexual experiences with both sexes at all times. You need to discuss this question with your partner as you would any other issues related to your relationship about sexuality or fidelity.

the word homosexual is widely identified with the purely clinical language of former—and, in some cases, existing—laws criminalizing homosexual activity.

From the Middle Ages to the twenty-first century, Western governments and religions demonized and criminalized homosexual activity, with convictions resulting in imprisonment, or even death. However, with the advent of modern psychology, the weight of empirical data gradually overwhelmed many of the medieval views.

Bisexuality

Bisexuality is a sexual orientation that directs a person to seek sexual fulfillment with partners of both sexes. Although Kinsey's research showed that 46 percent of those studied had engaged in both homosexual and heterosexual activity, and his scale indicates that the majority of people are bisexual to a certain extent, bisexuality is often the least understood orientation by members of the other groups.

Many people, at some point in their lives, become what are called *exploratory bisexuals.* This means they

are predominantly homosexual or heterosexual but choose to experiment with the opposite orientation out of curiosity. These experimental phases normally don't last very long, and become part of an individual's lifelong collection of sexual experiences, sometimes reinvigorating their "regular" sexual life.

Other people may be what are called *transitional bisexuals.* This means a person is at a point in the long, emotionally complicated, and sometimes confusing process of realizing his or her homosexuality. For many, that process includes a period—which can be very short, or last several years—in which they identify themselves as bisexual. Their

experimentation with bisexuality allows them to maintain a connection to the heterosexual identity that has been imposed on them by their environment while coming to grips with their true, inborn homosexual orientation.

Although it is possible for a person to transition from a homosexual to heterosexual orientation, it is rare because few children are raised to identify themselves as gay. As it stands today, most cultures around the world do not support homosexuality in the way that they support heterosexuality.

In addition to these "temporary" conditions, there are many people who identify themselves as having a true, permanent bisexual orientation. This concept is relatively new to Western culture. With the sexual revolution of the 1960s, an environment was created in which a true bisexual could pursue intimate relationships with partners of either sex.

Today, people who identify themselves as bisexual are more accepted in society than ever before, but still struggle with their own particular social stigmas.

Q: Do bisexual people go back and forth between relationships with individuals of each sex?
A: Not necessarily. Although Kinsey's research found that 11.6 percent of the men studied were equally sexual with men and women, the majority of bisexual people tend to have a more dominant tendency. Some bisexuals are only sexually active with one sex during their adult life, never acting on the desires for the other sex. Research on this subject is still young, but bisexuals are just as unpredictable as anyone else in terms of faithfulness and ability to commit to one monogamous relationship.

Sexually Transmitted Diseases

Sexually transmitted diseases (STDs) include a broad range of disorders, each caused by a unique organism, accompanied by a unique set of symptoms, and requiring a unique mode of treatment. Once referred to as venereal diseases (which generally meant only gonorrhea and syphilis), STDs have always carried a social stigma that has made detection and treatment challenging.

Sexually transmitted diseases can be passed from an infected person to a recipient through vaginal or anal intercourse, oral sex (including contact between the mouth and anus), kissing, and contact between genitals and infected patches of skin. STDs often affect not only the genitals but also other parts of the body, including the mouth, the skin, and even entire systems, such as the nervous system or the immune system.

In the past twenty-five years, the most devastating STD worldwide has been human immunodeficiency virus (HIV)—specifically its advanced stage, acquired immuno-deficiency syndrome (AIDS), which can lead to death.

HIV/AIDS is an epidemic that affects tens of millions of people worldwide. Like hepatitis, HIV can be transmitted from person to person through nonsexual contact, but is often transmitted sexually.

One of the biggest barriers to fighting STDs has been the cultural shame and stigma attached to them, which prevents many people from getting tested or seeking treatment and even stops people from telling their sexual partners that they may be infected. An understanding of potential risk, an ability to identify symptoms, and a willingness to seek testing, diagnosis, and treatment, are all essential to protecting yourself and your partner from STDs.

Who Is at Risk?

If you are sexually active and have more than one partner (or your partner has more than one partner), you are at risk for sexually transmitted diseases. Typically, the people most at risk are those ages fifteen to thirty, the age range during which most people engage in sex with multiple partners. Rates of infection drop significantly after age thirty and again at thirty-five, because most people in their late thirties and older have established stable monogamous relationships. No matter the age, it is always important to discuss STDs with a prospective sexual partner, including informing them of any infections you might have (a nonnegotiable ethical obligation), and asking them whether they have been tested and diagnosed themselves.

Preventing Infection

Unlike infectious diseases such as influenza, most STDs have no preventive vaccine (Hepatitis A and B are exceptions, and a vaccine for the herpes virus is being tested as this book goes to press). Consistent and disciplined preventive action is the only reliable method of halting the spread of STDs. The following measures should be taken by anyone who is at risk for STDs.

Use a Condom

Although not entirely effective in preventing the spread of all STDs, a latex condom will prevent the spread of most STDs through genital and anal intercourse.

Get Regular Checkups

For anyone with multiple sexual partners, or whose partner has multiple partners, a routine checkup is essential to detect asymptomatic STDs that can lurk in seemingly healthy bodies.

Abstain from Sex and See a Doctor

It is essential that you refrain from sex and seek medical treatment immediately if you are displaying symptoms of an STD. Such symptoms can include bumps, sores, discharge, or any unexplained change in the appearance of the genital area or anus.

Common STDs

HIV/AIDS

Human immunodeficiency virus (HIV) infects blood cells that help to maintain the body's immune system, leading to a compromised immune system that leaves the body vulnerable to a wide variety of infectious diseases. Acquired immunodeficiency syndrome (AIDS) is the final stage of HIV infection, in which the body's immune system can no longer fight infections without the help of medication. Individuals with severely compromised immune systems can succumb to infections, such as pneumonia, that otherwise healthy adults can survive. At present, there is no cure for HIV/AIDS.

HIV is transmitted through bodily fluids, such as blood, semen, vaginal fluid, and breast milk. Areas of the body that are especially vulnerable to HIV infection are porous membranes such as the eyes, nose, mouth, vagina, penis, and anus. Any area of skin with an open cut, sore, or rash is susceptible to infection through contact with infected bodily fluid. HIV can be transmitted sexually through genital intercourse, anal intercourse, and oral sex involving either the genitals or the anus.

(HIV can also be transmitted through such nonsexual contact as blood transfusions, mother-to-baby transmission, and the sharing of contaminated hypodermic needles, usually by intravenous-drug users.)

Consequently, a sexually active adult with more than one partner can protect themselves from HIV only by ensuring that neither blood, semen, vaginal fluid, nor breast milk from a partner comes in contact with susceptible areas of their body. A condom during intercourse or oral sex performed on a man, and a dental dam during oral sex performed on a woman have been identified as the most reliable barriers to infected bodily fluids.

The rapid spread of HIV throughout the world is due partly to the fact that most infected people show no symptoms for years (some individuals have reported flu-like symptoms shortly after contracting the virus, but such reports are exceptional). Roughly 50 percent of infected people develop AIDS within ten years of infection. Nearly all people infected with HIV eventually develop AIDS. Because of the dormant nature of HIV infection, regular testing is recommended for anyone who is at risk for STDs.

Further complicating early detection and treatment is the fact that HIV antibodies will not show up in a blood test until twelve weeks after infection has occurred. If HIV is detected, a follow-up test will be administered after three months to confirm the infection.

As with all sexually transmitted diseases, an individual who suspects he or she may be at risk for HIV must overcome any shame and fear about it and seek immediate medical attention. A diagnosis of HIV infection was once considered a death sentence, but in industrial nations, where infected people possibly have access to adequate health care, there are now courses of treatment that allow people to live with HIV—and even AIDS—for years. Complex drug therapies, referred to as cocktails, as well as counseling to facilitate lifestyle changes, stress reduction, and overall wellness for patients now mean that those with HIV/AIDS can live in the same way people are now living with some forms of cancer. In developing nations—particularly those in sub-Saharan Africa, where HIV rates have skyrocketed and many children are now born with the virus—such implementation has yet to occur.

Q+A

Q: Before my husband and I could receive our marriage license, we had to take a blood test. Was it a test for STDs?

A: Yes. Many places require a blood test before marriage. The test, which is also given to women in the early stages of pregnancy, is used to detect STDs that show few or no symptoms. Increasingly, a blood test to screen for STDs is included in the annual physicals of people who may be at risk.

sexually transmitted diseases

Chancroid

Chancroid is a bacterial infection common in Asia and Africa and now widespread in the West. *Chancres*, or sores, may appear on the penis, the labia, or the anus, and the disease is spread through contact with the pus in these chancres. Although chancroid can cause painful swelling of the lymph nodes, it poses no long-term serious threat and can be easily treated with antibiotics. However, open sores can serve as a site for HIV transmission.

Chlamydia and NGU

Chlamydia is a bacterial infection that is most commonly transmitted through genital or anal intercourse. In some women, chlamydia causes a burning or itching in the vagina, but most women remain asymptomatic, although the disease still progresses internally and can cause inflammation of the cervix and of the Fallopian tubes, leading to potential complications in pregnancy. For men (in whom the infection is called *nongonococcal urethritis*, or NGU), it causes a watery discharge from the penis, difficulty in urination, and itching and burning of the penis. Often called the "silent STD" because many people show no symptoms at all, chlamydia is often spread by people who don't even know they have it. Chlamydia and NGU can be detected by regular STD testing, and are easily treated with antibiotics over a two-week period during which time infected people must abstain from sex.

Gonorrhea

Gonorrhea is a bacterial infection spread by vaginal intercourse, anal intercourse, and oral sex. Symptoms of gonorrhea in men include a milky discharge from the penis that becomes thicker over the course of a few days, and enlargement of the lymph glands in the groin. More than half the women who contract gonorrhea remain asymptomatic, although they are still at risk for pelvic inflammatory disease (PID), which can lead to infertility. If a woman does show symptoms, it is often the oozing of pus from the urethra. Anal or oral sex can lead to gonorrhea of the mouth, throat, or anus, and pregnant women who contract gonorrhea can pass the infection on to the eyes of newborns, potentially leading to blindness. Gonorrhea is easily identified by medical professionals and is treatable with a week-long cycle of antibiotics.

Herpes

Herpes simplex is a viral infection that affects mucus membranes and the skin. Extraordinarily common (affecting as much as 20 percent of the population over the age of twelve) and unfortunately incurable, herpes is characterized by cold sores and fever blisters in the mouth and on the lips and face (known as HSV1), and genital herpes (known as HSV2). The herpes virus is spread through contact with an infected person in a variety of ways: mouth to vagina or penis, finger to penis or vagina, penis to anus, and vice versa.

Outbreaks of symptomatic sores and blisters can occur several times a year in an infected person, or the disease can remain in remission for months or even years. HSV1 can be spread only when symptoms are present, but the HSV2 virus can be spread before symptoms begin to appear. It is not yet known why some people have frequent recurrence of herpes outbreaks and others do not. It is believed that a healthy diet and the reduction of stress can contribute to an outbreak-free maintenance of a herpes infection. Treatment is directed toward drying up sores and relieving pain, and there is hope that current research will lead to an effective herpes vaccine.

Candidiasis

Sexual intercourse is not a major transmitter of candidiasis, also called yeast infections, but it does happen. Itching, cracking of vaginal tissue, and a thick, white discharge are the symptoms most women experience. Nonprescription, over-the-counter vaginal suppositories can easily treat this fungal infection.

Q+A

Q: Is it possible to contract an STD somewhere other than your genitals?
A: Yes. Oral sex can lead to gonorrhea of the throat, and anal intercourse can lead to gonorrhea of the anus, both treated with antibiotics. Herpes sores can be spread from mouth to mouth, and genital warts can be spread to the mouth through oral sex.

Q: Can I contract two STDs at the same time?

A: Remember, anyone who engages in sex with more than one partner is at risk for a number of STDs, and, yes, two or more STDs can be contracted simultaneously. Furthermore, having contracted and undergone treatment for an STD doesn't immunize you from the disease—you could contract it again—if you engage in the same behavior.

Pelvic Inflammatory Disease

Pelvic Inflammatory Disease (PID) is a condition brought on by other STDs and affects the Fallopian tubes. Bacteria are the culprits, often from gonorrhea, but possibly from other, nongonococcal infections. Aches, pains, chills, fever, and bloody discharges from the vagina are frequent symptoms of PID. It can cause permanent damage to a woman's reproductive system, increasing the risk of ectopic pregnancy and even infertility. A woman experiencing the symptoms of PID should get a blood test, have a doctor examine any discharge, and possibly undergo a laparoscopy to confirm the diagnosis. Once diagnosed, PID can be treated easily with antibiotics and bed rest.

Pubic Lice

More commonly known as *crabs*, pubic lice are tiny insects that live in hair. Any contact with an infested genital area, and also by contact with infested towels, clothing, bedding, and even toilet seats can transmit them. The moment of discovery can be traumatic, because pubic lice can be observed and their bites felt in the pubic area. Crabs may be efficiently dispatched with medicated creams, lotions, and shampoos.

Syphilis

Syphilis is a bacterial infection that is highly contagious and potentially very dangerous. It is spread through vaginal or anal intercourse and oral sex. The first stage of syphilis is the appearance of a chancre on the infected area within a few weeks of transmission, usually on the penis, labia, anus, mouth, or throat; during this stage the individual is highly contagious and contact with the chancre can transmit the infection to a sexual partner. The second stage of syphilis, which occurs several weeks later, is characterized by the fading of the chancre and the appearance of rashes on the palms and the soles of the feet, a sore throat, low-grade fever, loss of appetite, and loss of hair. A latent stage, in which the bacteria settle throughout the body and remain dormant for some time (possibly years), is followed by a noncontiguous final stage in which the nervous system, heart, and bones may come under attack. Depending on which organs have been compromised by the bacteria, a person can suffer mental incapacity, heart trouble, paralysis, blindness, and damage to facial cartilage. If treated in the first two stages or early in the latent stage, syphilis can be cured with penicillin or other antibiotics. The final stage also requires treatment, but is much more serious because, if left untreated, it can lead to death.

Trichomoniasis

Trichomonas vaginalis is a single-celled parasite that is spread through sexual contact, and infects the vagina and urethra in women and the urethra and prostate in men. Within a month of infection, symptoms such as a greenish discharge, pain on urination, itching, and abdominal pain, will appear. Trichomoniasis is treated with an antibiotic.

Vaginitis

Vaginitis is an umbrella term that takes in any number of conditions that cause inflammation and irritation of the vagina, usually characterized by itching, burning, and discharge. A bacterial infection, irritation from feminine-hygiene products, and sensitivity to contraceptive creams are among the causes of vaginitis. Over-the-counter vaginal suppositories or prescription antibiotics are a usual course of treatment.

Human Papilloma Virus

Human Papilloma Virus (HPV), also called *genital warts*, is a viral infection that takes the form of cauliflower-like bumps on the genitals. Transmitted sexually, warts may appear on the penis, vagina, anus, or cervix within six months of infection. Warts can be removed through simple surgery. Recent research has demonstrated that HPV can be transmitted from the genitals to the mouth through oral sex, and that HPV in the mouth poses a risk for future oral cancers.

Sexual Assault

Rape is a violent crime, an assault on the victim's body and psyche. Because the violence takes the form of a nonconsensual sexual act, the victims of rape are almost always faced with a variety of issues related to intimacy, self-esteem, and trust. For that reason, a brief look at rape or sexual assault and its varied repercussions is appropriate in any discussion of sexuality.

Rape is usually a crime against women characterized by the forceful, nonconsensual penetration of the vagina, anus, or mouth by the penis, the hand, or an object. When the rapist does not use violence, he finds other means of coercion: either the threat of violence or the incapacitation of the victim by drugs or alcohol. Rape is less commonly committed by men against other men, and rarely by women against men.

Whether the sex is consensual or not, any sexual act with a legal minor is considered rape (usually called *statutory rape*), and is punished harshly by most societies. The stereotype of the rapist as a crazed, violent loner is largely a myth. Many victims are raped by a man they already know. Also, rapes often occur in familiar surroundings (e.g., near or in the woman's home or workplace), making a healthy emotional recovery from the assault more difficult because a basic feeling of comfort and safety has been shaken.

A woman who has been raped, regardless of the circumstances, has been severely traumatized and will have trouble processing her feelings over the following days and weeks. Women have reported fear and anxiety, flashbacks and nightmares, the inability to get back to normal activities, feelings of low self-esteem, and a loss of religious faith. If a woman has been in a loving monogamous relationship, she may have trouble accepting the physical comfort and intimacy her partner has to offer.

There are steps a woman can take, starting at the moment she is assaulted and continuing for as long as it takes, to secure her physical and emotional well-being. Reporting the rape to the police immediately and undergoing a physical examination (before bathing) is necessary in order to apprehend and punish the rapist. It can also be a first step in taking control of a situation that often feels chaotic and hopeless. No matter what questions a woman is asked by the police or the health care professionals who administer the physical exam, she must remind herself that no victim of rape is ever to blame for what has happened to her.

Although the rape has taken the form of a sexual act, it is in fact a crime of violence against women, an attempt to dominate, shame, and even cripple the victim emotionally. Seeking the immediate support of other rape survivors may buttress a victim's self-esteem and help her to understand that although she may feel vulnerable and alone, in fact there is a vast support network available to help her to take back her life.

The partner of a woman who has been raped has the opportunity to be a source of support and understanding. He should remind himself that his partner has been the victim of a violent crime and that she is probably experiencing a flood of difficult and contradictory emotions at which he can only guess. If he is not already a "good listener,"

Q+A

Q: What kind of physical exam is performed on a woman when she reports being raped?

A: A woman who has been raped will typically be introduced to health care professionals who are specially trained in the handling of rape cases. A careful examination of her vagina, rectum, and mouth (depending on where penetration took place) for damaged tissue, swelling, and semen is necessary to gather evidence. They will also look for evidence of physical abuse and forcible restraint on other parts of the body. Traces of hair, blood, or semen from the assailant will be gathered from the woman's body and clothing. The experience will be difficult, no matter how sympathetic and well trained the caregivers are, and many survivors have recommended suggesting a friend or family member to accompany you to the hospital for support.

he must cultivate the ability to hear what his partner has to say about her experience; to continue to offer physical intimacy when she is comfortable with it and refrain when she asks him to; and to seek the help of a psychological counselor so that he, in his role as caregiver, feels supported.

Protecting Yourself

It is important to remember that, contrary to popular belief, you are more likely to be assaulted by a sexual predator whom you already know—in or near your home, school, or place of business—than you are by a stranger in an unfamiliar location. Keeping your home, workplace, and car secure; being alert to suspicious behavior; and being prepared to defend yourself or flee are the most commonly recommended steps you can take to protect yourself. Don't walk alone in lonely places—especially after dark. Don't allow a man whom you know only slightly to lead you into an isolated location where you will have difficulty defending yourself or fleeing.

It is also important to remember—especially for those who have been the victims of a sexual assault—that the victim is never to blame for an attack, and that no woman "asks for it" by dressing a certain way, going to particular locations, or behaving in an open and trusting manner—or even a sexually provocative manner—in the company of a man.

If You're Attacked

The chances of a woman being raped are not great. However, if a woman is attacked, there are some

Q+A

Q: My wife was recently raped and I'm afraid this is going to change our relationship. What can I do?
A: Your relationship has changed, at least for the near future. Your instinct to help your wife is the first step toward helping her rebuild her damaged psyche and restoring her ability to trust other people. You can help by listening to what she has to say. Offer physical comfort and intimacy (she may be feeling ashamed of her body and unwilling to reach out physically to you), but remember that she may not be ready for any intimacy for some time, particularly physical intimacy.

rules she can keep in mind. Some women have reported that being able to protect themselves physically—because they had been trained and used some sort of martial arts, for example—allowed them to escape being raped. Others report that just being trained in the martial arts has given them a feeling of empowerment that helps them feel prepared for any possible attack. If you are attacked, the first thing to do is get to a safe place, away from your attacker. Next, go immediately to a hospital—don't bathe or change your clothing before doing so. Call the police (or have someone call for you) from the hospital. At the hospital, you'll be examined for injuries. Evidence, in the form of saliva, hair, or semen, will also be collected.

Date Rape

Date rape occurs when a sexual predator (almost always a man) participates in a traditional date, and then takes the opportunity to force a woman to have nonconsensual sex. Women who have been the victims of date rape should remind themselves that rape is rape, and the

temptation to excuse rape when it is committed within the context of an otherwise consensual night out plays into the hands of those who would blame the victim. A woman has the right to engage in kissing, fondling, and still say "no" to intercourse.

Date Rape Drugs

These are drugs that are used to assist a sexual assault. The can leave the victim physically helpless and unable to refuse sex. They can cause memory loss and unconsciousness. Date rape drugs often have no color, smell, or taste and are easily added to flavored drinks without the victim's knowledge.

Rohypnol (flunitrazepam), for example, is a potent nervous system depressant that is becoming the date rape drug of choice. The drug comes in pill form, and dissolves in liquids. The drug causes amnesia and severe muscle relaxation, leaving the victim sedated for hours.

Alcohol use is involved in many date rapes. Drinking may loosen inhibitions and impair judgment. But even if a victim of rape drank alcohol, he or she is not at fault.

A Lifetime of Sex

Many believe that the sexual time in a person's life begins in adolescence and extends primarily into middle age, with the periods at the beginning and end of life empty of sexual interest and activity. However, research shows that sexual learning and expression begins in infancy and that sexual activity can be enjoyed throughout life, including during the years of late life. This section looks at the eight commonly accepted stages in life, exploring the unique components of sexual development and expression in each stage.

Infancy

Infancy is an extremely sensual period in a person's life. Touching and discovering are key elements in the incredible learning curve that developing children experience. One of the first things an infant discovers is his or her own body. A boy typically discovers his penis at seven to eight months, while a girl will commonly discover her vulva around nine to ten months. These discoveries occur along with the realization that the feet, hands, ears, and every other part of the body belong to the infant. In other words, it is natural and normal. Research indicates that an infant who is allowed to explore his or her body freely, without negative reactions or scolding about touching the genitals, develops a more positive self-image, and is less likely to have anxiety or guilt about sexual expression later in life.

Infant boys commonly have erections, and erections have even been observed in the womb. Although infantile erection is not a response to sexual stimulus, it can be a sensual response to touching or rubbing (it can also be a response to a need to urinate). Vaginal lubrication has been observed in infant girls. Additionally, infant boys and girls typically engage in rhythmic movements—often a rocking motion while on their stomachs—that are sensually stimulating to the genital area. Some researchers claim that these movements can create a near-orgasmic result.

Toddler Years

A toddler's fascination with his or her own body can often create confusion for parents, but it is natural for a child to have a heightened curiosity about the human body. Many toddlers engage in some form of play that involves "you show me yours, I'll show you mine," in which they reveal their genitals to one another. These games are a manifestation of normal curiosity about their body and the bodies of others. Parents should be concerned only if such play takes place with children who are well past toddlerhood (two years or more).

The toddler often has a love of nudity. During this period, parents must strike a balance between introducing the concept of privacy—that nudity and genital touching are not public activities—while making sure to avoid instilling a sense of shame about the naked body.

The sexual development of the toddler years also includes a growing awareness of gender and the discovery of gender identity. By the time they reach the age of two, most children recognize the difference in genders, and can identify who is a "boy" and who is a "girl."

Childhood

As children begin attending school, their understanding of gender identity grows deeper. In addition, children (ages five to eight) develop an awareness of *gender constancy* (or *gender stability*)—an understanding that gender is a permanent condition. Until this time, a young boy, for instance, may think he could grow up to be a mother. Children also develop a sense of *gender consistency,* an understanding that circumstances do not change one's gender (i.e., if Uncle Jim puts on a dress, he does not become a woman).

During childhood it is common for sexual play with other children to continue. Because concepts of privacy have probably been taught and learned, however, these games are often carefully kept out of view of parents. These games and explorations are grounded in curiosity, not sexuality, and are a natural part of development. As such, the gender of a child's playmate in these games is no reliable indication of the child's sexual orientation: Girls playing with boys are not necessarily heterosexual, and boys exploring the bodies of other boys are not necessarily homosexual. It would be troublesome, however, if the children are clearly mimicking adult sexual behavior—such as oral-genital contact—which could be an indication of sexual abuse. A child is likely to develop an awareness that all people are not heterosexual (if the child is not already being raised by a same-sex couple). Whether prompted by images in the media, friends and relatives, or the family structure of a child's classmates, parents may be asked questions about family structures different from theirs as well as about same-sex relationships. It is appropriate to explain that some children have two mothers or two fathers instead of one of each. As with any sexual issue, children are subject to school-yard misconceptions, so the more honest and open parents are (without offering unnecessary details), the more trusting and informed the child will be.

Childhood can also bring the first signs of puberty for some children. Some girls experience early menstruation at ages eight or nine.

Preadolescence

In the preadolescent years, most young people experience the onset of puberty. For girls, this typically occurs around the ages of ten or eleven, and for boys, eleven or twelve (although variations within a few years in either direction are considered normal). During this time, the sexual organs begin to grow and mature.

For girls, this includes the development of the internal reproductive organs, and an increase in size of the external sexual organs, including the labia and clitoris. The breasts also develop, creating the most obvious physical manifestation of a young girl's development. For boys, the

penis and scrotum grow markedly in size, and facial hair can begin to appear (although it is not unusual for that to follow later). Both sexes develop pubic and underarm hair.

For parents, it is important to explain these upcoming developments before they occur, as puberty can be a time of extreme insecurity and anxiety over the sometimes traumatic physical and emotional changes that take place seemingly overnight.

Preadolescence is a period when genital play moves from being rooted in curiosity to being sexual in nature, and leading to pleasure and orgasm. Many preadolescents begin masturbating. Also, it is not uncommon for preadolescents to experiment sexually with members of the same gender (although not all do), and this type of exploration is not a reliable indication of a child's sexual orientation.

A recent Canadian study reported that 5 percent of boys and 1 percent of girls had experienced sexual intercourse by age twelve. Children in this age group are more likely to be experimenting with kissing and fondling, including genital touching.

Adolescence

For most people, the teenage years are the period of greatest change in terms of sexual development (see Her Anatomy, pages 198–213, and His Anatomy, pages 214–225). Puberty hits with full force, causing growth spurts, hormonal changes, and extremely heightened self-consciousness. Adolescents can be virtually obsessed with sex and sexuality. And why wouldn't they be?

Many boys experience nocturnal emissions (or wet dreams), with involuntary erections and ejaculation. Girls can also have sexual dreams and experience vaginal lubrication while sleeping. During puberty, the body is literally taking over and making sure the adolescent understands that adulthood—with all

Q: My five-year-old daughter just asked me where babies come from. How should I respond?

A: Children around ages five or six have a strong fascination with pregnancy and birth. Although this is often an awkward subject for parents, it is best to deal with it simply and honestly, without worrying about sexual or biological details. Child development experts encourage parents to use correct terms like "uterus," instead of "belly." Answer the question the child asks, without elaborating more than necessary—but be prepared with an answer before the question is asked, knowing that from the age of three onward, children can be inquisitive about pregnancy. The more comfortable parents are answering such questions, the more likely the child will feel safe and comfortable asking questions in the future. Once they begin school, children are exposed to misconceptions and misinformation about pregnancy from other children, so it becomes that much more important for parents to be a source of honest, reliable answers.

a lifetime of sex

Q+A

Q: I am a mother of three. How do I juggle raising my kids and being intimate with my husband?
A: Many people find that raising children changes their sex lives dramatically, which can create problems in adult relationships. It's important for adults to make time for each other outside of child-rearing activities. Whether you are a single parent or part of a couple, remember: Your children will be happier and healthier if you teach them to take care of themselves—by showing them that you take care of yourself. Make time not only for adult activities, such as sex, but also for exercise, self-enrichment, and friends.

of its sexual implications— is around the corner. It's important for adolescents to explore these changes.

Almost all adolescents experiment to some degree with masturbation. By this age, genital play is sexual, with orgasm being the primary purpose. Studies differ, but at least 90 percent of adolescent males and almost 70 percent of females admit to masturbating before the age of eighteen. In addition to its sexual gratification, masturbation is also a way of exploring and discovering the seemingly new body that the adolescent inhabits. Pubic hair and significantly larger sexual organs are a source of tremendous fascination for the adolescent. Getting to know these new parts of the body is an important part of the adolescent experience, and can lead to the formation

of healthy physical relationships with others down the road. Masturbation—even if it is done frequently—does not cause physical or psychological damage unless it interferes with regular daily tasks (e.g., a student stays home from school to masturbate).

One way in which the adolescent's fascination with an increasingly sexual body can manifest itself is sexual exploration with friends of the same gender. Boys and girls may masturbate together. This is not necessarily an indication of sexual orientation, but is often a matter of sharing enthusiasm for their emerging sexuality and even "showing off."

As adolescents mature, they are increasingly likely to engage in sexual intercourse. Although statistics differ widely from country to country, a recent international survey polled teenagers from fifteen different countries. Researchers found that girls

reported having their first experience of sexual intercourse at an average age of sixteen, while boys lost their virginity at the average age of fifteen. Recent studies in the US indicate that at least half of American teens are sexually active. A 2003 US survey showed that one-third of teenage boys admitted to feeling pressure to have sexual intercourse. So, in addition to nature's own encouragement, many of today's teenagers experience strong pressure from their peers to be sexually active.

All of this leads to the issues of pregnancy (see pages 262–271) and sexually transmitted diseases (see pages 282–285). Because so many adolescents are sexually active, it is vital that they be armed with information about the risks and consequences of that activity. A recent study in Britain found that a full 40 percent of boys ages ten to fifteen had never heard of AIDS or HIV.

Q+A

Q: I have a six-year-old son who has discovered his penis. I stopped him from masturbating a couple times in the last week, but it doesn't seem to work. I don't know what to say to him except to wait until he is older. Is this normal, and is there something I can say to him to make him stop doing this until he is older?
A: All boys are fascinated by their genitals and the pleasurable sensations they can get from them, and no harm will come from a boy masturbating, even as a baby. When a parent tells a child not to touch himself there, the child gets the idea that doing so is somehow wrong. If your boy rubs himself in public, or even around the house, the best approach is to take him aside and say you understand that what he's doing feels wonderful—but that giving yourself pleasure is something that should be done privately, and that some people would rather not see a person doing that activity. Be careful not to be judgmental in your tone. It will do wonders for your son's future attitude toward sexuality if you tell him that self-pleasuring is a beautiful gift but that there is a time and a place to do it.

Although the rates of teenage sexual activity are similar in the US and many European countries, the rates of teenage pregnancy and STD diagnoses are much higher in the US, where condoms and information about the consequences of sexual activity are not as freely available to students. Parents should be diligent in talking openly with adolescents about the realities and consequences of sexual activity, and how best to protect themselves if they are engaging in it (see Birth Control, pages 242–257).

Adolescence is also the period when a young person's sexual orientation is most likely to become clear to him or her. Many homosexual or bisexual adolescents experience fear and guilt over sexual desires that they don't understand. It is important for all adolescents to be instructed that there is a range of sexuality, and that their personal desires and fantasies may fall anywhere between exclusive heterosexuality and exclusive homosexuality (see pages 280–281).

Adulthood

From ages eighteen to forty, adults can experience a wide range of sexual expression, depending on relationship status, orientation, family structure, and personal circumstances. Career pressures, health issues, pregnancy, and family obligations are just some of the factors that impact adult sexual behavior. This entire section is an examination of adult sexual expression, so it is enough to say here that a "normal" or "fulfilling" adult sex life can mean many different things.

Q+A

Q: My wife is going through menopause and she seems to be drawing away from me. We've always had a good sex life, but she's not as interested in sex as she used to be. Should I be doing something differently?
A: Your wife is going through physical changes that, in some ways, rival the changes caused by puberty. She may be feeling different physically, and her body image and self-esteem are probably vulnerable right now, all things that can influence sex drive. The best thing you can do is talk to her about your concerns, and ask her how she feels and what you can do for her, sexually and otherwise. Showing her that you still find her attractive and that her degree of fertility does not affect your love for her—things you may think are obvious, but she may not be able to see clearly right now—will help her and your relationship. And if your children have recently moved out, take advantage of your freedom to try new things, explore your changing bodies, and—most importantly—talk to one another.

Middle Age

When a person reaches the middle years (roughly forty to sixty-five), it is common for a host of outside issues to affect their interest in and enjoyment of sexual activity. If the person is parenting, his or her children—no matter their age—demand (and deserve) care and attention. If children are reaching adolescence, which is a time of tremendous upheaval, they can demand significant attention from mothers and fathers, thus drawing energy and time away from personal sexual fulfillment. Career obligations play an important part in this period of life as well. It is a time when many professionals are at the height of their working life, devoting much of their waking energy to work-related projects and problems. Additionally, middle-aged adults often have aging parents to care for, and find themselves having to contend with such stressful issues as the cost of medical care and the ability of an aging parent to continue to live independently.

Besides being unable to find the time and energy for sexual satisfaction, it is common for men and women to experience internal challenges to sexual expression during these years, including a diminished sex drive or libido. In middle age, both sexes experience some form of physical and psychological change, known as *climacteric* (from Greek, meaning a *rung on a ladder* or a *critical point*). For women, this critical point includes the biological reality of menopause—or the end of ovulation and fertility—while for men it is a less concrete but sometimes equally distressing change marked by a decrease in testosterone and a period of psychological stress sometimes referred to as a midlife crisis.

Sex and Menopause. Menopause marks the end of a woman's ability to ovulate and reproduce. It is a gradual process, in which egg production decreases and eventually menstruation stops. For most

a lifetime of sex

women this occurs sometime around the age of fifty; however, some women remain fertile into their fifties while others (approximately one in a hundred) experience premature menopause in their thirties. (For a detailed explanation of menopause and its effects, see pages 208–209.)

In terms of midlife sexuality, the effects of menopause are varied. The end of ovulation is accompanied by significant decreases in the production of estrogen, the female sex hormone. The decrease can severely curb a woman's interest in sexual activity, although this is not the case for all women. Lower levels of estrogen production also affect sexual function, as vaginal lubrication lessens and the walls of the vagina thin, making sexual intercourse sometimes painful and orgasms more difficult to achieve. Other physical changes associated with menopause— including an increase in body fat (particularly around the abdomen), and a thinning of the hair—can adversely affect a woman's self-image, further lessening her desire for intimacy with a partner.

Some women undergo *hormone replacement therapy* (HRT) to address some of the changes associated with menopause. However, HRT can cause other health risks and requires close monitoring by a doctor (see page 209). Some women find that water-based lubricants can assist in overcoming vaginal dryness. If that is not effective, doctors can prescribe estrogen creams to facilitate intercourse, but women should understand the health risks associated with these hormonal creams.

Menopause is far from a death knell for sexual activity. One recent Australian study discovered that only 10 percent of women found menopause's effects "severely distressing," while 70 percent found them to be a "mild to moderate nuisance." A recent study of 1,001 women reported that more than half of the women from ages fifty to sixty-five found their sex drive the same or increased following menopause. For some, the elimination of the risk of pregnancy, accompanied by other lifestyle factors (adult children leaving home, greater financial freedom) freed them sexually.

Male Climacteric and Sexual Drive. Although men do not experience anything as concrete and final as the end of ovulation, midlife brings physical and psychological changes that affect a man's sexual desire and function. Sometime around age forty, testosterone production begins to fall, and gradually slows over the next two decades (until it stabilizes at a lower level). This can mean it takes longer for a man to achieve an erection, and can diminish the intensity of ejaculation. Although the male remains physically fertile, his psychological virility can be affected. Other physical changes may damage a man's body image and, consequently, have a negative effect on his interest in sexual activity. Baldness, diminished muscle mass, and even something as seemingly minor as graying pubic hair can aggravate a midlife depression or sense of longing for the past.

Some heterosexual men during this period have fantasies of being sexual with a younger, fertile woman. As their own potency seems to be waning, there is a temptation to prove their virility one more time. If the man is in a marriage, acting on these fantasies can have devastating consequences. If the man is single, there can be a shift in dating patterns as he pursues women outside of his age group.

Post-Climacteric Sex. As is the case throughout life, communication is the key to a satisfying sexual life for midlife couples. Many women feel shy or ashamed to discuss menopausal changes with their partners, but communication can lead to adjustments in sexual expression that accommodate life's shifting physical realities. By midlife it may take both partners longer to become aroused and to achieve orgasm. Some midlife couples find that making time for lingering lovemaking can lead to a fulfilling sexual life. Whereas earlier in life, couples may have had to steal time for a "quickie," now they can slow down their sexual encounters and give each other more physical attention. Midlife couples might also consider adjusting their sexual practices, exploring new sexual territory with each other to deal with physical changes. If vaginal penetration becomes painful or less pleasurable for a post-menopausal woman, couples can experiment with mutual masturbation, oral sex, and sexual toys or other aids. These new paths can reawaken and reinvigorate interest for both parties.

Q: My grandfather is in an assisted-living facility and has recently taken up with a woman who is a fellow resident. I think they may be sleeping together. Is this safe?

A: With an increasingly elderly population in many Western countries, retirement homes and even nursing homes are making adjustments to accommodate new realities of intimacy among the elderly. For elderly couples, conventional medical wisdom advises that as long as both partners are able to make conscious decisions, and the actions are consensual, physical intimacy is to be encouraged throughout life.

Late Life

With lifestyle and medical improvements prolonging life and health, there are more sexually active seniors than ever before. Senior sex is no longer a taboo subject. Although cultural influences still inhibit some individuals from enjoying late-life sexual activity, and physical and psychological realities can impede performance, many people are discovering that sexual pleasure—in an array of forms—can be enjoyed throughout a long life.

Individuals in their sixties and seventies face physical challenges similar to those of midlife sexual partners: decreased hormonal production causes vaginal dryness and thinness in women, and can make achieving an erection more challenging for a man. And both sexes face societal and self-imposed challenges to satisfying sexual expression. Guilt and shame can force potentially active seniors to remain sexually idle. Widows often feel an obligation to be faithful to their deceased spouse. Occasional impotence is normal for a man over sixty-five, but many men let an isolated (but nonetheless embarrassing) failure to achieve an erection affect future opportunities for sexual gratification. The anxiety produced by a single failure to perform can cause *secondary induced impotence*, an inability to achieve an erection due to excessive stress and pressure.

There are other causes for sexual impotence in older men, such as depression. Ill health, retirement, and death are difficult for older adults to live with, particularly if they have not learned to cope with these life changes. If the depression is severe, the man can withdraw from physical contact and stimulation altogether. This is especially difficult for those who have had a good sex life in the past. But a good psychologist or sex therapist can recognize that the impotency exists because of the depression. If new interests are aroused, then the ability to perform sexually will also be aroused.

Overcoming these challenges can allow people to enjoy sexual activity for many years after menopause and middle age. Although vaginal penetration may not be pleasurable or practical, the clitoris and nipples remain highly sensitive in women well into late life. Manual stimulation of these areas by a partner can create prolonged and intense sexual pleasure. An older man's penis probably requires much more direct stimulation to achieve an erection, but for many late-life couples this is an opportunity for attentive and extremely sensual contact. As is the case throughout life, communication with your late-life sex partner is vital to ensuring a fulfilling sex life. Sexual contact later in life may be gentler, and may take longer, but it can remain a powerful component of a loving relationship for people into their eighties and beyond.

Among the greatest predictors of late-life sexual fulfillment is a person's history of exercise and diet. People who exercise regularly in middle age and eat well are much more likely to be sexually active in their later years. Some studies suggest that this correlation has as much to do with body image as it does with physical health. Alcohol consumption is also an important factor. Alcohol depresses the central nervous system, aggravating any preexisting challenges to physical arousal.

Late-life sexual relations, particularly for heterosexual couples, face demographic challenges. A recent study showed that 42 percent of women between ages sixty-five and seventy-four were widowed, while only 8.9 percent of the men were. This leaves many more women than men late in life. But for couples who have been together for years, or those who get together in their seventies or eighties, a little imagination can result in a fulfilling sex life.

Index

Index

Index

Index

P

Panties, **17,** 84

    kissing, **45**

    removal of, 112, **113**

    sliding hand under, **76**

    worn during sex, **35**

Pap smear/test, 201, 252

Paponicolaou, George, 201

Paraphilia, 275–279

Patch, the, 252–253

Pearl thongs, 12, **146**

Pectoralis major muscle, **211**

Pedophilia, 275, 278–279

Pelvic inflammatory disease (PID), 249, 251, 267, 282, 284, 285

Penectomy, 215, 216

Penis

    anatomy of, 214–218, **215–218**

    artificial, 216

    blow jobs and, 63, **63,** 65, **65**

    cancer of, 215, 217, 218

    circumcised, 72, 75

    cock ring for, **141**

    complications related to, 215–216

    corona, 215, **215**

    corpora cavernosa, 214, 216

    corpus spongiosum, 214, 216, 225

    development in preadolescence, 289

    foreskin, 65, 72, 75, 214, **216**

    frenulum, **63,** 63, 75, **75,** 189, 215, **215**

    g-spot in contact with, 88, 132, 133

    hand-jobs and, 72, 75, **75**

    size of, 215

    sliding against clitoris, 128

Performance anxiety, 160

Perfume, **16**

Perineum, 201, **201,** 270

Pessary, 204

Phalloplasty, 215, 216

Phone sex, 170

Phylogenetic normality, 238–239

Pill, the, **251,** 251–252

Pillows, as props, 144, **144**

Placenta, 262, 265

Plateau, 231

Police uniform, 145

Polyamory, 259

Pomeroy, Wardell, 238

Pornography, 272

Positions

    Arrow, the, 128, **128–129**

    Classic (missionary), 114, **114–115, 132,** 133

    Cobra, the, 104, **104–105**

    Cowgirl, 88, **88–91**

    "Crabwalk," 94, **95**

    Dog style, **54–55, 126–127,** 127, **132,** 133

    Jackknife, **124–125,** 125

    Lap dance, **96–99,** 97

    Rabbit, the, 118, **118–119**

    Ramp, 103, **103**

    rear-view, 92, **92–95**

    Rock, the, 100, **100**

    Sidewinder, **130–131,** 131

    69 positions, 66, **66–69**

    Slide, the, 101, **101**

    Stand and deliver, **120–121,** 121

    Superhero, **122–123,** 123

    Victory, **116–117,** 117

    Wraparound, 102, **102**

Pre-ejaculatory fluid, 225, 243

Preadolescence, sexuality and, 289

Preeclampsia, 268

Preemies, 270

Pregnancy

    age of woman and, 264

    birth control pills and, 251

    children's questions about, 289

    complications in, 266–268

    conception, 262, **263**

    ectopic, 249, 266–267

    endometriosis and, 202

    infertility, 264

    intrauterine devices and, 249, 250

    labor and delivery, 268–270, **269**

    miscarriage, 266, 267–268

    ovaries and, 205

    preeclampsia, 268

    prolapsed uterus and, 204

    signs of, 262–263

    stages of, 264–266, **267**

    termination of (abortion), 271

    tests for, 263–264

Premature birth, 270

Premature ejaculation, 197, 233–234, 244

Prepuce (clitoral hood), 79, 200, **201**

Priapism, 217

Privacy, masturbation and, 177, 179, 288, 290

Progesterone, 209, 265

    in intrauterine devices, 249, 250, 251

    in Mini-Pill, 252

    Rhythm Method and, 255

Prolapsed uterus, 204, 208

Props, 144, **144–147**

Index

acknowledgments

Illustrations on pages 59, 63, 65, 75, 77, 79, and 133 by Jason Lee.

Illustrations on pages 198–293 by Adam Raiti.

Photographs on pages 11, 13, 17 (top left), 84 (top right), and 86 (bottom left) from the Image Source.

Photographs on pages 18 (right), 20 (top), 85 (bottom left), and 152 from Digital Vision.

All other photographs, including front cover, by Philip James.

Philip James would like to thank Ester, Vickie and Julie for great assisting, Mandy for allowing the space and freedom to create, and having a great sense of humor, and all the models and crew for their endless patience.

Studio Cactus would like to thank: the models—Natasha, Mark, Jamie, Charlee, Steve, Lena, Michael, Carrie, Katie, Charles, Alan, Coralie, Oreke, Annaleigh, Jodie, Ken-e, Mutia, and Emma; the agency reps—Carlos from Shades of Ebony, Rachel from The SugarGroup, Hayley from Supermodel Ltd, and Michelle and Carina from Max Locations; the Lemonade Factory; Sam and Megan for hair and make-up; Lorna and Kate; and Karsten.

The publishers would particularly like to thank Morgan Rees of *Men's Health* magazine for his invaluable advice.